Managing Complexity in Global Organizations

Managing Complexity in Global Organizations

Ulrich Steger
Wolfgang Amann
Martha Maznevski

BICENTENNIAL
1807
WILEY
2007
BICENTENNIAL

John Wiley & Sons, Ltd

Other Wiley Editorial Offices

John Wiley & Sons Inc., 111 River Street, Hoboken, NJ 07030, USA

Jossey-Bass, 989 Market Street, San Francisco, CA 94103-1741, USA

Wiley-VCH Verlag GmbH, Boschstr. 12, D-69469 Weinheim, Germany

John Wiley & Sons Australia Ltd, 42 McDougall Street, Milton, Queensland 4064, Australia

John Wiley & Sons (Asia) Pte Ltd, 2 Clementi Loop #02-01, Jin Xing Distripark, Singapore 129809

John Wiley & Sons Canada Ltd, 6045 Freemont Blvd, Mississauga, ONT, L5R 4J3, Canada

Wiley also publishes its books in a variety of electronic formats. Some content that appears in print may not be available in
electronic books.

Anniversary Logo Design: Richard J. Pacifico

Library of Congress Cataloging in Publication Data

Managing complexity in global organizations / Ulrich Steger, Wolfgang Amann, Martha Maznevski [editors].
      p.   cm.
Includes bibliographical references and index.
ISBN 978-0-470-51072-8 (pbk.)
1. International business enterprises—Management.   2. Corporate culture.   3. Technological innovations—
Management.   4. Business logistics—Management.   5. Diversity in the workplace—Management.   I. Amann,
Wolfgang.   II. Maznevski, Martha L.   III. Steger, Ulrich.
HD62.4.M3655 2007
658'.049—dc22

                                                                                               2007004235

British Library Cataloguing in Publication Data

A catalogue record for this book is available from the British Library

ISBN 978-0-470-51072-8 (PB)

Typeset in 10/13pt Kuenstler by Integra Software Services Pvt. Ltd, Pondicherry, India
Printed and bound in Great Britain by TJ International Ltd, Padstow, Cornwall, UK
This book is printed on acid-free paper responsibly manufactured from sustainable forestry in which at least
two trees are planted for each one used for paper production.

Contents

Contributors

Editors

Wolfgang Amann

Wolfgang Amann worked for DaimlerChrysler and subsequently in top management consulting, before pursuing his PhD in international management at the University of St Gallen. He subsequently joined Institute for Management Development (IMD) in Lausanne to carry out further research in the areas of managing complexity, corporate strategy and governance, and family business. He also held visiting academic appointments at the Wharton School of the University of Pennsylvania, the Indian Institute of Management (IIM) in Bangalore as well as Hosei University in Tokyo.

Wolfgang Amann's primary expertise and interests relate to successful internationalization based on developing strategic success positions (SSP), choosing the right paths for growth and internationalization and managing complexities in globalizing companies. He has a particular interest in how ownership (family businesses, private equity, and venture capitalist companies, etc.) and lifecycle stages impact these aspects. Now a Professor at Henley Management College in the UK, he directs the Henly Centre for Creative Destruction, which innovates strategies for driving markets. He has directed, delivered, and contributed to open and in-company programmes as well as courses on complexity, strategy, internationalization, and governance in the US, Europe, China, India, and Japan. He has (co-)authored more than 60 case studies for these programmes. In 2006, his course 'Corporate Strategy and Governance' was chosen as the CEMS course of the year among all CEMS business schools in 17 European countries.

Martha Maznevski

Martha Maznevski is Professor of Organizational Behaviour and International Management at the International Institute for Management Development in Lausanne, Switzerland. She teaches courses and modules on topics spanning a broad range of organizational behaviour topics, including teams and leadership in global and virtual contexts, diversity and inclusiveness, and the relationship between organizational and national culture. She has served as a consultant and advisor to public and private organizations in North America, Europe, and Asia on issues of managing people in the complexity of globalization. Professor Maznevski has presented and published numerous articles on these subjects. Recently she published *The Blackwell Handbook of Global Management: A Guide to Managing Complexity* (2004) and she is a co-author of the popular textbook *International Management Behaviour* (Blackwell), now in its fifth edition. Her current research focuses on the on-going dynamics of high-performing teams and networks in multinational organizations, and managing people in global complexity.

Ulrich Steger

Professor Ulrich Steger holds the Alcan Chair of Environmental Management at the Institute for Management Development (IMD) and is Director of IMD's research project on Corporate Sustainability Management (CSM). He is Director of Building High Performance Boards and other major partnership programmes, e.g. the DaimlerChrysler and Allianz Excellence Program. He is also a member of the supervisory and advisory boards of several major companies and organizations. He was a member of the Managing Board of Volkswagen, in charge of environment and traffic matters and, in particular, the implementation of an environmental strategy within the VW group worldwide.

Before becoming involved in management education, he was active in German politics. He was Minister of Economics and Technology in the State of Hesse, with particular responsibility for transport, traffic, and energy. Before that, he was a member of the German Bundestag, specializing in energy, technology, industry, and foreign trade issues. Previously, Professor Steger was a full professor at the European Business School, a Guest Professor at the University of St Gallen and a Fellow at Harvard University. He holds a PhD from Ruhr University, Bochum. He is the author or editor of numerous publications including, most recently: *Corporate Diplomacy* (2002),

Sustainable Development and Innovation in the Energy Sector (2003), *Managing Complex Mergers* (2004), *Mastering Global Corporate Governance* (2004) and *In the Mind of the Stakeholder* (2006).

Authors

Arturo Bris

Arturo Bris has been a Professor of Finance at IMD since July 2005. Prior to joining IMD, he was the Robert B. and Candice J. Haas Associate Professor of Corporate Finance at the Yale School of Management (USA). A Research Associate of the European Corporate Governance Institute and a member of the Yale International Institute for Corporate Governance, he has worked extensively on issues of Corporate Governance, Financial Regulation, and International Valuation. His research and consulting activities focus on the international aspects of financial regulation, and in particular on the effects of bankruptcy, short sales, insider trading, and merger laws. He has also researched and lectured on the effects of the euro on the corporate sector, as well as on the valuation impact of corporate governance changes. His work has been published in the *Journal of Finance*, the *Journal of Financial Economics*, the *Review of Financial Studies*, the *Journal of Legal Studies*, and the *Journal of Business*, among others. He has been teaching Corporate Finance and Investment Banking at Yale since 1998, where he has received the Best Teacher Award twice. His consulting experience includes companies in both the US and Europe. He ranks among the top one hundred most-read social scientists in the world. Arturo graduated in Law and Economics from Universidad Autónoma de Madrid and received an MSc from CEMFI (Foundation of the Bank of Spain). He holds a PhD in Management from INSEAD (France). He is married to Eva Abejón, a music teacher, and they have two children.

Carlos Cordon

Professor Cordon's areas of special interest are supply- and demand-chain management, manufacturing management, process management, and outsourcing. Other interests include speed-based competition and project management. He is currently developing research and cases in the following areas: leading customer supplier relations, supply-chain configurations for speed, fast project execution, and types of supply-chain structures per industry (pharmaceutical, electronics, fashion, food, and transportation). He is the author of numerous articles and case studies in these fields, and over the past few years has won various prizes for his cases and articles on supply-chain management, outsourcing, and process management. Professor Cordon is also currently a consultant to multinational companies in the electronics, food, chemical, pharmaceutical, car, and other manufacturing industries. He has designed and directed numerous executive development programmes in the areas of supply-chain management, outsourcing, and purchasing. Professor Cordon studied civil engineering at the Escuela Politecnica de Barcelona (Spain) and holds a PhD in Management from INSEAD. Prior to the completion of his schooling, he was Manager in the manufacturing and distribution consulting group of Accenture, and later MIS Manager of Grupo Español General Cable (now a subsidiary of BICC).

Georges Haour

Georges Haour is Professor at IMD, where he teaches Technology and Innovation Management and directs executive programmes for managers from companies worldwide. He is also a partner of the innovator–investor company Generics (formerly Sagentia), in Cambridge, UK, on business innovation and new technology ventures and start-ups. Dr Haour acts as an adviser to organizations in Europe, North America, and Asia, in the area of R&D/Innovation management for effective value creation. Born and raised in Lyon, France, he graduated from the Ecole Nationale Supérieure de Chimie de Paris (ENSCP). He has undergraduate training in Law and Economics (Paris), holds a Master of Sciences (New York), and a PhD in Chemistry and Materials Science, from the University of Toronto, Canada.

Prior to joining IMD, Dr Haour was manager at Battelle, in Geneva, where, for nine years, he led a business unit carrying out innovation projects on behalf of companies in Europe, Japan, and the USA. In this capacity, he significantly grew his unit's sales up to $4 million annually and hired professionals from six different countries. Several of his innovations have been licensed to firms, resulting in substantial new business for the client companies. Earlier, he was a researcher at ATT's Bell Laboratories, in Murray Hill, New Jersey. He also worked with Marshall McLuhan at his Centre for Culture, Society and Technology, in Toronto. Dr Haour has 8 patents and 90 publications. On his research theme of 'creating value through technological innovation', his latest book is titled *Resolving the Innovation Paradox-Enhancing Growth in*

Technology Companies (Palgrave, London, reprinted in 2005). The Japanese version was recently published by First Press (Tokyo, 2006). The website of the book is www.innovationparadox.com. He is on the boards of several organizations, including start-ups. He founded the IFTM (International Forum for Technology Management) for managers and academics to debate issues specific to leading and managing technology firms. Forum venues include Bangalore, Kyoto, Paris, Istanbul, and, in 2007, Shanghai.

Amy Hykes

Amy Hykes is a research associate at IMD. Prior to joining IMD, Amy worked as a Senior Product Marketing Manager at Stellent, a content management software provider located in Minneapolis, Minnesota. Prior to Stellent, she was an equity research associate at William Blair & Company in Chicago, where she covered the computer software sector. Amy began her career as a business consultant at Accenture, first in Washington DC and later Chicago. Amy has a BA in Economics from Georgetown University and holds a Masters of Business Administration from the University of Chicago Graduate School of Business, with concentrations in strategy and marketing.

Kazuo Ichijo

Kazuo Ichijo is Professor of Organizational Behaviour at IMD. He is also Professor of the Graduate School of Social Sciences, Graduate School of International Corporate Strategy, both at Hitotsubashi University in Tokyo. He received a BA (social sciences) and MS (social sciences) from Hitotsubashi University and a PhD (business administration) from the University of Michigan. Professor Ichijo's research interests are concentrated on innovation through the process of organizational knowledge creation. His work on organizational knowledge creation is well known around the world. His areas of expertise are the development of knowledge-based competence of a firm, the management of innovation, and corporate transformation. He has published a number of papers in these research areas. His book, *Enabling Knowledge Creation: How to Unlock the Mystery of Tacit Knowledge and Release the Power of Innovation*, published by Oxford University Press in May 2000, is praised as a much-anticipated book providing practical tools into the hands of managers and executives who are struggling to unleash the power of knowledge in their organization. This book has won the Best Business Book of the Year award for 2000 from the Association of American Publisher's Professional and Scientific Publishing Division. Professor Ichijo has also received a wide range of academic recognition. His paper presented at the annual conference of the Strategic Management Society held in Barcelona, October 1997, was selected as one of the best papers. His book titled *Management by Values* (in Japanese) received the '1998 Best Book Award' from the Japan Management Association.

Professor Ichijo has also been actively providing consulting and training to a number of global companies. He has been actively working to help leaders of companies transform their companies and develop future leaders with global perspectives. He has been involved in many corporate transformation activities initiated by leading companies as a consultant and an advisory board member.

Jean-Pierre Jeannet

Jean-Pierre Jeannet is Professor of Global Strategy and Marketing. His areas of special interest are global business and marketing strategies, and market orientation. Professor Jeannet has been a consultant to several international companies and organizations including: ABB, Ciba-Geigy, Coutts & Co (ex-Handelsbank Natwest), DSM, ICI, Johnson & Johnson, Nestlé, Nokia, Polaroid, SMH, Siemens, Sulzer, Swissair, and Zeneca. Professor Jeannet resides part of the year in the US at Babson College and the remaining part of the year in Switzerland as a faculty member at IMD. He received his MBA and PhD from the University of Massachusetts at Amherst. Since 1974 Professor Jeannet has been on the faculty of Babson College, Massachusetts, where he is F. W. Olin Distinguished Professor of Global Business, teaching global marketing and strategy courses at various levels, including MBA and executive programmes. He has also been a Visiting Lecturer at Keio University Graduate School of Business in Japan. In 1981 he became a visiting Professor at IMEDE – one of the two founding institutes of IMD – and has regularly participated in a large number of programmes and in-company seminars. Since 1993, he has had a full-time dual appointment at IMD and Babson College. He has written numerous books and articles, and some 75 cases, on these subjects; most recently: *Global Marketing Strategies*, with H. Hennessy, 5th edition, Houghton Mifflin, 2001; *Cases in Marketing Management*, with D. Dalrymple and L. Parsons, John Wiley & Sons, Ltd, 1992; *The Global Mind, Die Unternehmung*, 1991; *Cases in International Marketing*, with C. Gale, K. Kashani, and D. Turpin, Prentice-Hall, 1995; *Managing with a Global Mindset*, The Financial Times/Prentice-Hall, 2000; *Pathways to Global Success*, Deloitte/ IMD, 2000.

Karsten Jonsen

Karsten Jonsen is Researcher of Organizational Behaviour and International Management at the Institute for Management Development (IMD) in Lausanne, Switzerland. Before coming to IMD in 2002 he held various management positions in the IT industry. He earned his Bachelor and Masters Degrees in Organizational Behaviour and Economics from Copenhagen Business School and an MBA from ESCP-EAP in Paris, France.

Karsten Jonsen is directing a global research project comparing culture between nations. His research interests and publications cover a variety of issues in Human Resource Management, including team performance, executive education, virtual teams, stereotyping, and workforce diversity.

Jean-Pierre Lehmann

Jean-Pierre Lehmann has been Professor of International Political Economy at IMD International Institute for Management Development since January 1997. His main areas of expertise are the socioeconomic and business dynamics of East Asia, the impact of globalization on developing countries, and the government–business interface, especially in respect to the global trade and investment policy process. In 1994 he launched the Evian Group, which consists of high-ranking officials, business executives, independent experts, and opinion leaders from Europe, Asia, and the Americas. The Evian Group's focus is on the international economic order in the global era, specifically the reciprocal impact and influence of international business and the WTO agenda. Jean-Pierre Lehmann acts in various leading capacities in several public policy institutes and organizations.

Prior to joining IMD, Jean-Pierre Lehmann has had both an academic and a business career, which over the years has encompassed activities in virtually all East Asian and Western European countries, as well as North America. He was (from 1992) the founding director of the European Institute of Japanese Studies (EIJS) at the Stockholm School of Economics and Professor of East Asian Political Economy and Business. From 1986 to 1992 he established and directed the East Asian operations of InterMatrix, a London-based business strategy research and consulting organization. During that time he was operating primarily from Tokyo, with offices in Seoul, Taipei, Bangkok, and Jakarta and was concurrently Affiliated Professor of International

Business at the London Business School. Other previous positions include: Associate Professor of International Business at INSEAD (European Institute of Business Administration) in Fontainebleau (France), Visiting Professor at the Bologna Centre (Italy) of the Johns Hopkins University School of Advanced International Studies, twice in the 1970s Visiting Professor and Japan Foundation Fellow at the University of Tohoku, Sendai (Japan), and Founding Director of the Centre for Japanese Studies at the University of Stirling (Scotland), where he also taught East Asian history in the University's History Department. From 1981 to 1986 he directed the EC-ASEAN 'Transfer of Technology and Socio-Economic Development Programmes', held in Singapore, Bangkok, Jakarta, Kuala Lumpur, and Manila. Jean-Pierre Lehmann obtained his undergraduate degree from Georgetown University, Washington DC, and his doctorate from Oxford University (St Antony's College). He is the author of several books and numerous articles and papers dealing primarily with modern East Asian history and East Asia and the international political economy.

Peter Lorange

Peter Lorange has been the President of IMD since 1 July 1993. He is Professor of Strategy and holds the Nestlé Chair. He was formerly President of the Norwegian School of Management in Oslo. Before this, Dr Lorange was affiliated with the Wharton School, University of Pennsylvania, for more than a decade, in various assignments, including director for the Joseph H. Lauder Institute of Management and International Studies, and The William H. Wurster Center for International Management Studies, as well as The William H. Wurster Professor of Multinational Management. He has also taught for 8 years at the Sloan School of Management (at MIT). Dr Lorange is Norwegian. He received his undergraduate education from the Norwegian School of Economics and Business, was awarded an MA degree in Operations Management from Yale University, and his Doctor of Business Administration degree from Harvard University. Dr Lorange has written or edited 15 books and some 110 articles. His areas of special interest are global strategic management, strategic planning, and entrepreneurship for growth. He has conducted extensive research on multinational management, strategic planning processes, and internally generated growth processes. He serves on the board of directors of several corporations including: Christiania Eiendomsselskap, S. Ugelstad Shipowners, StreamServe, Zaruma Resources Inc., Preferred Global Health, and Seaspan Corporation. He is also a board member of IMD and of the Copenhagen Business School.

Donald A. Marchand

Donald A. Marchand is Professor of Strategy and Information Management at the International Institute for Management Development (IMD) in Lausanne, Switzerland. His special interests include managing information and knowledge to drive superior business performance, internet strategy for established companies, demand/supply chain management, and the strategic use and deployment of information systems and technology in companies operating in local, regional, and global markets. Dr Marchand is also Founder, Chairman, and President of enterpriseIQ®, the first global business analytics company offering proven metrics that link superior performance to how effectively a company manages and uses knowledge, information, people, and technology. Professor Marchand was Director of the IMD/Accenture Partnership Research Project entitled Navigating Business Success, which was completed in December 1999. This three-year study examined the perspectives of senior managers on the use of information, people, and IT in achieving superior business performance. The study involved 1200 senior managers and over 200 senior management teams from 103 international companies as well as selected case studies. Oxford University Press published the research findings in *Information Orientation: The Link to Business Performance* (2000), and the management implications were published by John Wiley & Sons, Ltd in *Making the Invisible Visible – How Companies Win with the Right Information, People and IT* (2001).

Professor Marchand is an advisor to senior executives of leading service and manufacturing companies in Europe, North America, and the Asia Pacific. He was a principal researcher in IMD's seven-year research program Manufacturing 2000, and has directed national studies of information technology management in the federal, state, and local governments in the United States. Professor Marchand is the author/co-author of eight books and over 140 articles, book chapters, cases, and reports. He was the senior academic advisor for the 12-week *Financial Times* Series, 'Mastering Information Management', from February to April 1999. The series was published as a book by FT/Prentice-Hall in January 2000. He has also edited the book *Competing with Information*, published by John Wiley & Sons, Ltd in May 2000. The book was the first volume of the IMD Executive Development Series. Professor Marchand is a frequent and acclaimed speaker at corporate seminars and conferences worldwide. For more information, see www.enterpriseIQ.com, www.speakers.co.uk, and www.donaldmarchand.com. From July 1987 to June 1994,

Professor Marchand was Dean and Professor of information management at the School of Information Studies at Syracuse University. In his earlier career, he founded and directed the Institute for Information Management, Technology and Policy in the College of Business at the University of South Carolina, where he also taught information systems management in the Master's International Business Program. Professor Marchand is American. He received his PhD and MA at UCLA and his BA at the University of California at Berkeley, where he was elected to Phi Beta Kappa. He has also served as Vice President of Worldwide Chapter and Alliance Development for the Society for Information Management (SIM International), the leading global association for senior executives, academics, and consultants in IT management.

Karin Oppegaard

Karin Oppegaard is a Research Associate at IMD specializing in ethical leadership, sustainability, and corporate social responsibility. She is equally a doctoral student at the University of Lausanne; her thesis focuses on the role of mindfulness in leadership development. She has previously worked as a research assistant for INSEAD in the context of RESPONSE, a European-wide study of Corporate Social Responsibility. She has also worked as a dissertation fellow at the Imagination Lab Foundation in Lausanne, Switzerland, on the role of Aristotelian Practical Wisdom in leadership.

Ralf W. Seifert

Ralf W. Seifert is Professor of Operations Management at IMD. His primary research and teaching interests relate to operations management, supply-chain management, and technology network management. He is also interested in entrepreneurship, industry analysis, and international project work. Professor Seifert is director of the Mastering Technology Enterprise (MTE) programme, a six-week management development programme for technically trained managers. The MTE programme is jointly offered by the Alliance for Technology-Based Enterprise, formed by IMD, EPFL and ETH Zurich. Professor Seifert has also designed and directed a variety of company-specific partnership programmes at IMD and served as consultant and speaker to leading multinational companies.

Before joining IMD in 2000, Professor Seifert studied and worked in Germany, Japan, and the US. He consulted for Hewlett-Packard Company, Booz Allen, and McKinsey & Company, and worked for Freudenberg & Co. In parallel with his role at IMD, Professor Seifert holds a tenured professorship at the Swiss Federal Institute of Technology (EPFL) in Lausanne, where he directs the Chair of Technology and Operations Management (TOM). Professor Seifert earned PhD and MS degrees in the Department of Management Science and Engineering at Stanford University, a Diplom-Ingenieur degree in Mechanical Engineering from the University of Karlsruhe (TH) and a Masters degree in Integrated Manufacturing Systems Engineering (MIMSE) from North Carolina State University. In addition, he spent one year as a Visiting Scholar in Operations Research at Waseda University in Tokyo.

A member of INFORMS and POMS, Professor Seifert regularly presents his research in leading international journals and conferences. He serves as referee for several peer-reviewed periodicals and supervises doctoral student works as principal thesis advisor. Professor Seifert has co-authored about 30 case studies and teaching notes. These efforts have been recognized by a number of international case awards, granted by ECCH in 2006, POMS in 2004, and EFMD in 2003. Professor Seifert has been awarded three scholarships: an ERP Scholarship by the Federal Ministry of Economics and Technology of Germany; a Japan Scholarship by DaimlerChrysler AG and McKinsey & Company, Inc.; and a Fulbright Scholarship by the Fulbright Commission, Germany. Formerly he was a member of the German National Merit Foundation and the Siemens International Student Circle. He is a recipient of the Grashof Prize and of the Honors of the Jubiläums-Staats-Stiftung of the University of Karlsruhe (TH). He is married and has two children.

Thomas Vollmann
Thomas Vollmann is Professor (Emeritus) of Manufacturing Management at IMD. His areas of special interest are: manufacturing planning and control, performance measurement, supply-chain management, and enterprise transformation. He is a consultant to numerous companies in manufacturing, benchmarking, and supply/demand-chain management and a lecturer in executive development programmes throughout the world. He has been actively involved in executive education, notably as Professor of Business Administration at Indiana University, as Professor at INSEAD, as Professor of Operations Management at Boston University, and as Professor at the University of

Rhode Island and Dartmouth College. He graduated from the University of California, Los Angeles, where he later gained his MBA and PhD. He is the author of numerous books and articles, most recently *Manufacturing Planning and Control Systems*, 5th edition, with W. L. Berry and D. C. Whybark (McGraw-Hill Companies, 2005) and 'The Next Game in Purchasing', with Carlos Cordon, *The Smart Manager*, July–September 2004.

John Ward

John Ward is The Wild Group Professor of Family Business at IMD, and also a professor at the Kellogg School of Management (USA). He is co-director of IMD's renowned 'Leading the Family Business' program, in which he has taught since its inception in 1988. He is also co-director of the Lombard Odier Darier Hentsch Family Business Research Centre at IMD. His teaching and research interests are in family enterprise continuity, governance, company culture, philanthropy, and sustainable strategy. John Ward has authored several books, including the bestselling *Keeping the Family Business Healthy, Creating Effective Boards for Private Enterprises, Strategic Planning for the Family Business*, and the just published *Perpetuating the Family Business*, as well as the *Family Business Leadership Series*, many cases, and numerous articles. He serves on the boards of four companies in Europe and North America and three nonprofit boards.

Michael Yaziji

Michael Yaziji is Professor of Strategy and Organizations at IMD. His primary interests are in the areas of strategy formulation and implementation, nonmarket strategy, stakeholder management, and change management. His current research focuses on relationships between corporations and nongovernmental organizations (NGOs), e.g. Greenpeace, Friends of the Earth, PETA, and WWF. He studies both campaigns by NGOs against corporations as well as collaborative partnerships between corporations and NGOs. His recent publications on the topic include 'Turning Gadflies into Allies' in *The Harvard Business Review* (2004) and 'Toward a Theory of Social Risk: Antecedents of Normative Delegitimation' in *International Studies of Management and Organization* (2005).

Michael's articles have been translated into many languages and he is also a contributor to *The Financial Times*, *INSEAD Quarterly*, and *The European Management Journal*.

He was recently awarded a contract with Cambridge University Press for a book on NGO-Corporate relationships as part of a series edited by Ed Freeman. He has consulted for leading corporations such as Microsoft, Cisco, and AP Moller Maersk in the areas of market and nonmarket strategy formulation and implementation, corporate values, and stakeholder management. In addition to being a keynote speaker at various think-tanks including L'Institut Français des Relations Internationals and The Copenhagen Centre, Michael is a Visiting Fellow at INSEAD. He is also a member of the World Economic Forum Roundtable on Public–Private Partnerships in Health whose report is being studied at the 2005 UN high-level meeting. Michael was the founding director of the Business and Society Forum at INSEAD, which included notable speakers such as Robert Reich (US Secretary of Labor under Clinton), Dan Esty (Yale), David Vogel (Berkeley), and Robert Frank (Cornell). With a PhD in Management from INSEAD, Michael's educational background also includes a PhD in Analytic Philosophy from the University of California. His INSEAD Management dissertation research focused on NGO campaigns against corporations. It was based on the largest global survey of campaigning NGOs. The research provided insights into the goals, tactics, target selection criteria, dynamic interactions, and effects of these campaigns against corporations. Michael's doctoral research in Analytic Philosophy focused on the epistemological and ontological status of ethics.

Foreword by the Editors

'Managing complexity' is fast becoming the metachallenge for managers and one of the latest business buzzwords, often more a diffuse synonym for 'complicated'. On a heuristic level, parallels can be drawn with system or even chaos theories. However, the stories do not extend very far, because in social organizations where there are no natural/scientific/mathematical laws at play, it is all about human interaction.

As we were mainly interested in management application, we largely skipped these parallels and tried to establish in Chapter 1 a conceptual framework, to which managers can relate based on their experience. As tested in several executive programmes at IMD, it helped participants to understand better the often confusing, contradictionary, and rapidly changing conditions, which shaped their work and constantly force them to adapt in order to survive. Especially in global, 'boundaryless' organizations, which are for us the incarnation of complex organizations, the complexity drivers of interdependence, ambiguity, and diversity in a fast flux match the experience of executives working in such organizations.

In the complexity debate, reference is often made to 'Ashby's Law of Requisite Variety', stating that the internal complexity has to meet the external one. We disagree as organizations can easily be overwhelmed by a high internal complexity. For us it was therefore vital to identify 'simplifiers', which can help managers to cope with complexity on a practical level. We identified shared values, decentralization, and (standardized) processes as the three main levers that managers can apply to cope with the uncertainties and develop a robust strategy.

In the 'good old days', the confrontation was between workers and capitalists, a conflict increasingly moderated by state intervention after the Great Depression in 1929. However, this 'triangle' has given way to a much more pluralistic stakeholder landscape, which is described in Chapter 2. From financial analysts to environmental and social pressure groups, a vast number of stakeholders place their demands on companies, which developed special functions to manage these demands, but to set priorities correctly and respond effectively and in a timely manner remains an ongoing challenge.

The complexity increases again dramatically, if one moves from the corporate micro-perspective to the political macroperspective, as done in Chapter 3. The sheer number of players with different interests – and no simplifier at hand – makes the international negotiations very cumbersome, slow, and unpredictable for companies.

In Part II we 'return' to the industry level, because – as explained in Chapter 4 – the complexity drivers are mainly shaped by the industry dilemmas and competitive inter-dependencies, complemented by the existence of fast flux and uncertainty. This can be seen in the shipping industry (Chapter 5), which has become a much more integrated global market, where dynamics in one area (e.g. demand in China) shape the interde-pendent market conditions and force competitors' fast reactions, which increase the cyclicality.

Another industry-specific constellation is described in Chapter 6. It could thus be in highly consolidated markets as, for example, the auto industry, where competitors try to balance a set of dilemmas (please note a managerial dilemma is defined as the simultaneous existence of goals, which are all legitimate, but not complementing each other, or which could not be reached in a given time or with given resources). Moving from one priority to the next, the interdependency of competitors in a narrow oligopoly drives a series of rapid responses, which has a high probability of destroying profit margins.

Chapter 7 looks at the complexity of the supply chain as it is generated by the deepening global division of labour (usually described as outsourcing) and how the resulting interdependency in a sector driven by rapid technological progress can be managed.

As seen already in Chapter 6, complexity leads to the permanent search for a viable, sustainable business model, an issue that is explained in Chapter 8 with the Financial Service Industry as a representative example.

In Part III we move from the external market and political environment to the internal organization of global companies and look at the complexity generated in different functions or areas of corporate actions. As explained in Chapter 9, the functional complexities are often driven by the challenges triggered by diversity, heterogeneity in the presence of fast flux, and uncertainty.

This can be seen in Chapter 10, where the inability to find a 'one size fits all' approach to diverse markets leads to an unseen complexity in the strategy design and implementation, which are very difficult to manage. The need to simplify is as obvious as the obstacles that need to be overcome.

Chapter 11 carries this a step further into the high-tech area, R&D, and innovation. Here, the fast flux is even more rapid than in other areas and thus creates the need for different solutions. The next four chapters focus on the specific functional contributions needed to manage the diversity of global organizations more effectively. Humans – and their brains – are probably the most complex biological design on Earth; no wonder that humans contribute considerably to complexity. Chapter 12 outlines how managing diversity beyond a very narrow understanding of HRM can add value.

Chapter 13 describes how IT can shift from a complexity driver to a simplifier by designing processes accordingly and in an effort to change the behaviour, how information is managed in a global organization. This is a theme which is extended in Chapter 14 to include the issue of knowledge management, especially managing knowledge-based competences in a global organization. Chapter 15 deals with the external battle between marketing, generating diversity by following specific customer demands, against manufacturing and the supply chain, and by seeking economies of scale through standardization (some say 'uniformization').

Part IV enlarges our focus on complexity management again. Chapter 16 and the subsequent chapters explore the resulting learning needs, while simultaneously remaining sensitive to special contingencies, such as different ownership structures. It is shown how complexity negatively affects the 'bottom line', but the ability to cope with it in turn enhances profitability. M&A should often help companies leapfrog, but complexify the life of managers if not handled properly, as outlined in Chapter 17. As mentioned before, one of the key simplifiers are shared values; everyone can learn from the family business how they are managing their dilemmas, as described in Chapter 18. In Chapter 19 we have wrapped up the key learning and gaze a bit into the crystal ball.

Ulrich Steger, Wolfgang Amann, and Martha Maznevski

Acknowledgements

L ike every work in academia, this book builds on many contributions. We learned a lot not only from the cooperation with individual contributors but also from the insights of other colleagues, in particular Joe DiStefano and Philip Rosenzweig, who inspired us and provided great stimuli.

Special thanks must go to the executives in IMD executive programmes and board retreats, with whom we discussed the concept of complexity and its application in many brainstorming sessions (we are still sure that some must have felt a bit like guinea pigs!). We owe special thanks to Marcus Rettich and the DaimlerChrysler Corporate University for an in-depth reflection on the methodological and deductive design of complexity teams in learning events.

This book reinforced our conviction that IMD is a great place to conduct relevant, cutting-edge research. Special thanks to Peter Lorange, Jim Ellert, and Benoît Leleux for creating an encouraging framework and making resources available. We are also grateful to those who supported us in the background: Lindsay McTeague, Michelle Perrinjaquet, Beverly Lennox, and, last but not least, Kathy Schwartz. All shortcomings and omissions, however, are the sole responsibility of the editors who put this all together.

The Editors
Lausanne, October 2006

Part I

Conceptual Framework and Trends on the Macro-level

1
Managing Complexity in Global Organizations as the Meta-challenge

Martha Maznevski, Ulrich Steger, and Wolfgang Amann

How it all began

'Complexity' is currently often considered the latest business buzzword – it reflects a current common reality, but not a lasting one. Whenever the complexity concept is introduced to executives in globally operating companies, the response is: 'Yes, complexity is the real leadership challenge that I face. How can I focus on my area when everything else is connected? How can I be held accountable when everything is interdependent? How can I sort this out? It's overwhelming.' These are good questions with few answers. 'Complexity' is much more than a buzzword – rather a reality that is here to stay. Therefore the origin and generators of complexity will first be considered before presenting some of the answers that some companies have found to respond to complexity.

Complexity was multiplied to its current heightened level because globalization entails a far-reaching erosion of boundaries, a process that is still ongoing. Many types of boundaries have faded: trade liberalization has substantially alleviated the flow of goods, capital, people, and knowledge around the globe. The world has clearly moved beyond the key triad markets. Internationalizing companies from developed and developing economies try to tap the benefits of globalization to an unprecedented degree and therefore face – as well as contribute to – the complexity of eroding boundaries. Various motives rank high on the list of possible drivers of foreign expansion, such as learning, spreading risk, gaining access to new customers, realizing economies of scale and scope, or optimizing a value proposition with partners. However, the road to the 'Promised Land' turns out to be more demanding than expected, and complexity is the most common and pervasive challenge that arises.

Complexity is seen as a core challenge of present and future companies. Complexity cannot just be made simple and will not disappear in the near future. Managing complexity must therefore become a core competency of top executives and management. As a first step, it is crucial to understand what drives complexity.

What generates complexity?

In this research, four major sources of complexity have been identified that interact together to create today's environment. Each of these sources of complexity was created by the erosion of boundaries, but their effects differ.

1. **Diversity**. Global organizations face a complex set of challenges characterized by diversity both inside and outside the organization. This is more than just diverse sets of people as is often thought, but rather diversity across every aspect of the business itself. Inside the organization, for example, executives must manage and respond to more diversity in the (internationalizing) human resources (HR) pool; more variety in the management systems; more variety in the means and ends, ranging from simple financial goals to a more comprehensive view; and different business models for different types of business units. Outside the organization, there is also higher diversity, e.g. heterogeneous customer needs; differing cultural values; a plethora of stakeholders with different claims (investors, customers, employees, regulators, etc.); various political, economic, and legal environments; and, finally, competitors' differing strategies. While diversity on these dimensions used to be

limited within a firm, most firms increasingly face each of these types of diversity. Managing differences is not trivial, and reducing the diversity often means being less responsive.

2. **Interdependence**. In addition, companies must manage the effect of global inter-dependence within business to an unprecedented degree: everything is related to everything else and the impact is felt both more quickly and more pervasively. Value webs have replaced traditional value chains. Reputation, financial flows, value chain flows, top management, and corporate governance issues have reached advanced levels of interdependence. Managers have to take the effects of nonlocal events into account. The less clear-cut the boundaries of a company become, the more it is exposed to impacts on the value chain flow through mistakes, frictions, reverse trends, or even shocks. Risks appear as quickly as opportunities are captured or missed. Interdependence creates opportunities for globalization, but taking advantage of these opportunities raises difficult challenges.

3. **Ambiguity**. The business world today is characterized by too much information with less and less clarity on how to interpret and apply insights. A diversity of accounting standards renders financial figures ambiguous. Studies, scenarios, survey results, and reports become less reliable due to an ever-increasing uncertainty. Cause–effect relationships become difficult to determine; e.g. many businesses find it more and more difficult to discover what their clear value drivers are. Are they image, price, related services, privileged relationships, speed, knowledge, or something else? Cause–effect relationships have become blurred.

4. **Flux**. As if these three complexity drivers were not enough, managers have to face yet another – flux, in other words change that has a changing nature. Even if (temporary) solutions regarding interdependence, diversity, and ambiguity have been figured out for a specific company, industry, and personal situation, the situation may change the next day. Today's solutions (and especially those of the past) may be outdated tomorrow. Changes occur in many directions at once, and at faster and faster rates.

What are the repercussions?

Everything is diverse and nothing is stable; everything is in 'fast flux'. Interdependence is flowing in changing directions. The future is no longer the prolongation of the past – industry 'breakpoints' that fundamentally alter the value proposition in industries occur more rapidly. Any prediction could occur through sheer luck, as multiple influencing factors can materialize in different ways. The variety of options could overwhelm traditional decision making, as information often lacks clarity and is ambiguous. Multiple interpretations of the same facts are possible, depending on the prospective or cultural framework. No shared understanding can be assumed per se, whether inside or outside the organization. Thus, interdependence, diversity, and ambiguity – all in flux – are the building blocks of managerial complexity and explain why global companies have often been perceived as the most complex of organizations.

Many people have tried to simplify the complexity, and most contemporary management literature is misleading in this regard. As our colleague Philip Rosenzweig has argued in detail in his book, *The Halo Effect and Other Business Delusions*, current developments have grave impacts on management theory. Much has been written to cater to managers' desire for certainty. Studies typically examine successful companies to see what managers 'did' and then conclude that all managers should act similarly. Since unpredictability makes people uncomfortable, delusions are created regarding performance as a voluntaristic matter of choice (companies can choose 'to be great'); they like the certainty promised by these solutions. However, in an interdependent world, much depends on contingencies that have no clear distinction between input and output. Managers' accountability therefore contains an arbitrary element: yes, they are responsible, but results are influenced by factors beyond their control. This does not, however, mean that 'blind destiny' or 'luck' rules, but that navigating through this complexity requires a different way of thinking, acting, and organizing than the typical 'control' mentality.

Is management doomed, or are there solutions?

A long list of advantages lures companies into globalizing. Geographic expansion abroad offers the vast potential benefits of a much larger market arena, spreads risks, gives scope-, scale-, and location-based cost advantages, and provides exposure to a variety of new product and process ideas. However, without the ability to cope with the associated complexities, managers risk having reality lagging behind their expectations.

The practical consequence of complexity is that a dilemma often shapes the decision-making process. A managerial dilemma occurs, when:

- there are two or more conflicting legitimate goals to meet demands;
- both cannot be simultaneously achieved with the given resources.

For example, companies in the financial service industry set up competing distribution channels, but expect far-reaching cooperation across the company (e.g. shared services and product platforms) to reap economics of scale. In manufacturing, one ongoing dilemma is between global standardization and response to global market needs. Any required priority decision results in tension. As dilemmas cannot be solved, they need to be managed – continuously.

Global companies first reacted to this complex business environment by creating complex organizations. This was consistent with Ashby's law of requisite variety that an organization's internal complexity should match the complexity of its external environment. Multiple axes of management have been seen along product lines, geographical dimensions, customers, functions, and projects – one global company had a six-dimensional matrix structure (for a short time, at least). The simple relation between headquarters as strategic decision makers and subsidiaries as implementers is further blurred by centres of excellence or competence, market responsibilities, joint ventures, etc. To bind all of this together formally, companies often resort to sophisticated corporate policies on nearly everything: from strategy formation to anti-harassment. Add all of this together and it can be seen that it easily matches the volume of a federal law register.

However, structures and policies alone are not the solution. The more complex structures and policies become, the more complex they are to manage. The organization eventually implodes, spending more time managing the internal complexity than interacting with the environment, where real value is created.

Companies that are beginning to grapple with complexity in effective ways interpret Ashby's law differently. They harness the complexity already inherent within the organization – in people, their relationships, and so on – to work for the company rather than against it. They add Thoreau's advice to the recipe: simplify, simplify! However, they carefully choose what they simplify, without making the organization or its processes too simple.

The overall advice recommended in this book is to focus on the professional quality of decision making and to simplify organizational processes in specific ways, rather than predicting the outcome and simplifying a personal picture of the environment.

Simplify a few key issues: use complexity as an opportunity elsewhere

Four key issues have been identified around which companies must simplify: purpose and values, core processes and decentralization, early awareness systems, and leadership. Once these are clear and consistent throughout the company, managers in different parts of the company can respond to complexity in their areas according to their needs and realities.

It starts with purpose and values as fundamental issues. The purpose, the reason for being in this business, is a 'guiding star' on the horizon, a framework for prioritizing goals. Every business book mentions the importance of purpose and values, so perhaps this is nothing new. In simple and stable environments, the vision, even if it is a wishy-washy vague statement not clearly understood by everyone, can provide enough guidance for people to manage well. In a complex environment, however, the guidance provided by a clear statement of the purpose and values is critical. Every manager in the company should understand clearly and deeply what really drives the business, what the fundamentals of the business's profitability are, and why the company is in business. Once this is understood, it leads to the values, the business 'shoulds and oughts', that determine priorities in dilemmas, help focus the actions, and provide consistent patterns of behaviour over time. The companies best at dealing with complexity never have more than three or four core values, i.e. values that are never to be compromised and are consistent with a compelling business logic that explains why they are so important. A longer 'laundry list' of values is confusing at best and at worst is a rationale for any action. At the same time, it is helpful to have a few behavioural values beyond the core that guide the 'how' of the execution; behavioural values can be compromised, but every deviation must be explained. A clearly defined and well-accepted set of core values plus a guiding set of behavioural values therefore allows diversity at the periphery, empowerment for local adaptation, learning and experimentation, the existence of additional values per region, unit, profession, etc., as long as they do not contradict the core values.

Besides alignment according to values, another key lever to manage complexity is a combination of standardized core processes and decentralized authority. Core processes are those used by the entire company. Core processes vary from business to business, but most managers know what is vital. For example, in a consulting firm, the core processes might be knowledge sharing and recruiting; in a heavy manufacturing firm, they might be capital budgeting and logistics; in a pharmaceuticals firm, they might be research and development and go-to-market processes. A firm's core processes should always be standardized (not necessarily centralized) and based on comprehensive, accessible information platforms. Such processes might change over time, and more often than the business model or the core values. It is therefore important to erase old processes when introducing new ones (often complexity is mistaken for legacy – the idea that one just piles everything new on to the old). Only standardized processes generate the transparency that is key for accountability on the levels further down the organization. With such transparency and accountability, decentralization is possible without the company breaking down into political silos and bickering fiefdoms. In turn, decentralization that is consistent with the core processes allows local managers to address complexity in a way that is most effective for them.

As complexity creates many unpredictable situations, managers need an early awareness system. This sounds like a contradiction, but it is not. Chaos is simply a degree of complexity with rules and drivers that are not fully understood. It is comparable to a weather-forecasting system: never completely right, but rarely completely wrong. Early awareness does not need sophisticated systems or much workforce. It is a mindset, a sensitivity that allows 'weak signals' indicating emerging change and foresight to be understood. To deal with complexity, the variables that create predictable outcomes should be identified when they are within a specific range and unpredictable outcomes when they are not. As one executive recently said, 'We track hurricanes. As long as they stay outside this range, we don't pay much attention or put anything into action. But as soon as they hit inside this range, we start to put our contingency plans into place.' When facing complexity, managers need to identify which 'hurricanes' they need to track and which levels or ranges should trigger contingency plans.

Leading a complex organization requires an entirely different mindset. A hierarchy works if every level is doing something distinct and specific. However, due to the interdependence in complexity, this is impossible in today's organizations. By simplifying and clarifying vision and values, core processes and decentralization, and early awareness systems, the hierarchy can give way to 'heterarchy', a networked organization in which every part reflects a different perspective of the whole. The boss need no longer 'tell' the team members what exactly to do (in high complexity a 'telling' style does not lead to responsiveness), but can depend on their initiative, creativity, and competence for success. Leadership in a networked organization means not only providing different leadership roles and styles depending on the situation (but always consistent with the purpose, values, and core processes), but also means leading the different parts of a networked organization so they can work together to create value. The leader of a complex organization must create and communicate understanding of the different roles that managers, teams, business units, and bosses play in the interdependent structure; otherwise, the confusion is intensified. Leadership cannot be repetitive, but should be predictable. Permanent communication is therefore *the* leadership survival tool in complex organizations, but much more in terms of 'storytelling', interpreting context and meaning, and investing in relationships than in transferring dry facts or ultimatums.

How does it work in practice? The authors have not yet come across a company that has mastered global complexity – perhaps there are none; perhaps there will never be any! However, the various sections of this book identify several global companies that highlight various aspects of managing complexity, or the effects of not managing it well. The decade-long difficulties of General Motors (GM) – and to a lesser degree, Ford – clearly have their roots in the company's traditional control mode, which has led to GM's vast bureaucracy and a typical outcome: mediocre products due to risk aversion, mistrust of management (reflected in the high degree of unionization), high-transaction costs, and slow response. A counter-example is Toyota with its very clear value set (which is being challenged as the company becomes truly global) and its simpler worldwide core business processes and standardized processes model (the famous notion that every Toyota engineer can work in any Toyota factory around the world without encountering adaptation problems is probably slightly exaggerated, but only slightly. . .).

A similar set of elements is found in many other global companies: family businesses, a luxury goods business (due to identification with the product), and Dupont (known for its strong values). Research and development (R&D)-driven industries, such as the pharmaceutical industry, are known for focused business models. Energy companies, especially Exxon Mobile, are driven by standardized global processes, whereas fast-moving custom goods and the food industry are known for their strong regional decentralization, but are bound together and have shared processes across business lines. In the following, a real world, real learning example is provided to illustrate complexity drivers and simplifiers further.

Complexity drivers and simplifiers in action – a case study

Allianz, Europe's largest insurance provider, had integrated all the previously separated and more-or-less fragmented parts of its global insurance industry into a new division called 'Allianz Global Corporate & Speciality (AGCS)'. The complexity drivers were all in place: different cultures, different processes, different client focuses with different product offers, and high uncertainty about the portfolio of contract values (surprises had previously led to losses being incurred in some units). This happened in a cyclical market with fragmented regulation and a nature-driven chance of significant risks like storms and floods.

The new CEO (Chief Executive Officer) of the division, Dr Axel Theis, realized that he had no chance of success if he were to let all the complexity drivers continue to work in the new, much bigger company. He also realized that he was caught on the horns of a dilemma: to offer more comprehensive customer-focused solutions, he needed to remove silos and push for an increasingly boundary-less company, although this would increase the interdependence between the units and, thus, the internal complexity. Without a new approach, complexity would overwhelm the organization. Creating boundaries would also limit the impact on a specific organization if an event were to occur. Boundaries would, however, make it impossible to serve clients globally, while the elimination of boundaries would allow the impact of any event to 'travel' throughout the organization, triggering many responses and interventions as the organization became increasingly interdependent. How could this cycle be broken and the dilemma managed?

After deciding on the basic structure of and appointments to the key management functions, the new CEO arranged a three-day retreat for his executive team and most of their direct reports (underlings who prepare reports). The challenge was clear: understand what it means to work in one global company and draw the necessary managerial conclusions to make the new division a sustainable success.

The group's first focus was to identify what it meant to be a global company. This was emphasized as being the only option given the current market conditions, the clients' demands, and the portfolio risk diversification. The latter was important, as in order to have sufficient risk diversification, certain products in this segment of insurance can only be offered globally. After consensus had been reached, the big question was: what did globalization mean for the the unit's operation? The top team had identified four complementary building blocks that followed from the core decision that the unit needed to be global: focus on the global processes, a specific approach to client focus, excellence in risk management, and being an 'Employer of Choice'.

In the Financial Services industry, any product innovation can be copied easily and immediately. Therefore the entire value proposition to the customer is critical, as is excellence in risk management (which not only influences the prices to be charged but also the products that can be offered). Customers in this segment are professional and it is extremely important to understand their specific risks and to speak their 'language'. Tailoring solutions would definitely increase complexity, but a sure solution was to have standards and modules regarding underwriting, client relations, and claims handling besides the additional technical services. Units could then cooperate seamlessly and innovative solutions would not be a barrier to consistency in service quality. This meant that the risk management system would have to be improved, so that decisions regarding whether, and at what price, risk could be underwritten were taken quickly – additional advice might also help to mitigate or reduce risks.

However, without global processes and a qualified and dedicated workforce, even a good value proposition and excellence in risk management could not produce sustainable results. A set of criteria was developed to determine the most effective processes for global application and to implement them rapidly throughout the organization. As usual, a huge challenge was to overcome the information technology (IT) 'legacy systems', and the restrictions that they imposed on the organization. The management team again faced a dilemma: making life easier for customers could make it more complex for the organization. 'Where do you need to embrace complexity to add value for customers?' was the critical question raised by Axel Theis.

To avoid 'airy-fairy' visions (which are sometimes difficult to distinguish from hallucinations), the top management team's next focus was the three key stakeholder groups: clients, shareholders (in this case, headquarters), and employees. It was important to identify what these stakeholder groups expected from the new division and what could be offered them. For example, with respect to the employees, the team defined what they were promised (e.g. international career opportunities, high rewards for high performance, etc.) and also what the organization expected from them (e.g. result orientation, openness to change, etc.). Once this had been determined, the management team developed an easy-to-tell but compelling 'strategy story', which included the goals and vision for the following three to five years and the actions that were needed to move in that direction. Optimizing the communication to the three stakeholders was essential in terms of reducing the complexity to ensure that there would be no difference between expectations and delivery.

This formulation of the strategy, based on the building blocks, brought about a push in alignment and helped to reduce the internal diversity. It created a focus on global, standardized processes that further reduced internal complexity and made interdependence more manageable. Furthermore, excellence in risk management reduced ambiguity and uncertainty in key value-creation areas. Together with the 'Employer of Choice' strategy, it allowed for a more decentralized organization that could experiment and test new ideas to respond to the ongoing changes in the environment. The implementation does, of course, now need some time, but it is no longer an impossible mission – it is building on key simplifying processes. The alignment within the company helps to prevent the complexity outside the company from being overwhelming. The AGCS management is convinced that building the competencies of managing such complexity is creating a competitive advantage for this global insurance division.

2

The Complexity of Managing Corporate Social Responsibility in Multinationals

Michael Yaziji and Karin Oppegaard

Introduction

What are the roles and responsibilities of the corporation? What should corporations do and not do? Where does the boundary lie between moral obligation and discretionary corporate action to improve societal well-being? How are managers to deal with the complexity that surrounds these issues of corporate social responsibility?

As well as facing all the complexity involved in simply navigating toward a single goal of sustained profitable growth, managers are simultaneously being challenged about the appropriateness of such a singular goal. There are seemingly ever-increasing calls from various sectors for businesses to take on additional social or economic goals beyond mere firm performance; i.e. there are calls for greater corporate social responsibility (CSR).

Managers who have begun to dabble in – or even take a deep dive into – issues of CSR quickly find that 'doing the right thing' is neither easy nor obvious. Discussions with hundreds of executives concerning CSR have underscored just how difficult and complex – from both ethical and strategic standpoints – the issues are.

There is deep complexity along at least two different dimensions: ethical complexity and institutional complexity. In this chapter we will focus on how these two forms of complexity impact on the understanding and efforts of multinational corporations to pursue CSR and sustained profitable growth.

Ethical complexity is the result of difficulty in establishing clear ethical truths. As an academic field, ethics is filled with ambiguity and uncertainty. As a result, in many situations figuring out with certainty what constitutes the responsibility of the firm is, it will be argued, impossible. Managers who are personally motivated to do the right thing can easily be overwhelmed with various ethical conundrums. Even the best professional ethicists will be the first to admit that they have no ready 'pat' answers. Managers clamor for answers and it is tempting for ethicists to oblige. Often, the best that ethicists can do is to provide ethical guidance which sounds good in the abstract, but which is exceedingly difficult to apply in practice.

Simultaneously, managers face a great deal of institutional complexity. Corporations – especially multinational corporations – have resource dependencies on a large number of stakeholders whose different ideological and ethical perspectives are often competing or conflicting. These stakeholders can question whether a firm is living up to its responsibilities and whether it is acting legitimately. Powerful stakeholders that question the legitimacy of the firm or its actions can generate *social risk* for the firm, as will be seen in more detail below. Managers who are simply attempting to keep the firm profitable will find challenges in navigating this institutional complexity and the incompatible demands that it generates.

In this chapter we will first discuss the ethical complexity of CSR and its consequences for everyday decision making and interpersonal dynamics in the workplace. We will then move on to discuss the institutional complexity of CSR and its consequences for managers. It will be seen that ethical and institutional complexity are fundamentally related and tend to reinforce each other. We will close with a discussion of how managers may want to deal with these multiple levels of complexity, in order to come up with viable solutions for both the firm *and* society.

The ethical complexity of corporate social responsibility

Underlying dynamics

Any issue that has implications for people's welfare necessarily concerns norms and values. When norms and values are involved, there are no clear-cut guiding principles for the decision maker, who is often torn between different values and ethical principles. As a result, such issues frequently generate cognitive dissonance and emotional ambivalence for the person who is responsible for taking action.

Festinger's theory of cognitive dissonance specifies how individuals may hold inconsistent beliefs and how they attempt to resolve this dissonance.[1] While Festinger specified cognitions in his theory, individuals also experience emotional ambivalence, i.e. 'having mixed emotions and being torn in their attitude toward an object'.[2–4]

Emotional ambivalence and cognitive dissonance become salient in contexts where moral judgement is required. Most people simultaneously hold multiple and conflicting moral beliefs and sentiments. They might, for example, feel or believe that killing an innocent being is always wrong, but simultaneously feel or believe that they may be morally obligated to kill innocents for the greater good or to prevent more killings of more innocents in the future. This ethical tension and conflict within a person is magnified by the inherent complexity of moral evaluations.

Moral reasoning, from specific moral claims about a particular action down to the most foundational moral principles, is hierarchical, in that specific moral evaluations are built upon increasingly general and fundamental moral principles and values. This is witnessed whenever a justification for a specific moral claim is given. For instance, I might claim that it is morally appropriate to fib to a child about the existence of Santa Claus. Asked to defend this, I might say that it brings the child happiness and that is why it is morally good. Pushed further, I might resort to a utilitarian argument that supports the claim that the right action is that which maximizes overall utility and that fibbing, therefore, is morally appropriate in this context.

Moral philosophers have long recognized the distinction between different levels of moral thinking (moving from abstract to concrete or, in other words, from fundamental to issue-specific). Scholars have made the distinction between narrow applications of moral principles and the general principles upon which they are based.[5] For example, social contract theorists have noted the difference between reasoning about what general social contract is to be adopted (e.g. hypernorms) and how to apply this contract in specific everyday situations (micro-norms) (see References 5 to 9). Consequentialists recognize distinctions between what defines the 'good', how maximization of the good is to be calculated, and everyday moral evaluations using this maximizing principle.[10,11] Rights theorists recognize the distinction between rights (e.g. a negative right to life) and applications of the rights (e.g. what type of beings have this right). In the following analysis, we will focus on examples of how a single moral judgement is incredibly complex in terms of the number of levels at which there may be uncertainty.

Table 2.1 illustrates how different moral reasoning may look, depending on the level of abstraction and generality. The example is drawn from the human rights campaign claim, which stated that workers at Nike's suppliers' factories in Vietnam were being mistreated.[12]

This table shows different levels of generality of reasoning and possible beliefs/sentiments and counter-beliefs/sentiments associated with it. These sets of beliefs, norms, and values are 'nested' in that some of them are more general and fundamental than others. If we start at the top of the table, at Level 1, we find a belief that 'respecting rights' is an inviolable moral principle. As suggested above, although many people in Western cultures agree that rights are sacred and inalienable, many of the same people also support the 'counter-belief' that, for example, it is unfortunate, but morally acceptable, to unintentionally kill innocents in a justifiable war. There is some moral dissonance and ambivalence within individuals between beliefs/attitudes and counter-beliefs/attitudes at the same level of abstraction. One level down, even if one fully believes at Level 1 that respecting rights is an inviolable principle, one could be ambivalent about whether the application of this principle (Level 2) is enough to ensure that no rights are violated. At Level 3, the reasoning becomes more concrete, since it is applied to a specific societal context. However, the same phenomenon persists, in which a given belief and its counter-belief might coexist within an individual. Finally, when the fundamental principle is applied to a specific case (here, a Nike plant in

Table 2.1 Hierarchy of moral reasoning

Level of generality	Issues of dissonance or ambivalence	Example of belief/sentiment	Counter-belief/sentiment
1. Basic principles	Foundational moral principles (e.g. rights-based, consequentialist, social contract, virtue theories)	Respecting rights is an inviolable moral principle	Respecting rights is not an inviolable moral principle. Rights may be violated if doing so substantially increases overall social welfare and/or minimizes future rights violations
2. Application of the basic principles	Theories of free choice; economic theories; definitions of 'free market' and 'mutual consent'	Free market arrangements are a form of mutual consent. As such, agreements made in the free market do not constitute violations of rights	Free market arrangements are not a form of mutual consent because the differences in market power make free consent illusory
3. General facts about the context	Facts about standard Vietnamese employer–employee relationships; categorization criteria of free market arrangements	Standard Vietnamese employer–employee relationships are free market arrangements	Standard Vietnamese employer–employee relationships are not free market arrangements because the government prevents unionization and distorts bargaining power
4. Specific facts of the case	Facts about the firms; categorization criteria of standard Vietnamese employer–employee relationships	Nike suppliers use standard Vietnamese employer–employee relationships	Nike suppliers do not use standard Vietnamese employer–employee relationships

Vietnam), the tension between mutually exclusive but coexisting beliefs remains. If we add up the issues and counter-issues of the various levels as we move through the table, we see how the complexities build upon one another. Complexity and dissonance at one level carry over to complexity and diverging opinions/beliefs at the next level.

In this way, as we move down the table, the question of 'What is the appropriate application or specification of the underlying principle?' becomes increasingly difficult to resolve with certainty.

Most individuals have dissonant beliefs and ambivalent feelings within different moral systems. Most people draw on the various moral systems that constitute their cultural heritage and it can be seen that things get even more complicated when an attempt is made to apply general principles to concrete situations. Importantly, various stakeholders, and particularly social movement organizations (SMO's) such as NGOs (nongovernment organizations), typically leverage this moral ambiguity or conflict within the audience of critical players to delegitimize a particular organization or undermine a particular institution. They often do this by first picking an extremely morally egregious action and then assigning responsibility for it to the targeted organization or institution. This tactic serves to intensify feelings of uncertainty in managers and employees and impede action.

Consequences

This great moral complexity has consequences for the individual manager, as well as for the relationship between various actors in the organization and their performance. First, for the individual, the cognitive dissonance, emotional ambivalence, and uncertainty resulting from ethical dilemmas can slow down or entirely prevent decision making. Second, once a decision is made, these psychological states can quickly and powerfully dissipate the energy, commitment, and effort toward a given course of action, since the individual will be constantly dogged by lingering doubts about the appropriateness of the action. Third, conflicting ethical considerations, if played upon, can lead to inconsistency and misalignment across actions. Just as strategies cannot be switched too frequently for risk of dissipating momentum and failing to build on prior gains, decisions that are inconsistent as a result of following first one ethical principle and then another can lead to poor performance. Fourth, the complexity might lead to a refusal to accept responsibility for ethical deliberation and decision making. When a manager faces too many conflicting opinions in his or her mind, he or she will tend to dismiss the morality of the subject altogether and replace the moral evaluation with some other standard or criterion of judgement. Typically, this means referring to a principle of profit maximization, or industry best practice, or the effect the decision will have on a performance evaluation, or a combination of these. In the example outlined above, instead of trying to figure out the morally correct thing to do regarding Vietnamese factory workers, the manager might rather refer to what other companies in the region are doing or to what is best for the 'bottom line'.

On a more interpersonal level, when a leader is perceived over time to be morally inconsistent or to lack integrity (which can be the perceived result of the ethical complexity and conflict within the leader), his or her influence over followers is threatened, and this can have disastrous effects on productivity (for recent evidence in leadership research, see References 13 and 14). Similarly, in teams, lack of alignment or agreement on what principles and values are going to be the basis for collaboration will have consequences for the performance of the team. In effect, the importance of value congruence in organizations is beyond doubt,[15] and when latent moral conflicts persist, this will have clear negative effects on the organization's long-term performance.

Solutions

What can you as a manager do, given this moral complexity and ambiguity and the conflicts that will necessarily derive from this? A first step is simply to recognize that conflicting values and norms exist and that you have to live with this fact. Further, you have to accept that ambiguity and conflict are unavoidable in daily work and that a manager who claims to have found a clear-cut, objective, and straightforward solution to a given ethical dilemma might be doing more harm than good.

Having accepted and recognized this ambiguity, you should attempt to figure out what *you* believe. What is your own ethical stance in a given situation? What key principles can you willingly adhere to in decision making that involves ethical issues? Such principles or heuristics could, for example, be to 'maximize welfare without violating rights'. This introspective process will not only help to raise your awareness of ethical issues but it might also enable you to avoid ducking the whole issue by referring to overly-simplistic principles or heuristics, as outlined above.

Raising your awareness in this way might also have positive repercussions for your capacities as a leader. In order to avoid the downside of 'amoral' leadership as outlined above, a leader can communicate explicitly (verbally) and through example that there are some clear moral imperatives that he or she will not renounce. It is important, however, that a company does not announce too many such principles, since it risks becoming more of a 'laundry list' that has no real practical value and is impossible to enforce or refer to in daily decision making. Thus you as a manger can acknowledge complexity and announce the simple guiding principles or heuristics you expect subordinates to respect (including a limited number of principles that subordinates are never to violate).

It is vital in this communication process to act upon the principle oneself, i.e. to be a role model for ethical behaviour.[16] This also implies actively illustrating your commitment, e.g. by firing an employee found to have displayed unethical behaviour. Such action conveys an unambiguous message about what behaviour is clearly unacceptable, and can constitute an exemplar to which employees can subsequently refer.

The institutional complexity of corporate social responsibility

In addition to the moral ambiguity inherent in issues of CSR described above, the institutional context adds additional complexity to the picture. Companies exist in increasingly complex environments due to the ever-more globalized nature of their operations and markets. In these environments, various stakeholders often have conflicting demands in terms of what they expect of a company. In other words, their ideas of what constitutes the social responsibility of a given firm might vary to a great extent. How is an individual manager to deal with these conflicting demands? Given the high and growing relevance of various stakeholders to firm performance, how can their demands be balanced to develop a coherent strategy that is both ethical and effective?

Underlying dynamics

Current realities intensify the uncertainty

Current societal realities, particularly globalization, are making it easier for stakeholders to more effectively voice their demands:

1. The vast anti-globalization movement is increasingly powerful and has developed strategies and tools that can seriously hurt corporations.[17]

2. Information flows ever more freely thanks to the media and the internet. This in turn leads to better coordination between aligned interests and ideologies, as well as the possibility for anyone to observe and evaluate firms' actions.
3. The spread of democracy has set the context for stakeholders to voice their demands more effectively, and increasing awareness following democratization in developing countries has led to an increase in the number and power of stakeholders.

It is important to note that, although conflicting *interests* are a serious risk to the company (as will be seen in more detail below), the diverging *ideologies* of the different stakeholders are even more important for the issue developed here. When we speak of ideology, we are in the domain of norms and values, and automatically depart from the domain of certainty, objectivity, and predictability. For a company, this has implications similar to those derived from moral ambiguity. Therefore, as if the complexity due to diverging institutional demands were not enough, institutions are, in addition, suffused with value systems. In effect, core to institutions are the sets of beliefs, norms, and values that characterize them.

Figure 2.1 illustrates the complexity managers face in terms of multiple, often conflicting, stakeholder demands. Stakeholders like NGOs, consumers, government agencies, international organizations, and unions, by their nature, have diverging opinions on what a corporation should be doing for society. These opinions relate to the interests of the various stakeholders, as well as to more fundamental beliefs regarding

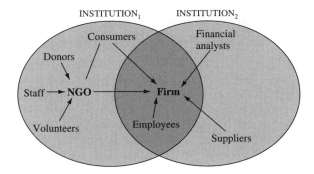

Figure 2.1 Firms operate in multiple institutional contexts simultaneously

what the role of business in society should be (i.e. its normative role). However, before looking more closely at this institutional and normative complexity, there is first a need to understand the notion of legitimacy of the firm and the role it plays in the context of CSR.

Legitimacy

When a company does not live up to its stakeholders' expectations of what is morally right, its legitimacy is challenged. Legitimacy is the quality or state of being perceived or understood to be in accordance with a set of norms or values concerning what is desirable, proper, or appropriate.[18] Legitimacy lies in the domain of social values[19] and is indicative of the degree to which a firm complies with its society's moral evaluation of what the norms and values, means and ends of an organization should be.

Legitimacy has some distinctive attributes that are critical to the way managers must deal with the dilemmas arising out of challenges to the legitimacy of their firm. *Legitimacy is a resource but is not 'owned'* in the same way as most other resources. It has a special attribute of external control that distinguishes it from most material resources. Ownership of property usually 'consists of a bundle of rights which the owner of the property possesses with regard to some thing – rights to possess, use, dispose of, exclude others, and manage and control'.[20] Given that legitimacy is essentially granted and revoked by individuals, organizations, and institutions beyond the focal organization, organizations do not have this 'bundle of rights' over their legitimacy as they do over their physical property. *Firms do not own or fully control their own legitimacy;* it is granted and revoked by those who evaluate the firm. The most difficult type of legitimacy to manage is normative legitimacy: Is the firm acting in a way that corresponds to the value-based expectations of its stakeholders?

While normative legitimacy is not fully controlled by the focal firm, it is also not usually fully controlled by any single outside individual or organization. *The sources and control of a focal firm's normative legitimacy are distributed or fragmented.* Normative legitimacy is a socially constructed, perpetually negotiated status conferred upon a focal organization and is dependent on many players' actions and evaluations. Some outside organizations, particularly those with a great deal of legitimacy and influence themselves, can affect others' judgement of a focal firm's legitimacy, but rarely do all the evaluators in the firm's environment judge it uniformly. Thus, normative legitimacy is inherently complex in nature, since different players have different opinions on what is the appropriate response of a company to a given social issue.

These complex, distributed, and often conflicting evaluations of the legitimacy of the firm are a great source of uncertainty for managers.

The competing and conflicting institutions surrounding multinationals

Firms simultaneously need to heed the demands of various institutions.[21-25] Meeting multiple *competing sets of institutional requirements* can place a heavy strain on the limited resources of a firm, particularly when there is a great deal of distance between the various institutions' demands.[26] The higher the number of competing institutions in a firm's operating environment, the greater the number of social demands it must meet in order to gain or maintain legitimacy with its various stakeholders. Given that stakeholders represent the values of various institutions, it is quite likely that the firm will fail to meet some of these demands fully and therefore will face social risk.

An even more intractable situation is found when different institutions demand mutually incompatible behaviour from the firm,[21] since satisfying one set of demands logically implies failing to meet another set of demands. *Conflicting institutional demands* can often arise in the context of pluralistic or liberal societies – as found in much of the developed world – and when a firm operates transnationally and therefore in differing cultural contexts. For example, an American car assembly firm attempting to decide whether to close down its US factory and set up a *maquiladora* just south of the border will face a host of conflicting institutional pressures concerning the appropriateness of laying off established American employees, maximizing shareholder return, meeting labour and environmental concerns, and the like. In such a context, there is no way for the firm to meet the inherently contradictory social demands; it will almost certainly face some stakeholder challenge. The greater the conflict between institutions in a firm's operating environment, the greater the probability of stakeholders challenging it.

As the discussion above suggests, the relationship between the various demands – from fully overlapping, to competing, to conflicting – affects the social risk of a firm.

For instance, a number of environmental NGOs (e.g. Friends of the Earth, Green-peace, Peasant's Confederation) may have overlapping demands concerning genetically modified organisms. A firm that is under attack for not meeting these demands faces a coalition with more resources with which to press their demands. However, since the demands are overlapping, multiple demands can be met simultaneously by, for instance, establishing sufficiently broad buffer zones around test plots of genetically modified crops.

When the demands are not overlapping, however, but are competing, multiple, and conflicting, the challenge of meeting them all is daunting. In the worst cases – those of conflicting demands – meeting one set of demands automatically precludes meeting another set. In sum, it seems almost impossible to resolve institutional complexity, and it becomes increasingly difficult for a manager to respond appropriately to all these demands at once. Choice, where possible, must be exercised based both on the strategic considerations of minimizing exposure to social risk and on the manager's own values.

Finally, institutions are inherently subject to change and evolution, creating a complex coevolution of ideas, actions, tactics, actors, and the like within the broader social system. This adds additional complexity and uncertainty to a manager's task of dealing with the conflicting and competing demands the institutional environment imposes.

Consequences

Social risk

In the past, strategy scholars have generally focused on four external risks: competitive, macroeconomic, technological, and political. Of these, political risk is closest to social risk in the strategy literature; both literature streams centre on firms' interactions with particular nonmarket players that can affect firm behaviour and performance. However, fundamental differences between social risk and political risk indicate that social risk is sufficiently unique to require and merit attention from managers.

Political risk can be distinguished from social risk in terms of actors, interaction dynamics, firm strategic behaviour, and consequences. First, apart from the firm, the primary actors in political risk are governments. These actors are clearly identifiable, relatively stable, and occupy distinct and mostly nonoverlapping domains. By contrast, the primary actors in social risk, such as NGOs, may not be readily identifiable, may arise and vanish relatively quickly, and may geographically overlap.

Second, the interactions between actors (evaluators, critical players, and focal firms) are fundamentally different in political risk and social risk. Governments primarily govern only what firms do within their borders, while social pressure groups challenge corporate actions carried out in other countries. The demands of governments are relatively clear, unitary, and coherent, while those of various NGOs may be unclear, fragmented, and contradictory. Governments have sovereign powers to impose their will; NGOs do not and have only indirect influence on firms via third parties (e.g. consumers, government, media).

Third, the strategic options of firms facing political and social risk are quite distinct. Strategies such as avoidance, defiance, or manipulation may be more feasible with NGOs, which have relatively less direct coercive power than governments.

Finally, the consequences of political risk centre on government actions including regulation, taxation, and nationalization. Social risk can lead to political risk – and thus have these consequences – but it also includes a market-size effect (as seen in areas such as hydroelectric dams, nuclear energy, furs, and tobacco in the United States and much of Western Europe over the last 20 years,[27] a firm's market share, reputation, etc.).

These fundamental differences between social risk and political risk emphasize the strategic importance of managers paying heed to the role of legitimacy and its relevance to decision making in the field of CSR. In sum, the managerial consequences of institutional complexity and social risk must not be underestimated. In the field of CSR, if a manager stays exclusively focused on abiding by the law and complying with regulations (i.e. ensuring legitimacy under one institution), this does not mean that he or she has avoided all social risk to the company's reputation and performance.

In the remainder of this chapter we will focus our attention on (partial) solutions to the problems of legitimacy and social risk arising out of the increasing institutional complexity facing firms.

Solutions

It should be clear at this point that it is not easy for firms to manage the institutional complexity of their environment, but some guidance can be provided. In this section, the suggestions will be divided into two basic categories: what the manager must do to understand this environment and what actions the manager should consider in attempting to retain a firm's legitimacy prior to or during a challenge put forward by a set of stakeholders.

It is worth underlining before this discussion that the action is built on the assumption that a manager has first consulted his or her own conscience, values, and principles. Simply being an effective 'hired gun' willing to do whatever is in the interests of one's organization is unworthy of anyone who considers himself or herself an autonomous moral person.

Understanding

First, managers must remember that not all the key variables are within their control since legitimacy is ultimately a distributed and fragmented property controlled by numerous stakeholders. Thus they may not have much freedom in choosing, for example, the social, economic, or institutional environment in which they operate.

Second, social risk must be weighed against other factors driving a firm's performance. Having a strong brand is a risk factor for attacks by NGOs, but a strong brand can be a great asset in the marketplace. McDonald's is repeatedly attacked by various stakeholders at least partially because of the strength of its brand and what the brand stands for. However, letting the prominence of the brand drop simply to reduce social risk is probably unwarranted. A manager should take decisions with as holistic a perspective as possible. McDonald's should perhaps seek a more nuanced approach, which reduces its social risk without damaging the salience of its brand in the mind of consumers. For instance, it might consider how it could create a less glaringly 'foreign' and impersonal façade to the public in countries outside the United States.

Third, managers should understand social risk as a continuously evolving phenomenon, not a static characteristic of the environment. Stakeholders' evaluations of the legitimacy of a company are as volatile and ephemeral as any other societal trend. In order to reduce uncertainty, managers must therefore develop tools for environmental sensing and interpreting of current demands, as well as regularly analysing social, political, economic, environmental, political, and legal trends in order to predict better what the future holds. A snapshot understanding is simply insufficient.

Fourth, managers must identify and minimize exposure by considering what risk factors their firms face, such as working with new technologies or working across different institutional contexts (see Reference 17 for a complete discussion of these risk factors).

Fifth, managers must remain mindful of the distinction between what is *legal* and what is *legitimate*. As already seen, NGOs engaged in efforts to change industry-wide practices, laws, or institutions often attack a firm regardless of whether it is law-abiding. Meeting legal requirements does not imply meeting all stakeholders' expectations and demands.

Acting

Beyond understanding the institutional complexity underlying social risk and challenges to the legitimacy of the firm, managers must actively manage social risk. Given the complex and conflicting interests and ideologies of the different players, a move to satisfy one stakeholder often leads to the dissatisfaction of another. Many market transactions involve two parties and thus finding win–win situations is relatively easy when compared with nonmarket transactions in which the multitude of stakeholders would require solutions that are win–win–win–win–win–etc. Nonetheless, here are a few key suggestions for actively managing social risk.

First, the earlier a firm comes up with an effective strategy to deal with social risk, the better. Trying to be a first mover is useful not only in terms of brand image and marketing but also in terms of profiling the company as having goodwill and interest in the various claims of stakeholders. In this way, the company can develop a positive image not only in its customers' and investors' minds but also in the minds of those who may have criticized this very company on the basis of moral misconduct.

While the focus of this chapter has primarily been on minimizing downside risk arising from the complexity surrounding CSR, this environment can also be a source of competitive advantage for firms that are well adapted to it, relative to their competitors, especially if they are robust first movers. For example, firms that respond as first movers to shifts in the social environment and to social risk may outperform firms that do not, because they may gain leads in innovation, meet latent demand, have a better brand image, and be better able to meet future regulatory demands at lower cost.

Second, an effective and proactive way to deal with the uncertainty of social risk is to actively communicate with stakeholders in order to identify their concrete demands as well as attempting to sense any underlying normative claims. Such engagement, especially if it is prior to any stakeholder campaigns against the firm, can increase the trust, respect, and flexibility of stakeholders with respect to the firm, as well as providing better information about threats and opportunities.

Third, the importance of announcing one's stance must not be underestimated. When a given position has been strategically elaborated, this position should be announced widely, clearly, and effectively. In this way, stakeholders will not be able to leverage contradictory messages from the organization in their attacks. If the normative dimension of the issue is addressed explicitly, this will also minimize the effectiveness of campaigns that leverage the moral ambiguity in their audience, since all parties would be quite clear about the values espoused by the focal firm. Espousing these values clearly and unambiguously gives stakeholders with whom the firm has voluntary, economic relationships (e.g. employees, suppliers, shareholders, etc.) the opportunity to exit, should they be dissatisfied with these values. If they remain engaged with the firm, they will be less likely to complain – effectively – against these values.

Fourth, firms under attack need to determine the goal of the attack – whether it is to change the firm's behaviour, change industry practices, or change the rules of the game. The optimal response could well depend on the goals of the attacking NGOs. Some researchers (e.g. Suchman[18]) have assumed that the loss of legitimacy was the result of failing to meet existing dominant institutional standards. However, since campaigns are often launched as a form of proxy war, more closely adhering to the dominant standards – what institutional scholars call isomorphism – is unlikely to satisfy the campaigning organizations.

Fifth, the short-, medium-, and long-term consequences of one's response to a campaign must be given due consideration. One of the reasons to resist any compromise with NGOs could be that this would only encourage more attacks on firms that show that they capitulate under pressure. The thinking is that although a compromise might bring some short-term relief, it would only bring longer-term heartache.

This reasoning only captures a partial truth and confuses the medium term with the long term. For very high-profile organizations, evaluation and critiques from many quarters are almost constant. Thus, close and ongoing cooperation, communication, and compromise with relevant stakeholders might be the optimal long-term approach, since the various stakeholders' demands are unlikely to disappear even if the focal firm initially succeeds in rejecting or ignoring them. Earning a good reputation and the trust of stakeholders might be difficult and costly over the medium term, but beneficial over the long term.

Conclusion

As multinationals come under increasing scrutiny and ethical evaluation, they face an explosion in the degree of complexity in their world. The familiar complexity of simply running a multinational profitably is crossed with the complex and ambiguous realm of ethics, which in turn is crossed with a broader range of increasingly vocal stakeholders expressing a range of institutional ideologies as well as interests.

No one said it would be easy! It is hoped that this chapter provides some insight into this complexity as well as some guidance on managing it.

References

[1] Festinger, L., *A Theory of Cognitive Dissonance*, Stanford, California: Stanford University Press, 1957.
[2] Jamieson, D. W., 'The Attitude Ambivalence Construct: Validity, Utility, Measurement', Presented at the American Sociological Association, Toronto, Canada, 1993.

[3] Priester, J. R. and Petty, R. E., 'The Gradual Threshold Model of Ambivalence: Relating the Positive and Negative Bases of Attitudes to Subjective Ambivalence', *Journal of Personality and Social Psychology*, 1996, **71**, 431–449.

[4] Priester, J. R. and Petty, R. E., 'Extending the Basis of Subjective Attitudinal Ambivalence: Interpersonal and Intrapersonal Antecedents of Evaluative Tension', *Journal of Personality and Social Psychology*, 2001, **80**, 19–34.

[5] Donaldson, T. and Dunfee, T. W., 'Towards a Unified Conception of Business Ethics: Integrative Social Contracts Theory', *Academy of Management Review*, 1994, **19**(2), 252–284.

[6] Hobbes, T., in *Leviathan* (ed. J. C. A. Gaskin), Oxford: Oxford University Press, 1996.

[7] Nozick, R., *Anarchy, State, and Utopia*, Oxford: Blackwell, 1977.

[8] Rawls, J., *A Theory of Justice*, Cambridge, Massachusetts: Harvard University Press, 1971.

[9] Rawls, J., *Political Liberalism*, New York: Columbia University Press, 1993.

[10] Hare, R., *Moral Thinking: Levels, Methods, and Point*, Oxford: Oxford University Press, 1981.

[11] Mill, J. S., *Utilitarianism*, Hackett, 1863.

[12] The table is a single, illustrative representation of sources of internal dissonance and ambivalence in moral belief systems. It is intended to be illustrative and not an exhaustive or exclusive representation of such ambiguity and contradiction. There are multiple plausible ways of dividing up the levels, and multiple ways of framing the issues.

[13] Antonakis, J., Cianciolo, A. T., and Sternberg, R. (eds), *The Nature of Leadership*, Thousand Oaks: Sage Publications, 2004.

[14] Bass, B., *Transformational Leadership: Industry, Military, and Educational Impact*, Mahwah, New Jersey: Lawrence Erlbaum Associates, 1998.

[15] Chatman, J., 'Matching People and Organizations: Selection and Socialization in Public Accounting Firms', *Administrative Science Quarterly*, 1991, **39**(4), 459–484.

[16] Trevino, L. K., Hartman, L. P., and Brown, M., 'Moral Persona and Moral Manager: How Executives Develop a Reputation for Ethical Leadership', *California Management Review*, 2000, **42**(4), 128–142.

[17] Yaziji, M., 'Turning Gadflies into Allies', *Harvard Business Review*, 2000, **82**(2), 110–115.

[18] Suchman, M. C., 'Managing Legitimacy: Strategic and Institutional Approaches', *Academy of Management Review*, 1995, **20**(3), 571.

[19] Selznick, P., *Leadership in Administration*, Berkeley, California: University of California Press, 1957.

[20] Votaw, D., *Modern Corporations*, Englewood Cliffs, New Jersey: Prentice-Hall, 1965, pp. 96–97.

[21] D'Aunno, T., Sutton, R. I., and Price, R. H., 'Isomorphism and External Support in Conflicting Institutional Environments: A Study of Drug Abuse Treatment Units', *Academy of Management Journal*, 1991, **34**(3), 636–661.

[22] Deephouse, D. L., 'Does Isomorphism Legitimate?', *Academy of Management Journal*, 1996, **39**(4), 1024.

[23] Meyer, J. W., Scott, R. W., and Strang, D., 'Centralization, Fragmentation, and School District Complexity', *Administrative Science Quarterly*, 1987, **32**, 186–201.

[24] Powell, W. W., 'Institutional Effects on Organizational Structure and Performance', in *Institutional Patterns and Organizations. Culture and Environment* (ed. L. G. Zucker), Cambridge, Massachusetts: Ballinger, 1988, pp. 115–136.

[25] Ruef, M. and Scott, W. R., 'A Multidimensional Model of Organizational Legitimacy: Hospital Survival in Changing Institutional Environments', *Administrative Science Quarterly*, 1998, **43**(4), 877–904.

[26] Kostova, T. and Zaheer, S., 'Organizational Legitimacy under Conditions of Complexity: The Case of the Multinational Enterprise', *Academy of Management Review*, 1999, **24**(1), 64–81.

[27] For example, according to the World Commission on Dams (*Dams and Development*, 2000, Earthscan), dam commissions in North America dropped by 90 % from the 1960s to the 1990s, primarily because of various stakeholder concerns. Similarly, per capita cigarette consumption in the US has dropped by more than 50 % (from 4345 cigarettes per person in 1963 to 2025 in 2000) according to the US Department of Agriculture (*Tobacco: Situation and Outlook*, various issues, URL: http://usda.mannlib.cornell.edu/reports/erssor/specialty/tbs-bb/2005/tbs 2005.pdf).

Further reading

Abelson, R., 'Computer Simulation of 'Hot' Cognition', in *Computer Simulation of Personality* (eds S. Tomkins and S. Messick), New York: John Wiley & Sons, Inc., 1963, pp. 277–298.

Aldrich, H. E. and Fiol, C. M. 'Fools Rush In? The Institutional Context of Industry Creation', *Academy of Management Review*, 1994, **19**(4), 645–670.

Baird, I. S. and Thomas, H., 'Toward a Contingency Model of Strategic Risk Taking', *Academy of Management Review*, 1985, **10**(2), 230–243.

Barley, S. R. and Tolbert, P. S., 'Institutionalization and Structuration: Studying the Links between Action and Institution', *Organization Studies*, 1997, **18**(1), 93.

Baumol, W., *Business Behavior, Value and Growth*, New York: Macmillan, 1959.

Becker, G. S., *The Economic Approach to Human Behavior*, Chicago, Illinois: University of Chicago Press, 1976.

'Biochips Down on the Farm', *The Economist*, 2001.

Bureau, U. C., *1997 NAICS Definitions*, Vol. 2003, US Census Bureau, 2002.

Clore, G. and Isabell, L., 'Emotions as Virtue and Vice', in *Citizens and Politics: Perspectives from Political Psychology* (ed. J. Kuklinksi), New York: Cambridge University Press, 1996, pp. 103–126.

Damasio, A. R., *Descartes' Error: Emotion, Reason, and the Human Brain*, New York: Putnam, 1994.

D'Emilio, J., *Sexual Politics, Sexual Communities*, Chicago, Illinois: University of Chicago Press, 1983.

DiMaggio, P. J. and Powell, W. W., 'The Iron Cage Revisited: Institutional Isomorphism and Collective Rationality in Organizational Fields', *American Sociological Review*, 1983, **48**(April), 147–160.

Drucker, P. E., 'Will the Corporation Survive', *The Economist*, 2001.

Edwards, K. and Smith, E. E., 'A Disconfirmation Bias in the Evaluation of Arguments', *Journal of Personality and Social Psychology*, 1996, **71**, 5–24.

Eisinger, P., 'The Conditions of Protest Behavior in American Cities', *American Political Science Review*, 1973, **67**, 11–28.

Elster, J., 'Emotions and Economic Theory', *Journal of Economic Literature*, 1998, **36**(March), 47–74.

Fazio, R., Sanbonmatsu, M., and Kardes, F., 'On the Automatic Activation of Attitudes', *Journal of Personality and Social Psychology*, 1986, **50**(2), 247–282.

Freeman, J., 'The Origins of the Women's Liberation Movement', *American Journal of Sociology*, 1973, **78**, 792–811.

Frooman, J., 'Stakeholder Influence Strategies', *Academy of Management Review*, 1999, **24**, 191–205.

Gale, R., 'Social Movements and the State: The Environmental Movement, Countermovement, and Governmental Agencies', *Sociological Perspectives*, 1986, **29**, 202–240.

Gargiulo, M., 'Two-step Leverage: Managing Constraint in Organizational Politics', *Administrative Science Quarterly*, 1993, **38**(1), 1.

Giddens, A., *The Constitution of Society*, Berkeley, California: University of California Press, 1984.

Hannan, M. T. and Freeman, J., 'The Population Ecology of Organizations', *American Journal of Sociology*, 1977, **82**(5), 929–964.

Jenkins, J. C. and Perrow, C., 'Insurgency of the Powerless: Farm Workers' Movements (1946–1972)', *American Sociological Review*, 1977, **42**, 249–268.

Karatnycky, A., *Freedom in the World: The Annual Survey of Political Rights and Civil Liberties 2001–2002*, New York: Freedom House, 2002.

Lodge, M., Steenbergen, M., and Brau, S., 'The Responsive Voter: Campaign Information and the Dynamics of Candidate Evaluation', *American Political Science Review*, 1995, **89**, 309–326.

Lorant, R., *Motorola & Philips Electronics Pulled Out*, Vol. 1996, Associated Press, 1996.

Lord, C. G., Ross, L., and Lepper, M. R., 'Biased Assimilation and Attitude Polarization: The Effects of Prior Theories on Subsequently Considered Evidence', *Journal of Personality and Social Psychology*, 1979, **37**(11), 2098–2109.

McAdam, D., McCarthy, J. D., and Zald, M. N., 'Social Movements', in *Handbook of Sociology* (ed. N. Smelser), Newsbury Park, California: Sage, 1988, pp. 695–737.

Meyer, J. W. and Scott, W. R., *Organizational Environments: Ritual and Rationality*, Beverly Hills, California: Sage, 1983.

Miller, D. and Friesen, P. H., 'Momentum and Revolution in Organizational Adaptation', *Academy of Management Journal*, 1980, **23**(4), 591.

Milliken, F. J., 'Three Types of Perceived Uncertainty about the Environment: State, Effect, and Response Uncertainty', *Academy of Management Review*, 1987, **12**(1), 133.

Morris, A., *The Origins of the Civil Rights Movement*, New York: Free Press, 1984.

Nelkin, D. and Pollak, M., *The Atom Besieged*, Cambridge, Massachusetts: MIT Press, 1981.

Oliver, C., 'Strategic Responses to Institutional Processes', *Academy of Management Review*, 1991, **16**, 145–179.

Pfeffer, J. and Salancik, G., *The External Control of Organizations: A Resource Dependence Perspective*, New York: Harper & Row, 1978.

Scott, R. W., *Institutions and Organizations*, Thousand Oaks: Sage, 2001.

Simon, H., *Administrative Behavior*, 3rd edn, New York: The Free Press, 1976.

Stark, D., 'Recombinant Property in East European Capitalism', *American Journal of Sociology*, 1996, **101**(4), 993.

Staw, B. M., 'The Escalation of Commitment to a Course of Action', *Academy of Management Review*, 1981, **6**(4), 569.

Thorngate, W., 'Possible Limits on a Science of Social Behavior', in *Social Psychology in Transition* (eds F. E. A. J. H. Strickland and K. J. Gergen), New York: Plenum, 1976, pp. 121–139.

Union of International Organizations, *Yearbook of International Organizations: Guide to Global Civil Society Networks 2002–2003*, Munich: K. G. Saur, 2003.

Vernon, R., *In the Hurricane's Eye*, Cambridge, Massachusetts: Harvard, 1998.

Weick, K. E., 'What Theory is *Not*, Theorizing *Is*', *Administrative Science Quarterly*, 1995, **40**(3), 385–390.

Wiley, M. and Zald, M., 'The Growth and Transformation of Educational Accrediting Agencies: An Exploratory Study in Social Control of Institutions', *Sociology of Education*, 1968, **41**, 36–56.

Winestock, G. and Cooper, H., 'How Activists Outmaneuvered Drug Makers in WTO Deal', *Wall Street Journal*, Eastern edn, 2001, **6**.

Zald, M. N. and McCarthy, J. D., 'Organizational Intellectuals and the Criticism of Society', *Social Service Review*, 1975, **49**, 344–362.

Zimmerman, M. A. and Zeitz, G. J., 'Beyond Survival: Achieving New Venture Growth by Building Legitimacy', *Academy of Management Review*, 2002, **27**(3), 414.

Zuckerman, E. W., 'The Categorical Imperative: Securities Analysts and the Illegitimacy Discount', *American Journal of Sociology*, 1999, **104**(5), 1398–1438.

3

Opportunities and Threats in the Global Political and Economic Environment

Jean-Pierre Lehmann

Introduction

Globalization is the incarnation of complexity, both on a political and a business level. There are many players with different interests acting in a world with less and less boundaries, higher interdependence, as well as fundamental uncertainties and dilemmas, making any extrapolation of trends based on the past meaningless. This chapter will focus on the important drivers of complexity in the sociopolitical environment of global companies, the newly emerging players and their impact, and the dilemmas and uncertainties ahead. The need for corporate action is emphasized to stabilize and evolve the basic framework conditions for open global markets, without which that complexity could well turn into chaos. The complexity and the threats and opportunities in today's globalizing world – with its open markets and increasingly open societies – is illustrated through impressions gathered from recent research journeys.

The opportunities

This section describes the opportunities in the current global political and economic environment. Vietnam serves as the first and possibly the best example.[1] The GDP figures and export growth that are reported are one thing, the observed dynamism behind them is another. Vietnam endured 30 years of virtually uninterrupted war – against the French, the Americans, and the Chinese successively – followed by a decade of Stalinist economic mismanagement.[2] Reform (or renovation, *doi moi*, as it is known) began in 1986, characterized perhaps more by errors but also by a lack of conviction on the part of the leadership. Vietnam had no Deng Xiaoping, no powerful, imperial, charismatic figure to own the reforms and drive them through. Vietnamese Communist leadership was more orthodox and more bureaucratic. In 1997, nine years after the reform was launched, the initial enthusiasm of foreign investors had mostly dissipated into disillusionment. At the turn of the century, however, things changed, mainly reflected in the way the government became more tolerant of private economic activity. This has resulted in that quite powerful compound, described by author Robert Templar as 'Market-Leninism'.[3] As for quite a few communist countries, including China, Vietnam has benefited not only from the boom being driven by the private sector but also from all the investment that has been made in education and human capital formation.

In order to situate ourselves and to project where we might be in the coming decades, we need to look back. The current Vietnamese scene would have been unthinkable just a few years ago. Things are far from perfect, of course; it is still a repressive state with too much bureaucracy and corruption, there are deep pockets of poverty and growing inequality, and some of the ills of growth and globalization – drugs, prostitution, crime – are becoming more malignant. However, there is hardly any visible misery, children are going to school, and the economy is booming. Vietnam is becoming far more open and there is the emergence of a middle class – currently estimated at only about 14% of the population, but growing quickly. Vietnam also benefits from the brainpower and capital of its quite large diaspora, the Viet Khieu, mainly in France, Germany, US, Canada, and Australia, many of whom have re-established strong professional, business, and family links with the homeland. Neither does there appear to be any resentment towards them and nor is there any visible resentment directed against the erstwhile enemies of France, the US, and China. That may be in part because the Vietnamese won!

Vietnam is a good example of early twenty-first century globalization, especially regarding the interdependence of markets through trade, investment, and enterprise, underpinned by enabling policies – reform and liberalization – and enabling information, communication, and transportation technologies. Globalization requires openness, with regard to both domestic and global markets; indeed, it is synonymous with openness. No matter how much regimes try to limit openness to the economy and continue to insulate society, ultimately they fail.

While Vietnam is a remarkable example, it is by no means unique. At the other extreme is Chile,[4] a country that is a paragon of economic, social, and political change. Emerging from the oppressive years of the Pinochet dictatorship, the Chilean establishment has very successfully manoeuvered reform in bringing about a quiet, but nonetheless profound, liberal democratic revolution. Spain achieved a similar feat after the death of Franco in 1975, but Chile's reform is all the more remarkable in that it continued during Pinochet's lifetime, so that by the time of his death, in December 2006, the Chilean political landscape had become unrecognisable. For those who claim that miracle growth economies are an Asian monopoly and cannot be achieved by Latin Americans, Chile proves them wrong. Take, for example, the recent election of Michelle Bachelet as president, the first woman in Latin American history to become head of state and government on her own merits.

Chile, however, does prove right those who argue that openness to globalization is a prerequisite to growth and development. Protectionism and import-substitution can drive growth for a limited period of time – as was the case in Brazil under military dictatorship in the 1960s – but under these conditions growth is not sustainable (as the Brazilian case proved) and socioeconomic inequality becomes both extreme and endemic. Although openness may generate inequality, this is temporary, but it also provides opportunities for socioeconomic mobility. While there have been reforms in many Latin America countries during the last decade, they remain for the most part too inward-looking.[5] Chile has a vibrant foreign trade sector, it has benefited from significant flows of inward direct investment, it has signed a number of prominent bilateral FTAs (free trade agreements), and it has been active in international and regional institutions, such as APEC (the Asia Pacific Economic Cooperation Forum). Mexico has also undertaken great change since it joined NAFTA (North American Free Trade Agreement) in 1994, but less so than Chile because it has put most of its eggs in the American basket and hence, while being open, it has been far less global.

Although nationalist populists such as Venezuela's Hugo Chávez get a lot of air-time, the story of the early twenty-first century is that most countries are moving forward, not backward. Whether enthusiastically or reluctantly, most states are in the process of undertaking the necessary reforms, albeit with varying degrees of pace and scope, to improve and thereby render more competitive their domestic economies. Former Malaysian Prime Minister Mahathir bin Mohamad may have used the podium for political reasons to denounce the evil conspiracies lying behind globalization, but Malaysia also stands out as an economic success story, much of which can be illustrated from the concentration of global semiconductor companies' investments in Penang. Malaysia, composed of Malay (*bumiputra*), Chinese, Indian, and other communities, is one of the very few multicultural societies – think of Lebanon, Cyprus, Sri Lanka, and Northern Ireland – that has not only endured but thrived. It is difficult to imagine that without the economic growth and rapidly growing pie that globalization has engendered in Malaysia, its intercommunal relations would have remained so stable.

Just as Chile disproves the claim that it is not possible for Latin American states to become 'tigers', so Malaysia challenges those who say that Muslim societies are doomed to remain 'the orphans of globalization'.[6] Although terrorist acts in Muslim countries, such as Jordan, Egypt, Saudi Arabia, Afghanistan, and Indonesia, continue to cause concern and consternation, in fact most Muslim countries are moving towards reform, liberalization, and openness, albeit extremely slowly.[7] Even Saudi Arabia, according to a recent survey by *The Economist*,[8] is undergoing profound change, resulting in more qualified opening. Pakistan is another example of a country that undertook market liberalization reforms a decade ago and has since experienced strong economic growth.[9]

There can be no doubt that the global market offers more opportunities today than the planet has ever witnessed. The entrepreneurial drive that is engrained in every society but which is often repressed has been enjoying a far more untrammelled environment in most parts of the globe. A fundamental lubricant of this explosion of entrepreneurship has been trade. Trade is vital for several reasons. The most important, going back to David Ricardo, is that on the basis of comparative advantage it allows societies to concentrate on what they are really good at, thus enhancing productivity, the essential ingredient to sustained growth.[10] Imports especially contribute to significant improvements in living standards, by offering more choice at lower prices. Western economies, for example, have benefited enormously from the import of cheap Chinese textiles and garments, which has reduced prices for basic clothes by as much as 30%. For the less affluent, knocking a few euros off the price of children's school clothes can be a godsend. From antiquity, trade has been one of the distinguishing characteristics of homo sapiens, reflecting people's natural inclinations and enjoyment. Think of the Silk Road and all the adventure and riches it evokes. As the fourteenth century Tunisian historiographer and philosopher, Ibn Khaldun, put it, 'Through foreign trade, people's satisfaction, merchants' profits, and countries' wealth are all increased.'[11]

The threats

Hong Kong may be less of a threat than most people may perceive. Once a British colony, Hong Kong, with its population of six million, now boasts a higher GDP per capita than the UK. It has been described, among other things, as a 'capitalist paradise',[12] and though this may sound like an oxymoron, there is no doubt that this is a place where the entrepreneurial buzz is more like a din!

Although Hong Kong's astonishing growth and development were primarily due to the energy and enterprise of Hong Kong entrepreneurs – assisted by an enabling institutional environment, especially in respect to the rule of law provided by the British colonial government – in the last quarter of a century it has also benefited tremendously from the opening up of its giant neighbour, China. Today, Greater China – encompassing the People's Republic, Taiwan, and Hong Kong – is the global economic locomotive.[13] The IMF (International Monetary Fund) calculates that in the last few years it has accounted for over 25% of global GDP (gross domestic product) growth and fully 60% of growth in global trade, a remarkable and, until recently, unexpected story. Thirty years ago, Mao had just died and China was emerging from the throes of the Cultural Revolution. There was plenty to celebrate, so what was wrong?

From 13 to 18 December 2005, Hong Kong was host to the World Trade Organization's (WTO) sixth ministerial conference.[14] The WTO was established as the successor institution to the General Agreement on Trade and Tariffs (GATT) in 1995. GATT sought to achieve multilateral trade liberalization among its members on the basis of certain fundamental principles – the most fundamental of which is 'nondiscrimination', or equal treatment, between members – and through a process of regular negotiations, known in GATT-speak as 'rounds'. The WTO adheres to the same basic principle, to which has been added a commitment (alas, only in principle) to fairer treatment to developing countries; it remains engaged in trade liberalization negotiations and in addition has acquired a judicial function, through its Dispute Settlement Unit (DSU). If one member country believes that another is acting in violation of the WTO and to the prejudice of their industries it can report it to the DSU. This has brought about a profound qualitative change in the world's trading institution. Another dramatic, more quantitative, change has been the increase in membership. Some 90 countries belonged to the GATT in 1990; today 150 countries belong to the WTO, the most recent being Saudi Arabia, with Russia also expected to join soon. A great step was taken when China joined in 2001, after 15 years of negotiation for accession, bringing with it 22 % of humanity and its huge dynamic market.[15] Not only are most countries throughout the world marching in the direction of a vibrant entrepreneurially driven global market but also there is a global institution to provide the legal, political, and administrative framework and the ideological underpinning through reference to its fundamental principles.

When the WTO was established, member countries committed to holding a ministerial conference (MC) every two years. With the benefit of hindsight, that was a mistake. Ministers should meet when they have something to discuss, not just for the sake of institutionalized procedures. Nevertheless, the commitment is there and must be respected. The first MC was the one that established the WTO in Marrakech. The second was held in Singapore, where a number of loose ends from the previous Uruguay Round (1986–1994) were tied up and a number of new issues were addressed. Throughout the GATT years, developing countries tended to have an arm's length relationship with the institution, to a great extent because most of them practised import-substitution policies. The Uruguay Round, however, took place simultaneously with the adoption by many countries (notably India, Brazil, Mexico, Argentina, and South Africa) of reforms resulting in the abandonment of import-substitution in favour of export-orientation.[16] Hence developing countries became much more interested, but they also felt that they had been dealt a rotten hand in the Uruguay Round. This was mainly the case in respect to agriculture, which the rich countries – the US, EU, Japan, Switzerland, and Norway – had managed to keep off the agenda. As this is one area, along with labour-intensive industries such as textiles, garments, and footwear, where a number of big developing countries have comparative advantage, not surprisingly they wanted agriculture on the agenda.[17]

Something else that has had a tremendous impact on the WTO was the rise of NGOs – the number of NGOs and their adherents exploded in the 1990s – and the emergence of the anti-globalization movement. The impact was most acutely felt at the next MC, which was scheduled for November 1999 in Seattle, where both the EU and the US were quite keen to launch a new round. This was partly in reflection of new areas needing attention, especially in services, as well as a desire to extend WTO jurisdiction to competition policy, investment, government procurement, and trade facilitation, as well as for reasons of prestige. Bill Clinton was quite pleased at the idea of having a round named after him, like former President Kennedy. Seattle was a fiasco of huge proportions. Although anti-globalization demonstrators stole the limelight, the main cause for the collapse of the Seattle conference was the growing rift between the rich industrialized countries of the North and the developing countries of the South, mainly over agriculture.

After Seattle, no country was keen to hold the next WTO conference, until a new member, Qatar, offered to host it in its capital Doha in late November 2001. Certainly that location would make it easier to hold the demonstrators at bay! People who were monitoring the progress (or lack thereof) of trade talks, and especially the continuously growing polarization between the North and the South, were pessimistic that any breakthrough could happen in Doha. Then came 11 September. In the wake of the terrorist tragedy, most nations felt impelled to make Doha a success. At the meeting, ministers decided to launch a new round with ambitious objectives and it was decided that not only should it seek to redress the discrimination suffered by developing countries but also, by naming it the Doha Development Agenda (DDA), it would do so explicitly.[18] The glow of global solidarity soon evaporated, including on the trade front, where shortly after Doha President Bush passed a farm bill containing a huge increase in domestic subsidies and then further poisoned the climate by unilaterally raising tariffs on steel.

By the time of the next MC in September 2003 in Cancún, Mexico, the poisoned atmosphere had become venomous. Although the matter is quite complicated, the nub is as follows. Developing countries contend that they are being treated unfairly, that they are being prevented from accessing markets in the North that are heavily tilted against them, and that this is depriving them of growth and welfare gains, which the World Bank[19] and other institutions have indicated would be very sizeable. All this is further compounded by the fact that they are at an unfair advantage due to lack of institutional and human capacity. Specifically on agriculture, there are three interconnected bones of contention:

1. In contrast to most industrial goods where the North has the undoubted advantage and tariffs are close to zero, tariffs and other forms of trade barriers in relation to agricultural goods are prohibitively high, thus depriving developing economies of lucrative markets.
2. Heavy domestic subsidies allow countries in the North to produce goods uncompet-itively and to thereby distort prices, while the developing countries are either not allowed to provide domestic subsidies (e.g. because of IMF conditionalities) or are not able to afford to do so.
3. Export subsidies on agriculture lead to countries of the North, especially the EU, dumping products on third markets, thereby unfairly undercutting developing country producers and in many instances driving them to ruination.

'Peak tariffs' are another measure of how unfair the system is, whereby tariffs increase in proportion to value-added, thus penalizing countries that seek to move from the export of basic commodities to processed products. Another contentious point is that devel-oping countries face much higher tariffs in the labour-intensive goods they produce than the countries in the North themselves charge for the capital-intensive or knowledge-intensive goods they produce.[20] Bangladesh, one of the world's poorest countries, pays as much in tariffs for its exports (mainly cheap garments, such as T-shirts) as does France, one of the world's wealthiest countries, which on a value basis exports over 30 times more.[21] In other words, a crude Bangladeshi 'I love NY' T-shirt pays proportionately far more duty than an Yves St Laurent silk handmade dinner jacket shirt.

All these forms of protectionism are, of course, highly political and in most cases have nothing to do with economics. Although in the EU, the US, and Japan the proportion of agriculture to the overall labour force and contribution to GDP is infinitesimal, the political clout of agricultural constituencies and lobbies is formidable.[22] Another example is Japan's footwear industry, which is heavily protected against its more competitive Asian neighbours, notably China. Working with leather has tradition-ally been carried out by Japan's outcastes (*burakumin*), of whom there are about three million, and it is far easier socially and politically to allow them to continue engaging in a protected monopoly than to seek an end to discrimination and bring the *burakumin* into mainstream Japanese society. In the case of the US, inefficient textile and garment workers are to be found in key electoral states such as the Carolinas, while probably the most contentious North–South issue is cotton, for which American domestic subsidies often exceed the total value of the market, but its roughly 25 000 cotton plantation owners (in contrast to the tens of millions of cotton farmers in poor developing countries) contribute significantly to political coffers.[23] It is the same pattern throughout the world: producers, who stand to lose something from open markets in the short term, are politically much better organized and outspoken than the potential longer-term winners and the customers. This asymmetry gives the political debate a clear bias towards protectionism.

At the Cancún MC, fed up with being marginalized, discriminated against, and isolated, a number of developing countries formed an alliance – the G-20 – led by Brazil, India, South Africa, and, nominally, China, though this trade powerhouse has been very silent in trade talks. The emergence of the G-20 alliance has caused a systemic jolt and one positive effect has been that the oligopoly of trading powers hitherto known as the 'quad', composed of the EU, the US, Japan, and Canada, no longer exists. The countries of the North do not deny that their subsidies and tariffs are distortions of trade (though they do not agree on the extent of the distortions) and economic arguments are not used to justify them; in the case of agriculture, reference is more often made to tradition, lifestyle, and 'multipolarity'. In return for their reduction and possible elimination and the 'burden' that they will have to endure as a result, they are seeking concessions from developing countries, partly in industrial goods but mainly in services.

The chasm between the North and South was so wide that Cancún collapsed among much recrimination.[24] The next MC was set for Hong Kong for 2005. In the interval, the trade talks have been marked by paralysis, procrastination, and squabbling over minor details and technicalities. The big picture and the great challenges the planet faces in seeking to generate sustained and inclusive growth amid a growing population – the labour force in developing countries is due to increase by one billion in the first decade of this century, more than the total workforce of the rich countries – have been set aside. As the date of the Hong Kong MC approached, one thing that ministers did agree upon was that it should not be a failure. In order to declare a success, however, it was essential that there should be, in the words of one WTO official, a 'recalibration of expectations'. In other words, by setting the goals to be achieved at their lowest possible level, success might be declared. For five days, several thousand officials from the four corners of the planet converged on Hong Kong ultimately to produce a crippled anorexic mouse. They therefore went off for their Christmas and New Year holidays and a month well-earned vacation.

The contrast between the enthusiastic and entrepreneurial hustle and bustle of the streets of Vietnam and the eerie paralysis, procrastination, and hostility of the Hong Kong convention centre where the talks were held was devastating. While entrepreneurs throughout the world are busily engaged in seeking the opportunities that the global market provides, the rule and policy makers may be in the process of eroding, certainly fragmenting and possibly destroying, the global market. While entrepreneurs think globally of a world without borders, politicians are promoting nationalism, mercantilism, and protectionism. Although Hong Kong is less than a three-hour flight from Vietnam, it seemed not only a different continent but also a different planet. There was no reference to the great benefits and dynamic effects of open liberal trade, to the drive and potential of many developing countries, and to the great gains to be had from closer interdependence between the young and dynamic developing countries and the rapidly ageing and mature post-industrial countries. Hong Kong evinced virtually nothing of what should bring humanity together, but dwelt on divisions. There was absolutely no sense of seeking to build a global community. It was extremely depressing.

Global corporate responses to parochial political paralytic postures

With all the excitement of the global marketplace, globalist corporate executives have little interest in trade talks and feel that their time could be more usefully spent entering new markets and developing new products. In spite of its many faults, the GATT did provide a framework for business that has proved highly beneficial and dynamic. Its successor, the WTO, should do even more and better. In sharp contrast to the lawless, indeed anarchic, and highly unpredictable global business environment that character- ized the pre-World War II era, the GATT provided an environment characterized by rules, principles, predictability, and an increasing degree of transparency. Of course it was not perfect and the rules were often violated, but the difference may be between the environment in, say, New York, where there are rules, even if crime rates are high, to that of Kinshasa, where there are no rules and brutal crime is endemic. In which city would you rather live?

At present the world trade system is located in New York. The WTO talks should be seeking to move it to Stockholm, one of the world's most law-abiding and civic-minded cities. Instead, however, it may be heading for Naples and once there further on to Kinshasa. This is not sheer alarmism. One of the most egregious errors committed by many in the 1990s was to refer to globalization as 'irreversible'. This is simply not true; it should be remembered from the tragic history of the last century that globalization was regularly and brutally reversed. Of course, in the very long run it may be irreversible, but, as John Maynard Keynes commented, in the long run we are all dead and our children and grandchildren may have suffered greatly and unnecessarily in the meantime. Those who forget the past are, as George Santayana said, forced to repeat it.[25]

The fact that the paralysis of the WTO and the collapsed conferences such as Seattle and Cancún had relatively little impact on business life and little effect on stock markets, that the world economy has continued to grow in reasonably robust form, and that many corporations' profits are at an all-time high have all combined in inducing a false sense of security. Rule-making policy bodies such as the WTO are least needed when things are going well, but they may be desperately needed when things take a turn for the worse. There are a number of mega-fragilities underlying the world economy that could trigger something akin to a world depression: as Economics Nobel Prize Laureate Joe Stiglitz has written, 'Today, the system of capitalism is at a crossroads just as it was during the Great Depression.'[26] The world economy is basically being driven by two engines, China and the US, both of which have some potentially huge, albeit very different, problems ahead. What happens if one or both engines stall? In fact, if one engine stalls, it is pretty certain that the other will too.[27] The WTO existing today would be pretty useless and its unprincipled and acrimonious atmosphere might even cause the situation to worsen as it did in the 1930s.[28]

There are two ways in which the global corporate world has contributed to the current miasma, even if partly inadvertently, both of which have to do with perceptions. Perceptions of reality are much greater determinants of policy than reality itself.

The impact of destructive corporate behaviour: Part 1

In this context, one of the great and bewildering paradoxes of today is that in public opinion – and not only that of the activist protest community – globalization should have such pejorative connotations. Type 'globalization' in Google and the results are almost overwhelmingly negative. Globalization is held responsible for abuse of human rights, decrease in labour standards, environmental damage, child labour, extinction of cultures, depletion of resources, and much else. A politician, not only in Europe, the US, and Japan but also, amazingly, in countries such as Korea that have so overwhelmingly benefited from globalization, is far more likely to attack globalization as a perceived means of political gain than to promote it, which could be political suicide. This kind of primitive visceral populist nationalism is by no means the preserve of people such as Hugo Chávez, but indeed has been used to a great extent by France's Jacques Chirac. Part of the problem is that the global corporate executive has been more conspicuously absent than present from the global economic policy scene. The trade agenda in the North has been essentially captured by uncompetitive parochial economic sectors, e.g. in the US cotton plantation owners, textile and garment industry unions, and the steel industry, and ideologically driven and highly media-effective NGOs. Religious, environmental, human and animal rights groups, along with farmers, unionists, and backward industries have dominated the platform and, consequently, the agenda. While more forward, international, and dynamic companies played a very important role in driving the Uruguay Round, they have been out to lunch for most of the Doha Round, mainly on the basis that only a handful of sectors, primarily in services, stand to gain a lot in concrete terms out of this Round.[29] It is surprising that the financial markets have not seen this risk. If this is another indication of their myopic view, they need to take a second look.

Companies are good at securing their private interests, but are mainly absent when it comes to public goods. This is very shortsighted. Ultimately, a deteriorating business environment will have severe repercussions on all companies, no matter how dynamic and global; profits, paychecks, and head counts will all be reduced significantly. This myopia is well-illustrated in the case of France,[30] a champion of rearguard mercantilist procrastination, which in Hong Kong had delegations with very strong representation from unions, farmers, and militant NGOs, but where highly successful global companies, of which France counts many, were either absent or hiding. To name but one small but nevertheless evocative sector, where would Cognac be today without Greater China? Indeed, Hong Kong is on a per capita basis Cognac's most lucrative market, yet in the din of protectionist rhetoric emanating from the French delegation to Hong Kong, the voices of Rémy Martin, LVMH (Hennessy), Camus, and so on were mute! It is not just alcohol, fashion, or luxury goods. French automobile companies have become spectacularly successful in global markets, as has happened with France's insurance industry, high-speed train (TGV), nuclear energy (Alsthom), food and beverages (Danone), and cosmetics (L'Oréal). Had Carlos Ghosn, the highly successful CEO of Renault and Nissan, made an appearance at Hong Kong and lectured the French delegation on globalization, this could have had a great effect. However, while Ghosn was not there, the McDonald restaurant-smashing, Monsanto GMO farm-invading militant activist José Bové was! Part of the reason for the global agenda having been hijacked by narrow vested sectorial interests and other protectionist forces is that the policy terrain was abandoned by the globalist corporate forces.

The impact of destructive corporate behaviour: Part 2

The second way in which global business has contributed to anti-globalization has been in the highly publicized cases of unethical and wealth destructive corporate behaviour by Swissair, Enron, Parmalat, Sumitomo, etc. A term frequently used by NGOs that seems to get strong resonance from the public has been 'corporate driven globalization' or, even more discrediting, 'corporate greed-driven globalization'. This accounts for the shift that has occurred in the last few years between 'anti-globalization' and 'alter-globalization', the 'alter' being short for alternative and hence an alternative form of globalization that would exclude or greatly limit the role of greedy profit-seeking labour-exploiting, environment-devastating multinational corporations. The fact that this is little more than pie-in-the-sky pure illusion is irrelevant. It has great appeal.

There is here a false dual, but deeply entrenched, perception. The first is that the sole beneficiaries of globalization are multinational corporations; the second is that multinational corporations are prejudicial to the welfare of ordinary citizens. Hence, 'globalization is evil'. Visit Vietnam and you will see that the main beneficiaries are the Vietnamese people. Sadly it is not yet *all* the Vietnamese people, but it is a growing number; more to the point, contrast the situation today with what it was ten years ago. Unless a scenario is preferred where everyone is poor with the exception of high-ranking political leaders, e.g. the Pyongyang scenario, it must be admitted that the Vietnamese people have significantly benefited from globalization. It is true that global companies also benefit from globalization, since both profits and procurement are spread across the globe in order to maximize economies of scale, economies of scope, and extract maximum advantage from their global supply chains, but it is also true that this is at the cost of much greater competition. Also, as a general phenomenon, direct investments by multinational companies tend to propel, rather than repel, domestic entrepreneurship through the opportunities for supply, procurement, distribution, consulting, servicing, and so on, that are generated. While in many poor countries there is virtually no middle class, the job opportunities provided by multinational companies offer the prospects of creating a middle class.

Of course it is critical not to embellish reality. Reality also includes some quite unedifying examples, such as the often-cited brutal exploitation of labour in factories producing for Nike in Asia. The Google globalization search provides a number of sites focused on sweatshops in developing country textiles, garments, footwear, sports goods, toys, etc., factories producing for household Western names, such as Gap, Wal-Mart, H&M, and Carrefour. Some of it is exaggerated and taken out of context. The sole temporary advantage many of these countries have, e.g. Bangladesh, is the cheapness of their labour; impose a 40-hour, let alone a 35-hour week, and a minimum wage commensurate with wages in the West and the jobs will rapidly evaporate.[31] Furthermore, in most instances workers engaged in textile factories are much better off than they were in the fields or if they worked in purely domestic industries, e.g. construction. The author was able to witness the contrast after having visited a number of textile factories in Economic Processing Zones (EPZs) outside Dhaka, where conditions were relatively spartan but by no means Dickensian. On the road back to Dhaka were many stone quarries and brick factories where women and children were working under brutal and exploitative conditions, not only in the burdens they had to carry but also all the dust they had to breathe. The protest community does not pay much attention to these cases as there is no political and media mileage to be gained from attacking Bangladeshi local companies or authorities.

Under no circumstances, of course, should the brutal onus of domestic industrial employment or the travails of agricultural work be used as an excuse for maltreating workers engaged in production for Western companies. However, it is important to put these things into perspective. In the meantime, companies must clean up their act and seek to ensure that cases such as the brutal maltreatment and sexual harassment that occurred in the Nike factories be eliminated. In doing so, companies must not go overboard.[32] At the garment factories in Bangladesh, which produce for high-brand Western companies, the author noticed that there were no children and was told that their corporate customers required that no one under the age of 18 be hired. This is stupidity bordering on criminality. It would be admissible if the majority of Bangladeshi girls could go on to secondary school, but that is not the situation at present.[33] The options are limited and not especially encouraging: the quarries, the fields, the very low paid and long hours jobs in the service sectors, and prostitution. Another high risk for the young unemployed in poor countries such as Bangladesh is falling prey to people traffickers – the fastest growing and most lucrative illegal industry[34] – and finding themselves engaged in slavery in places where they will not be seen, let alone saved, by Western civil society or international organizations, such as the International Labour Organization (ILO). A proper balance needs to be found. It is difficult, but its pursuit is one of the most fundamental and critical priorities in the current global era.

The global market, global community, global executives, and global citizens

It was Benjamin Disraeli, the great Victorian British Tory statesman, who in 1845,[35] three years before the publication of *The Communist Manifesto* by Karl Marx and Friedrich Engels, wrote of what he called the 'two nations' cohabiting in the UK: the rich and the poor. The Global Community is also composed of two entities: the haves (money, mobile phones, overseas travel, good schools, good medicine, etc.) and the have-nots (any or few of those things). The haves account for about 1.5 billion members of the human race, the have-nots for the remaining 4.5 billion. As C. K. Prahalad, Stuart Hart, Bala Chakravarthy, Anna Lindblom, and an increasing coterie of authors have demonstrated,[36] the greatest opportunities for companies' growth and profits in the future are to be found in the bottom layers of the global population pyramid. It is in the enlightened self-interest, therefore, of corporations that conditions in the overall global economic and administrative environment should be as conducive as possible to growth among developing countries.[37] By the middle of this century, Africa will have a population of 1.5 billion, about the same as China and India. Imagine an African market akin to China's! Here again, financial markets and especially the main players in institutional investment have to give up the 'numbers-only', short-term view and see the broader context of growth opportunities and the complexity, which needs to be managed, not only regarding markets, but also the political and macroeconomic context. These developments, however, will not happen on the basis of self-propelled momentum. It is not things that happen; it is people who make things happen!

Conclusion

The message is simple. In order for companies to reap the potential benefits of highly dynamic economies such as Vietnam, China, Pakistan, Chile, and the potential benefits to be gained from other emerging markets in the process of reform, the global institutional framework has to be in a good, solid condition; it has to have legitimacy, credibility, and impact; and it has to be driven by a spirit that is animated by a desire to create a genuine global market, not to its destruction or fragmentation into diminishing parts.

Global executives must play a crucial role in that respect. In order to participate in building a vibrant and lucrative global market, they must also contribute to creating a real and increasingly united global community. To that end, the global executive must be, and act as, a global citizen – nothing more, nothing less. As a conclusion, the complexity of the global economy and its political framework is huge and executives can ask themselves: 'Can I make a difference?' It is obvious that new players can make a difference, if they come with dedication and a clear message.

References

[1] The author wishes to thank his former MBA student, Roland Tschanz, with Nestlé in Vietnam, who, over an excellent luncheon in Ho Chi Minh City, provided him with many fascinating insights.

[2] Hanshaw, Natasha, 'Trade and Vietnam', Evian Group Trade Issue of the Month, December 2005, http://www.eviangroup.org/p/1181.pdf.

[3] Templar, Robert, *Shadows and Wind: A View of Modern Vietnam*, London: Abacus, 1997.

[4] The author was in Santiago de Chile in late October 2005 and wishes to express great gratitude to the members of the Chile IMD Alumni Association for having organized a fascinating workshop on the Chilean economy and its regional and global challenges.

[5] Lehmann, Jean-Pierre, 'Argentina Stuck on the Periphery of a Globalized World', *Yale Global Online*, 20 February 2004.

[6] Ajami, Fouad, *The Dream Palace of the Arabs: A Generation's Odyssey*, New York: Random House, 1999.

[7] Lehmann, Fabrice, 'Trade and the Arab Region', Evian Group Trade Issue of the Month; http://www.eviangroup.org/p/1116.pdf.

[8] 'A Survey of Saudi Arabia', *The Economist*, 7 January 2006.

[9] The author has become in recent years significantly more engaged in Pakistan and has been struck how, contrary to much of the media stereotypes, the Pakistani economy and society are on the move and increasingly opening up. Special thanks for interpreting Pakistan are due to Manzoor Ahmad, Huma Fakhar, Sheikh Inaamul Haque, Syed Babar Ali, Shafiq Ahmed Siddiqi, and Roland Decorvet, General Manager of Nestlé in Pakistan.

[10] Ricardo, David, *Principles of Political Economy and Taxation*, 1817.

[11] Khaldun, Ibn, *kitAb al-'ibAr*, 1380s.

[12] Woronoff, Jon, *Hong Kong – Capitalist Paradise*, 1980.

[13] Garrett, Michael W. and Lehmann, Jean-Pierre, 'The China Challenge', *European Business Forum*, December 2005.

[14] Two excellent summaries of the World Trade Talks in Hong Kong are Guy de Jonquières, 'All at Sea in World Trade Talks', *The Financial Times*, 9 January 2006, and Marcos Jank, 'Protectionists without Borders', *Telos-EU*, 16 January 2006.

[15] Panitchpakdi, Supachai, and Clifford, Mark, *China and the WTO: Changing China, Changing World Trade*, Singapore: John Wiley & Sons, Ltd, Asia, 2001.

[16] Lehmann, Jean-Pierre, 'Global and Domestic Governance and the Challenge of Peace and Prosperity in the 21st Century', Evian Group Policy Brief, October 2002, http://www.eviangroup.org/p/13.pdf.

[17] For the agricultural issue at the WTO, see Edward Gresser, 'Fate of the Farmers in Balance', *Yale Global Online*, 1 November 2005, Kevin Watkins, 'To Save Global Trade Talks, Act on

Agriculture', *Yale Global Online*, 7 October 2005; and Olivier Cattaneo and Valérie Engammare, 'Why Is Agriculture So Important and What Must Be Done?', Evian Group Policy Brief, February 2004, http://www.eviangroup.org/p/455.pdf.

[18] For the Doha Ministerial Declaration adopted on 20 November 2001, see http://www.wto.org/english/thewto_e/minist_e/min01_e/mindecl_e.htm.

[19] World Bank, *Global Agricultural Trade and Developing Countries*, 2005.

[20] See the section 'Hypocrisy of the Rich', in Martin Wolf, *Why Globalization Works*, New Haven, Connecticut: Yale University Press, 2004.

[21] Figures are taken from the Progressive Policy Institute, Trade and Global Markets, http://www.ppionline.org/ppi_ka.cfm?knlgAreaID=108.

[22] An excellent article on French agricultural policy and subsidies is by Pierre Boulanger and Patrick Messerlin, 'The Enemy Within', *Wall Street Journal*, 10 November 2005.

[23] Kilman, Scott, 'To Soothe Anger over Subsidies, US Cotton Tries Wooing Africa', *Yale Global Online*, 5 August 2005.

[24] Engammare, Valérie, 'What Has Happened Since the WTO Ministerial in Cancún – and What Does It Mean for the Doha Round?', Evian Group Policy Brief, March 2004, http://www.eviangroup.org/p/481.pdf.

[25] Santayana, George, *Life of Reason*, Vol. 1, New edn, New York: Prentice-Hall, 1905.

[26] Stiglitz, Joe, *Globalization and Its Discontents*, Basingstoke: Penguin Books, 2002.

[27] See Charlene Barshefsky and Edward Gresser, 'Revolutionary China, Complacent America', *Wall Street Journal*, 15 September 2005.

[28] Lehmann, Jean-Pierre, 'Ignorance of History Lies at the Roots of this Malaise in which We Find Ourselves', *South China Morning Post*, 13 December 2005.

[29] Beattie, Alan, 'Beneath the Bureaucracy Lie Rich Rewards', *Financial Times*, 25 September 2005.

[30] Lehmann, Jean-Pierre, 'Deconstructing France at the WTO', Evian Group Policy Brief, January 2006, and 'France and the Doha Debacle', Evian Group Policy Brief, January 2005.

[31] The author undertook a field trip in Bangladesh in 2004. He is grateful to Farooq Sobhan, President of the Bangladeshi Enterprise Institute, for his hospitality and many insights. He is also most grateful to his close friend Iqbal Quadir, visionary founder of the fascinating company GrameenPhone, who took him around parts of the magnificent Bangladeshi countryside to meet with villagers who had acquired his product. See 'Bottom-Up Economics: A Conversation with Iqbal Quadir', *Harvard Business Review*, August 2003.

[32] There is an excellent article by Ethan Kapstein, 'The Corporate Ethics Crusade', *Foreign Affairs*, September–October 2001, in which he warns companies not to allow the ethical agenda to be hijacked, with the result that often good intentions produced poor results.

[33] According to the gender-related development index of the UNDP's 2005 Human Development Report, http://www.undp.org/, out of 177 countries, Bangladesh ranked 139th in female combined primary, secondary, and tertiary education.

[34] See *World Migration Report 2005*, International Organization for Migration.

[35] Disraeli, Benjamin, *Sybil*, 1845.

[36] Prahalad, C. K. and Hart, Stuart, 'The Fortune at the Bottom of the Pyramid', *Strategy and Business*, 2002, and Chakravarthy, Bala and Lindblom, Anna, 'Serving the Poor: Identifying and Managing Win–Win Opportunities', *Perspectives for Managers*, June 2005.

[37] Lehmann, Jean-Pierre, 'Going for Global Growth', *World Today*, May 2005.

Part II

Impact of Changes in the Competitive Landscape and Business Models on Selected Industries

4

The Need to Look at Complexity at the Industry Level

Ulrich Steger and Wolfgang Amann

As seen in the previous chapter, on the macro-level, all drivers of complexity come into play. There are close to an unlimited number of players with different interests (diversity) in the global economy, but their actions are highly interdependent (e.g. protectionist retaliation, negotiation positions). These many actions and counteractions lead to an unpredictable outcome, which creates ambiguity. The number of unknown, but emerging, competitors from developing countries offering similar or even fake products is creating a feeling of unease. Simple events (e.g. the suspicion that Iran goes nuclear) can create a fast flux, changing pre-conditions and ambiguities.

The present thesis for this analysis is that, at the industry level, the dominant complexity driver is interdependence. That does not mean that other drivers are completely irrelevant, but it is known from classic industry analysis that the rivalry between firms – next to their way of organizing the value chain – dominates the profit level and therefore the tension among companies. At this level of analysis, there is less diversity as major global competitors often follow a similar business model and dominant logic of competing. This is true from the automotive to the pharmaceutical industries, even in the tool-making industry. At least in the perception of managers, there is thus less ambiguity as – from experience – the responses to competitive moves are clear. If company A reduces prices, increases advertising, relocates production, and even R&D to China, etc., companies B and C do the same. This experience-based approach, which is often less friendly, is called herd behaviour, and it has two disadvantages: first, it might miss important changes in the environment and, second, it often leaves everyone worse off. The price level in the industry has declined, but the relative position of each player remains the same.

Interdependence as a complexity generator has become more dominant for two reasons. First, a lot of global industries have consolidated in recent years and nowadays a couple of global companies lead or dominate the market. Their rivalry – often in a narrow oligopoly – is fierce as everyone watches everyone else and responds immediately. The interdependence is significantly lower in the atomistic competition of many small, fragmented players that can only adapt their behaviour to market conditions, not try to shape them (an ideal that still dominates textbooks). Second, information and communication technology, information brokers, and the media have done a lot to create much more market transparency, making it difficult to hide competitive moves. Supply-chain management and logistics experts have increased their capacity to react quickly. Many markets are therefore showing the features of a commodity market: they are becoming cyclical and price-sensitive. Companies are trying to avoid this 'commoditization' by differentiating, but this is an uphill battle; the market forces would soon erase any gains made.

However, even with less diversity and ambiguity, the interdependence is generating a fast flux in many industries. New competitors are appearing (currently firms globalizing from an Indian and Chinese home-base) and technology and customer behaviour are changing. Former growth markets will mature in three to five years and require very different rules of engagement. These general considerations are exemplified in the following chapters based on the idiosyncrasies in the shipping, automotive, electronic manufacturing, and financial services industries.

5
Shipping Organizations – The Ultimate Global Players

Peter Lorange

This chapter focuses on several critical issues that have been found to make shipping organizations more performance-oriented, especially in increasingly complex and dynamic environments. The question is explored of how to create a truly high-performance organizational culture in shipping organizations, which typically operate in one of the most open and globalized economic sectors in the world, and should thus be truly global. We also look at how they can achieve this without being overwhelmed by the resulting complexity. Still, many such firms are often conservative and traditional in their focus. One reason is the often heavy emphasis on the asset value of the ships, which is an understandable approach considering that ship owning is one of the most asset-intensive industries. However, it is important not to neglect other organizational issues.

An obvious focus for strategy making in shipping companies is good, market-related decision making: fixing the ships on long charters versus short and/or entering the charter market versus leaving it, i.e. operating in the spot market. Another key issue is to strive for noncommodity segments. A reasonable portfolio strategy is also critical, above all, for settling on an acceptable overall risk profile for the shipping firm.[1] The typical shipping organization itself is perhaps not sufficiently focused on these strategic issues. In order to be a winner, a strong global organizational platform is vital to ensure decision-making consistency. There are three critical strategic areas that will be discussed: the need to (1) excel with commodity-based strategies, (2) push for niche strategies, and (3) articulate an overall portfolio strategy for the firm. To succeed in this, a clear geographic strategy is also needed, consistent with the above three strategies. In particular, geographic growth is important – an area where China is currently centre stage.

A third set of issues – organizational strategies – are derived from this. A global focus is essential, to be addressed by creating an opportunity-driven organizational culture. There is also a need for internal entrepreneurs, for a focus on both cost and quality excellence, a robust strategy, and, finally, for the ability to be able to live with some key dilemmas. Let us now first discuss the key strategic issues, before continuing with one critical geographic issue – China – and, finally, moving on to discuss critical organizational issues – all interdependent, of course.

Strategic choices

Here the three major strategic options for shipping companies will be discussed: commodity strategies, niche strategies, and portfolio strategies.

Commodity strategies

Shipping markets are often supercompetitive. There tend to be few – if any – frictional barriers when it comes to moving shipping assets around the world to anywhere a particular demand might be – a rather unique situation, which fosters fast flux. This is in contrast to most businesses, which rely on fixed manufacturing plants, office networks, and/or distribution systems and structures. The volatility of market amplitudes is also higher than for most other industries, in the sense that oversupply of ships will drive the market down – fast – while overdemand will drive the market up – also fast, and high! The shipping market tends to be rather open to new entrants, as there are low or no barriers to entry, and also has typically relatively easy access to capital. Rapid increases in the number and diversity of players are easily possible.

How does one develop viable strategies in such commodity settings if, say, one is active in the bunker or the day bulk markets? A strong commodity strategy must take into account at least five classes of issues:

1. **The chartering strategy**, bearing in mind the need for good timing. How can one develop an understanding of the market, cutting through the paralysing ambiguity and uncertainty? When does one get in, by entering into time charters, and when does one get out, by going in the open spot market? If opting for time charters, how long should they be, i.e. long versus short? Above all, when does one see turning points in the markets, so that one can dynamically update the chartering strategy? Figure 5.1 gives a picture of several cycles in a shipping market, where the long/short and in/out decisions are made as a consequence of the turning points in the market development.

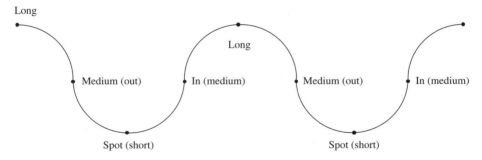

Figure 5.1   In/out, short/long chartering decisions at various phases of the ship market cycle

The shipping market forecasting firm Marsoft makes market predictions for the major size types and trade legs of the tanker market, the day bulk market, and the container ship market. Its approach is based on a careful analysis of factors stimulating both the supply side and the demand side.[1] Marsoft is also able to construct, for major markets and trades, a cumulative probability distribution regarding future expectations and extrapolations for spot rates. Figure 5.2 gives a picture of this, for

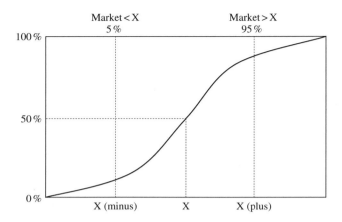

Figure 5.2 Future expectations – cumulative distribution of spot rates

one market and trade (say, day bulk from Brazil to Rotterdam). There is a 50% chance that the market will be either higher than X or lower than X. There is a 5% chance that the market will go lower than X (minus) and a 95% chance that the market will go higher than X (plus). This type of analysis thus helps the decision maker to get a better 'handle' on the turning points in the markets.

2. **The ordering of new ships** and the purchase and sale of second-hand ships. Many of the issues discussed above also apply here. Timing is, once again, critical. A counter-cyclical attitude towards the markets will be a key aspect.

3. **A low cost focus**. This is essential both for purchasing ships and for running them. By aiming to order and buy ships when the new building and/or second-hand markets are low, costs can be kept in check. Regarding operations, it is particularly important to keep related costs low, especially in view of the emergence of crews from less developed countries. Having a lower breakeven point than the competition means lower rates can be sustained. Similarly, maintenance and dealing must be undertaken systematically, in order to keep costs under control. A mentality of squeezing costs must prevail – proactively and not merely as a reaction to a crisis.

4. **Take advantage of the volatile environment**. It could be argued that it might be unrealistic to expect sustained high shipping markets unless there is an exceptional economic growth situation in one industry and/or geography of the world. China,

with its extraordinary annual GNP growth, is an example of this. It is dramatically fuelling the growth of most shipping markets and keeping rates at exceptionally high levels. It follows from this that shipping executives must also be sensitive to the risks associated with this situation. For instance, what about excessive congestion in Chinese harbours? What about terrorist attacks, say on a container ship? Is the political situation in China sufficiently stable, and so on?

5. **Operations or asset play**? Some companies have decided to adopt a simplified commodity strategy. Rather than emphasizing all the issues discussed above, they may focus primarily on, say, timing decisions for the purchase and sale of ships, with relatively less emphasis on the cost side. They may end up losing money on operating their ships, but making a lot of money on the appropriate asset play. Other firms, by contrast, may focus solely on running their ships, avoiding too many variations in fleet size, i.e. an operations focus. In the author's opinion it is the combination of the two approaches that will tend to yield the most potent commodity strategy – both asset play and an operational focus.

Niche strategies

Many shipping organizations will of course have seen that there may be ways to reduce exposure to global commodity strategies by finding specialized niches where competition is less fierce. Unique competences, critical for success in a given niche, will also create barriers to competition. The key would be for a shipping organization to be able to see business opportunities before they are obvious to everyone else. This would call for more unique customer relationships – being closer to the customer, understanding his or her needs more intimately, and developing real trust via continuing interaction. In this respect, possessing unique know-how that the customer can appreciate will be vital. Such know-how might be technological, e.g. relating to special cranes and equipment on the ships; systems-related, in terms of safety, health, and environmental policies; and IT-related, e.g. more precise scheduling of a customer's containers, and so on.

It seems important for a good niche strategy to be evolving all the time, building on already established strengths. Driving fast flux may then turn change into a problem for others. Potential competitors will typically want to copy one's niche strategy to gain benefits from enjoying such a niche. Here, it should be kept in mind that ships tend to be relatively easy to copy, and shipbuilding capacity tends to be ample. New buildings are coming out at ever-greater speeds. The fast flux of technological advances often leads to even more capacity. The implication is that niche-focused ships must evolve in their developments all the time to stay ahead. They must also be ordered at advantageous times, to keep costs down. Clearly, there are definite links between commodity strategies and niche strategies.

What, then, is the best way to protect against competition for a niche strategy? Huge investments in what might be seen as adjacent fields to shipping may be the key. Marketing and terminal organization of ferry ship companies; marketing, reservations, and logistics systems of cruise ship owners; terminal, transportation, and IT support systems for container line shipping companies; and engineering support for large, heavy-lift cranes all represent examples of effective ways to protect niche strategies. This is done by investing in broadening the strategies and not primarily by investing in the ships themselves.

Corporate portfolio strategies

It goes without saying that the concept of diversification – and the development of a portfolio strategy – may not have much validity when one is operating in the pure commodity segment. Admittedly, there could be some diversification by having different in/out, long/short profiles for ships, but this would in fact mean that management would be following a different policy for part of its fleet than what it actually believes to be optimal, based on its understanding of the market. Clearly diversification into niches can, however, be valid. Also, management may want to complement steel (i.e. ships) with paper (i.e. shipping stocks), perhaps as a hedge, by going short or long relative to the profile of the firm's own ship portfolio. A similar diversification can be done by doing freight hedges, say, via the IMAREX market.[1]

There seem to be three overriding questions when it comes to developing a portfolio strategy for a shipping firm:

- How many shipping niches (commodity markets, niche markets, others) can the firm handle? Here, it seems important to remember that too much diversification will tend to lessen the benefits of a portfolio strategy approach – strategy means choice!

• What is the nature/degree of interdependence between the chosen shipping market strategies?
• For each of these shipping market strategies what is the degree of maturity? Is it still a niche strategy or is it a commodity strategy?

Three types of strategies for shipping companies have been discussed: commodity strategies, niche strategies, and portfolio strategies. Modern shipping firms probably tend to pursue a mix of these, typically not seeing adherence to a single one as providing the right answer. Rather, they may see the overall strategic choice issue as a dilemma – each strategy will have pluses and minuses and it will be up to the leadership to find the best way to balance the dilemma! Such balancing capabilities will become increasingly crucial in the complex environments of the shipping industry.

Geographic issues

As stated earlier, it seems critical for the development of strong shipping markets that there is an exceptional economic growth driver of some sort underpinning them. The most recent contributor to the burgeoning development of most of the world's shipping markets is the exceptional economic development of China. Shipping executives may want to ask to what extent this exceptional growth will continue – and what are the chances of 'derailment'. For instance, will the development of China's infrastructure, when it comes to parts and roads, keep up? So far the answer seems to be 'yes'. Will the current political stability prevail? Again, so far this definitely seems to be the case.

Will continuing steel production and consumption drive ongoing growth? It is known that modern buildings are constructed with higher strength steel, especially for the more modern constructions taking place now. The same is true for the use of steel in infrastructure such as bridges. Automotive manufacturing also uses relatively less steel per car now than before. When taken together, this might lead to a reduction in steel growth in China, with a consequential lessening of general economic growth as well. So far, however, this negative growth scenario has not taken place.

Energy consumption growth in China could potentially represent another threat to ongoing economic growth. Can China actually get enough energy to sustain its position as the emerging manufacturing centre for much of the world's manufacturing activities? As a related issue, can the burning of fossil fuels continue in the same way in the future as it has until now, with its effects on pollution and CO_2 gas emissions? What about positive effects as a result of China's offshore exploration for oil, as well as its hydroelectric programmes? Again, the answer seems to be that – so far – China has been able to sustain its economic growth in the face of its energy shortage considerations, and its offshore oil exploration operations and hydroelectric programmes may well bear fruit.

What about potential fragility when it comes to the container shipping system that caters for the bulk of China's exports? Could, for instance, a terrorist attack or a particular container ship disrupt the flow of export goods? Again, so far any such risks and concerns seem to have been dealt with in a realistic way. There do not seem to have been any negative effects on China's growth momentum.

There are undoubtedly many more factors that could potentially have a dampening effect on China's continuing growth. What is important is that shipping company executives take all these factors into account – including those not mentioned above – when developing their strategies. There is no way to avoid coping with this diversity of factors; there are hardly any simple decisions left. A potential slowdown of growth in China would in all likelihood lead to a major drop in the world's shipping markets.

Organizational issues

Organizational culture

The optimum organizational culture is to be able to see business opportunities before everyone else sees them. Five interrelated aspects of such a culture will be discussed. First, the organization must function as a 'meeting place' where business problems can be aired in a networked environment, thus allowing various solutions to be proposed. The key factor is to make sure that the relevant people meet in a network context. In organizations that are now more typically 'flat' and project-based, it is essential that the network is broadly defined so that inputs, solutions, and inspirations can also be received from outside sources – shippers, brokers, banks, and the like. Truly creative solutions probably go hand in hand with a broad, open-minded network organization.

To allow for more experimentation, i.e. trying new things out quickly rather than ending up overanalysing and procrastinating, it is important here to realize that timing is everything and that a willingness to commit early is part of a winning organizational culture. Unfortunately, the desire to create a more professional organization has often been translated (wrongly) to mean more analysis, more scenarios, and more deliberations, even at the expense of maintaining a decision-making focus. To succeed in shipping, decisions must typically be taken early on.

Juxtaposing traditional and radically different business views is related to the need to maintain a networked organizational focus, where there should be no 'sacred cows'. The key issue is to continually challenge one's own business model with new thinking, always believing that 'good can be done even better'. While scenario planning is very important in shipping companies – in order to better understand the relevant upside as well as potential downsides of any strategy – such planning must not become a goal in itself.

Systematic learning is also critical. Learning means that one cannot think about certain outcomes as failures; rather, they must be seen as experience gained so that things can be done better next time. It is imperative to avoid a culture of stigmatization and to encourage learning by analysing what can be done better, rather than to focus on the negative side if things do not work out as well as hoped.

Having no silos, no 'kingdoms', no culture of 'not invented here' is also critical. This is closely related to the need to create a network culture, where the various organizational departments do not function as barriers against a free-flowing interaction. Internal politicking would thus be of no positive value.

Internal entrepreneurs

Doers are critical in all organizations – and shipping organizations are no exception – in order to get things done, accelerate actions, and the like. Often the owner and/or CEO is the most pre-eminent internal entrepreneur in a shipping company. The 'problem', however, is that there is then often such dominance at the top that there is no room for anyone else to play an internal entrepreneurial role. Typically, however, several internal entrepreneurs are needed for sustained success. To provide space for internal entrepreneurship is thus critical. An effective and successful internal entrepreneur must be able to:

- See business opportunities when they present themselves, i.e. show good judgement and strong creativity, and – in order to do all of this – must probably have a broad, outside-oriented network of contacts. This creates benefits beyond allowing for a mere early warning system.
- Draw on the firm's entire know-how base, not only the parts of it that he or she is particularly close to. There can thus be no silo thinking in the mind of the internal entrepreneur. The ability to mobilize the firm's capabilities in new, creative ways will be critical.
- Lead inspirationally, encouraging members of the specific project teams he or she is responsible for to perform well and give of their best. The classic power hierarchy, with classic control, is not the way to get things done for the internal entrepreneur.
- Be close to the CEO, while maintaining some distance. The internal entrepreneur needs to have the confidence of the CEO so that there are no 'surprises' for the chief executive and to have a platform to work from implicitly or explicitly provided by the CEO. At the same time, he or she must also have some distance from the CEO, i.e. some room to execute, some space to perform, so that excessive centralization does not hinder him or her from getting the job done. Unfortunately, many shipping companies have struggled with this, heavy centralization at the top often means that internal entrepreneurs are few and far between, or even nonexistent.

No-nonsense cost-driven delivery without sacrificing quality

The successful shipping organization must be the lowest-cost provider. It must also have the best possible way to provide value for its customers. It is not a matter of either/or, but both. How can this be achieved? Four issues will be indicated here.

First, it is necessary to identify the 'must-win battles' that are essential for success. What does the firm need to have in-house versus what can be outsourced? What is essential to create customer value? What is the customer willing to pay for? Total openness is important here. Everything else can be outsourced. Unfortunately, many shipping organizations are reluctant to outsource, based on traditional binds and on the fact that there might be a reluctance to move physical parts of the organization elsewhere to focus on new capabilities. One can, however, easily find a situation where one needs to dismantle/outsource parts of one's organization while simultaneously attempting to build/attract new members in other parts of the organization.

Second, it is important to go for the lowest-cost solutions in all respects and in all cases. It is essential here to leave nothing 'on the table'. Thus, efficient operations per ship as well as in headquarters needs to be coupled with efficient management of the financial side, to achieve the best possible finance costs to allow one to do one's best, coupled also with the most efficient utilization of one's marketing network. This needs to be done in such a way that the lowest-cost solutions prevail. This is a function of achieving all cost advantages; the lowest-cost advantage can in fact only be achieved through such an attitude.

Third, a positive control culture is essential – not a reactive, classic one, but a performance-driven one. It is important here to set realistic but stretch targets, to provide feedback (positive as well as negative) to those responsible on a regular basis, and to have clear performance-based bonuses associated with achieved performance.

Fourth, benchmarking of competitors will also be important. One obvious way to benchmark is to look at the cost side. A potentially much more relevant benchmarking has to do with how customers see the company – benchmarking one's value to the customer relative to competitors is essential.

Robust strategy

There are many aspects to maintaining a robust strategy, but four will be pointed out, some of which have already been discussed. It is critical that strategies be kept simple, as already noted, and to remember that strategy means choice! Complexity should normally be avoided. Unfortunately, however, many shipping companies have followed strategies where they have diversified into a large number of activities, often from a portfolio strategy point of view based on 'not putting all their eggs in one basket'. Such broad diversification leads to a lot of complexity, and it is perhaps more difficult than previously thought to maintain a realistic focus. A portfolio strategy with meaningful diversification is, of course, good. Such a strategy can still be kept simple.

Managing the firm's overall risk exposure will be as critical as ever. In this regard, shipping is different from many other industries in that each discrete investment decision, involving a particular ship, tends to be large. A well-thought-out portfolio strategy will be essential for this, with particular focus on a balance between longer-term contractual coverage versus operating in the spot market. Bringing in co-investors for a particular new project is another way of managing risk. Making use of futures contracts, such as through IMAREX, is a third. Investing in shipping company shares, rather than directly in 'steel' itself, is another way to manage risk.

A customer-centric focus is an absolute must. We have already touched upon aspects of this. From the customer's viewpoint, it is vital that a relevant know-how base is being established. The company must be willing to exchange knowledge with customers to satisfy new customer needs. Strategy thus means 'being prepared'.

As has previously been discussed, in order to be the lowest-cost provider, it is necessary to have a realistic, no-frills strategy.

At ease with key dilemmas

As noted, the shipping industry is both global and highly volatile. The resulting demands are full of paradoxes. Therefore shipping executives will have to live with dilemmas, not finite answers to their strategic issues. There are at least five such key dilemmas that cannot be resolved in one way or another. It is a matter of 'and, and, and' – not either/or. The first three have already been dealt with at length; the last two should be clear to the reader by implication.

Short-term and long-term

It is important here for much of the focus to be on short-term actions, keeping some ships in the spot market while also, at the same time, having other ships on long-term contracts, long-term charter parties. It is not a matter of either/or. This means that one must have the flexibility to utilize short-term market swings, as well as having longer-term stability from longer-term contracts.

Local and global

Customer-centricity means that one has to be close to the customer in his or her own environment, and thus have a local presence in many places. At the same time, one must have a global focus on how to run the fleet, how to keep a globally driven cost view, and the like. Here, too, there is a dilemma, i.e. to find a balance between local and global.

Commodity and niche

Clearly, much of shipping will always be commodity-driven. It is important that a firm has a strategy that allows it to be competitive. At the same time, it must also strive to establish itself in niches where a more customer-centric focus can prevail and where it can get paid for such customer-driven services. Unfortunately, such niches tend to be disappearing relatively quickly within shipping, where it is typically easy for others to copy what a particular pioneering company has developed. The key aspect here is always to push for new niches while, at the same time, being effective when it comes to commodity strategies.

Intuition and discipline

As seen with the internal entrepreneur, it is essential that he or she is given the room to take the initiative based on intuitive judgement. At the same time, a disciplined focus based on thorough analysis is also important. The trick here is to find a way to handle both, i.e. not to go overboard in relying only on intuition or on excessive analysis and discipline. The former can lead to too many 'trigger happy' decisions, while the latter can lead to no decisions at all.

Continuity and change

Finally, it is necessary to develop a balance between a stable focus and a dynamic one. Here it is important to realize which competencies need to be maintained in a stable way, while at the same time trying to develop a dynamic view of how to evolve these competencies. This means that continuity and change need to coexist harmoniously if a shipping company is to be successful.

Conclusions

There are many aspects to creating more effective shipping companies in complex environments. There will always be a critical need for crisp strategic thinking and execution in this perhaps most global of all industries: a strong understanding of the commodity strategy reality; a concrete ability to seek out niches; and a robust, focused portfolio strategy. In addition, a firm 'handle' on China – today's key growth inducer for global shipping markets – is essential. There are also at least five broad organizational issues that relate to the execution of the strategic and geographic challenges, and that thus need to be dealt with to gain more effectiveness. This would mean fostering an opportunity-driven organizational culture, having a cadre of effective internal entrepreneurs, following a focus that strives to achieve both the lowest cost and highest customer value, having a strategy that is indeed robust and does not change all the time, and, finally, putting on the table a number of dilemmas that the firm must face and developing a management approach that involves 'living' with these dilemmas. A successful shipping company is built around a good global organization benefiting from a global focus. It is not enough simply to make brilliant asset-related timing decisions based on a feel for the markets. This must be done with an organization that is 'up to speed' – global and professional!

Reference

[1] Lorange, Peter, *Shipping Company Strategies: Global Management under Turbulent Conditions*, Oxford: Elsevier, 2004.

6
Managing Complexity Caused by Industry Dilemmas: The Case of the Automotive Industry

Ulrich Steger

Dilemmas generate complexity

Beyond the rhetoric of 'win–win', 'outpacing', 'synergies', etc., the real life of managers is much more shaped by dilemmas. Although many are reluctant to admit it – as it sounds like an excuse – few reject the description. Dilemmas occur when there are conflicting goals or demands which cannot be met with the given resources at the same time (or a foreseeable time period). They are more common than not. Examples include cost saving versus customer satisfaction, 'partnership' along the supply chain versus cost pressure, employee satisfaction versus restructuring needs, etc. The eternal dilemma in global companies is between local responsiveness and global economies of scale, which leads to a type of matrix management, so typical for multinational companies.

Priorities have to be set, but other goals or demands cannot be neglected completely; otherwise this could generate too much friction or become counterproductive. In short, dilemmas cannot be solved (sometimes at best temporarily balanced), but they need to be managed – permanently.

Dilemmas generate complexity with several 'transmission belts':

- **'Law of unintended consequences' as a result of interdependence**. Decisions in dilemma situations create unforeseen situations (often those that one hoped could be ignored). The neglected demand could be stronger than anticipated and the friction higher than expected. This explains why short-term-driven companies often 'flip-flop', e.g. a cost-cutting initiative is chased by a follow-up in customer satisfaction. When the results of cost cutting are seen on the top line, seasoned managers know that this can be a never-ending cycle. In any case, reality cannot be ignored and a (counter-) reaction is needed. Therefore, to a certain degree volatility is unavoidable.
- **Multiplicity**. Dilemmas occur often, because goals or demands are backed up by specific stakeholders – internally (quality department, sales organization, etc.) or externally (from financial analyst to environmental or social pressure groups). They will continue to lobby, creating pressure and tension, which will often not go away without being satisfied to some extent, keeping things in flux.
- **The ambiguity often inherent in dilemmas**. There is not only an abundance of information but the information as such is too often ambiguous. Cause-and-effect relationships are blurred. Multiple factors lead to several consequences and vice versa, without clear and manageable variable relationships. As a consequence, the ambiguity defies simple decision-making criteria, making the decision process more complex.

Basically, not only are dilemmas complex situations in themselves but to manage them generates additional complexity. Therefore, it is vital for organizations to understand and deal with this 'complexity accelerator'; otherwise they can easily become overwhelmed (e.g. by paralysis through analysis) or turn more political as tensions mount.

Dilemmas in the global automotive industry

The car industry is one of the most global and most consolidated industries,[1] where six global players account for approximately 80 % of world production. All players employ a similar strategy:

- global presence;
- covering the full spectrum (including niches);
- accelerating new model development with new (mostly electronic) features;
- attempting to differentiate through services and apply an 'extended' enterprise concept (that means sophisticated managing of complex supply-chain and distribution networks).

Due to overcapacity and trends in commoditization, competition is fierce and every move a competitor makes is watched and reacted on. Few companies earn their cost of capital continuously (only Toyota and Porsche are constantly in that league), but many destroy value, e.g. General Motors for more than 20 consecutive years.

The industry is difficult to enter, but even more difficult to exit. High unionization, political attention due to its technological lead function, regional concentrated employment, and huge sunk costs are the main causes of the persistent overcapacity. The temptation to enter into 'price wars' in order to earn some cash flow on the heavy assets and employ the workforce seems to be irresistible. Suppliers are consolidating and the former tight grip on the distribution network is loosening (in Europe, for example, the result of a block exemption for distribution).

This situation is creating four distinct dilemmas:

1. **Standardization versus model explosion**. In one way or another, car manufacturers are trying to 'standardize' components (e.g. batteries, fuel pumps) through the model ranges, taking complexity cost out of the supply-chain and manufacturing process (e.g. the high variety of components is a major quality issue on the assembly line). Increasingly, different brands or models share a common 'platform' (basically, everything the customer cannot see – roughly 60% of the 20 000–30 000 components of a car) or add-on features are 'packaged' (e.g. climate control). In an attempt to decentralize supply-chain decisions, the manufacturers try to deal only with the 'first-tier' suppliers, which deliver ready-to-assemble modules (e.g. the whole dashboard), leaving them to the management of the supply chain further down, based on certain standards (e.g. quality).

   On the other hand, car manufacturers are confronted with an explosion of niche products (e.g. lifestyle cars, crossovers). Whereas in 1960 the average car buyer in Europe could choose from approximately 60 different models on the market, clustered basically in three segments, today over 40 segments exist and every one of the global six is producing between 250 and 300 different models. Regulations still differ across countries, so practically all of the several dozen markets served demand slightly different features (e.g. rear lights or heating systems). Cultural factors and infrastructure characteristics also play a role (e.g. cars for the US require a 'softer' suspension than in Europe and in Japan additional 'gimmicks' are important). In addition, the fierce competition and shorter lifecycles push car companies to upgrade the technology in their existing model ranges constantly during their lifecycles; otherwise they could appear to be outdated even in the early stages of a model's lifecycle. So far, sales have mainly won the battle in the name of top-line growth, leaving it to other functions (including after-sales) to manage the rapidly escalating complexity.

2. **Multibrand competition versus cooperation and sharing**. All of the global six have multiple brands (e.g. DaimlerChrysler has five brands in the car division and eight brands in the commercial vehicle division). Partly, they compete for the same customers, especially in the mass market. However, they definitely compete for resources and investments, timing of new model launches, and positioning of the project, which is closely guarded when in the more profitable upmarket. (As one executive put it, 'To be in a multi-brand car group means you are constantly at war.')

On the other hand, all units are obliged to cooperate in the back-office processes (e.g. the same logistic for spare parts), shared services (e.g. one HR function for all subsidiaries in one market), rapid transfer of technology and 'best practice', and bundling of demand in purchasing. More often than not, this pitches the interest of one unit against that of the group. A case in point is why should a research-intensive upmarket unit share its hard-earned competitive edge in technology with its lower-market brethren? If headquarters introduces remedies, e.g. in the form of transfer pricing for certain technologies, a leap in complexity is unavoidable. In the case of transfer pricing, the value of the shared technology has to be assessed and negotiated.

3. **Standardization processes versus local leadership**. One of the key common features across global automotive companies is the precision and sophistication of their standardized – some would say bureaucratic – processes along the value-creation chain. This drive towards repetitiveness is essential to ensure product quality and compliance with the many product regulations, but even more important is the

need to establish transparency and with that accountability in a value-creation chain, which otherwise would be far too fragmented and complex to be coordinated (remember the 20 000–30 000 parts per car).

On the other hand, local leadership is needed to operate successfully in the 100 or so markets and adapt to the specific local regulation, different driving and buying habits (both culturally deeply ingrained), widely varying market conditions and competitive pressures, and a hugely diverse workforce around the globe. Does a process that works in Detroit and probably in Cologne also work in Tianjin, São Paulo, or Kiva Masha? The tension between headquarters and the subsidiaries is obvious. Whereas the local units are calling for (partly far-reaching) adaptations, headquarters insists on standardization, knowing that every variation increases the complexity and thus its ability to control and access the local unit.

4. **Short-term profitability versus stakeholder demands**. The dire financial situation of the auto industry calls for urgent action to boost profitability, at least to a level where the risk-weighted costs of capital are earned, which boils down to a return on investment of 10–12 %. The market capitalization of even the biggest players in the industry is so low, e.g. General Motors, that they could easily be bought if the potential buyer had any idea of how to earn money under the current and foreseeable conditions in the industry.

On the other hand, the car industry is by the nature of its product a 'political' industry as it needs complementary public infrastructure and regulatory standards to prosper. This is further enhanced by the size of the often-regional concentrated employment and visibility of its product, and its involvement in a couple of 'hot issues'; e.g. as mobility by car and truck is increasing, so is its contribution to global warming. As the world moves to more and more people living in agglomerations, the future of individual mobility becomes more contentious, from local emissions to the speed of traffic flow, which in cities like Bangkok approaches the speed of a pedestrian. Last but not least, cars depend completely on oil, which in turn comes increasingly from unstable regions (mostly the Middle East) and new deposits seem to cluster in ecologically sensitive areas (e.g. rainforests and arctic wildernesses). Therefore a multitude of stakeholders is pressing – more or less gently – the car industry in different directions: invest in fuel efficiency (with limited prosperity by customers to pay for it) and nonhydrocarbon motor power (e.g. fuel cells), help decrease traffic congestion, reduce emission, increase safety, etc. Not everyone is pushing in the same direction and the customers, in particular, seem to be pretty uninvolved; they focus on driving pleasure, horsepower, emotional design, and convenience features.

This generates a high ambiguity in the industry and the future direction is by no means clear. Take fuel cells for example: which kind of membrane technology will succeed? Will hydrogen be used directly, and if so, will it be pressurized or liquefied? Will methane serve as an intermediate step, which in turn would require another membrane? Where will the electricity come from to generate the huge amount needed for hydrogen? In order to invest in the new fuel infrastructure, the service station industry needs to know how many fuel cell cars will be on the road in the years to come. However, to come up with a realistic projection, the car industry needs to know, among other things, how many service stations will be on the streets.

This brief description of the dilemmas in the car industry indicates how dilemmas are generating or increasing ambiguity, interdependence, and diversity/multiplicity. It also shows that this cannot lead to a stable dynamic, but a volatile 'fast flux'. There is an urgent need to understand these dilemmas better and also to look at possibilities for managing them successfully. 'Smart' is the concrete example chosen in order to discuss and from which to draw some general conclusions.

Managing the dilemmas of growing complexity: the Smart experience

The Smart story

Smart started out as the radical simplification of the automobile industry. The intellectual promoter (some say 'missionary') of this idea, Nicolas Hayek, envisioned a very simple, cheap, and handy car, sufficient for young city dwellers (two persons and a crate of beer). There would be only one model, but in many colours (and the colour could be easily changed), and it would be easy and fun to drive and ecologically friendly. In short, Hayek wanted to repeat his Swatch success in the watch industry, where he transformed time measurement into fashion by delivering a simple, inexpensive watch with a flashy design, thereby rescuing the Swiss watch industry in the lower price segments. The car industry, however, turned out to be different. A first joint venture with Volkswagen in the early 1990s failed completely.

In the second trial, Mercedes took the lead (and 51 %) as they had observed that many of Hayek's dreams (e.g. an electric train with four-wheel drive) could technically not be realized or were too expensive. The many regulations, especially safety standards, which govern the design and manufacturing of a car, along with customers' expectations of what a car should be and the values, traditions, and experiences of Mercedes, shaped the new 'Smart' more than Hayek's original ideas. Only the idea of a two-seater for city traffic survived. A sophisticated safety cell and other car standards drove the cost to double what Hayek had imagined (Smart started with a price tag above €10 000).

Nevertheless, after several crises and an ongoing cost escalation, the first Smart hit the road in 1998. It was still an innovative concept on four dimensions:

- No other car manufacturer offered a two-seater with safety standards equivalent to a compact car, 135 km/h speed and modern car features, such ABS (anti-lock breaking systems).
- The production concept was unique: suppliers settled next to the assembly line and delivered more than 70 % of the value by the time Smart left the factory gate – the highest ratio in outsourcing ever in the car industry.
- A unique distribution system with 'Smart-only' dealers was established, many new to the industry. Distinctive 'Smart Towers' signalled the departure from conventional car distribution.
- Additional 'mobility services' were offered, from special parking slots, special rates at ferries, and also car rental discounts if a bigger car was needed.

To be innovative, however, does not mean to be economically successful. As losses were mounting, DaimlerChrysler sent in troubleshooter Andrea Rentschler, who was sought to help solve Smart's problem through growth. Under Rentschler's leadership, the company:

- opened up a new distribution channel through Mercedes dealerships and extended the number of dedicated Smart dealers;
- accelerated the move into more countries (in 2004, 33 countries were served, up from 9 in 1998, which required – among other things – a right-hand drive version);

- extended the range of models, adding a Roadster, a four-seater, and (planned) an SUV (sport utility vehicle), all with typical Smart features (e.g. dual colours), a convertible, a diesel version, and more upmarket features (e.g. air conditioning), which were demanded by the customers who were older (and wealthier) than originally expected.

Currently, Smart is again in a restructuring period as the growth strategy did not deliver the expected financial results. As the issues are more on the market side (e.g. the more expensive four-seater nevertheless faces the 'shark competition' in the small car segment), a lot can be learnt from the way Smart approached the continuously rising complexity and tried to manage it through:

- deliberate complexity reduction;
- a stepwise learning approach;
- developing a 'complexity-robust' culture and organization leading to a 'phase-based' complexity management.

Complexity management at Smart

When Mercedes started the joint venture with Nicolas Hayek, its goal system was already complex:

- lower average fuel consumption of the Mercedes fleet;
- learn from the experiments and innovation at Smart for the whole group;
- lap into a new growth potential as the Mercedes brand reached its limits;
- attract especially younger customers.

Combined with Hayek's vision, it became clear that the goal system would become overly complex as the joint venture development progressed and, in the worst case, perhaps even contradictory. As a result, Mercedes decided to buy out Hayek in order to reduce complexity. Though it was an expensive move, it allowed Mercedes to focus on its own goal system.

In the first crisis in 1998, when Rentschler came in, complexity was dramatically reduced by basically postponing the mobility concept and focusing on just the car. On the product side, Smart has gained credit in the industry for being most skilful and successful in 'packaging' the add-on features into three model types, thus dramatically reducing the variations in the assembly process. Easy to add on features are even shifted to the maintenance workshops of the dealers (e.g. fog lights, all mobile phone installations).

However, the most skilful reduction of Smart's own internal complexity came from its cooperation with the Mercedes car group. Normally when a company grows to become a 'mid-sized OEM' (original equipment manufacturer) (Rentschler), a lot of internal services and knowledge are built up along the way (e.g. technical test facilities). Smart decided, instead, to tap into the resources of 'Big Brother' and pay for the services as needed. This kept Smart lean and simple, but it required skill to manage the increased external complexity – a web of sometimes difficult relationships.

A similar learning process was the seamless cooperation with its outsourcing partners. Although the high degree of outsourcing kept the internal development and manufacturing more lean and simple, it dramatically increased the external complexity. The 'law of unintended consequences' hit more than once. However, Smart took the time to learn, even if it was costly. The original product launch was postponed twice, rather than forced through, in order for Smart to learn and to get it right. Interfaces and interactions with suppliers were constantly 'streamlined' (e.g. now suppliers are paid without invoice, once the final car leaves the conveyer belt). Several times, expansion (e.g. into the Chinese and US markets) was postponed, because the leadership was not convinced that the organization was ready to cope with the increased complexity.

The third dimension of complexity management was the development of a 'complexity robust' culture and organization. Personal accountability was very high on the leadership agenda, leading to an unusual degree of decentralization (one of the main levers to cope with complexity). This also allowed for higher speed in reaction to the unavoidable volatility, resulting from the dilemmas described above, through horizontal rather than hierarchical coordination. Flexibility, informality, and fun did not contradict a performance and action culture; to the contrary, it blended into a 'solve the problem first' *Leitbild*. The trick nevertheless was to keep the focus on what an OEM really needs to do and what are the priorities on the agenda, not allowing the autonomy to branch into a noncore business or nonvalue adding activities.

To sum up, Smart could not escape the industry-specific complexity and the dilemmas that accelerated it. In hindsight, Hayek's vision was thus an illusion. It was unavoidable that the complexity grew with the number of markets and the product range. However, Smart did provide a couple of interesting examples of 'complexity-conscious' management, where in each phase of the development a couple of steps were taken in order to keep the organizational competence aligned with the growing complexity.

General lessons

The Smart case has been chosen as it has applied a series of very important 'simplifiers' (see Chapter 1), which can be used generally to manage industry dilemmas:

- Grow with focus. A certain industry-specific level of complexity is unavoidable, but you should grow it only if you can manage it appropriately. Many companies are trying to extend the range of products or services, but an honest check is always necessary. Do we master the current complexity sufficiently so that we can learn to handle the additional complexity?
- A permanent task is to simplify the corporate processes and standardize them as far as possible (which does not mean to centralize decision making, but to give it a frame for running the business). This cannot be decided at the 'expert level'; they know too many details and are always tempted to make it more complicated. Instead, it needs permanent leadership attention and ongoing dialogue with the subsidiaries – to reject their chains for differentiation politely but compellingly.
- Modularize with easy interfaces. Managing complexity through decentralization is not only a proven concept on the organizational level but also in product design and development. Here it works to delegate the complexity management to the next level (in this case, the supplier). However, it should be done in such a way that the newly generated complexity through outsourcing is really lower than the 'old' internal complexity.
- Build an 'I-am-responsible-and-get-it-done' culture, with incentives for knowledge sharing, personal communication across the stakeholders, and a readiness to take risk ('decide first, apologize when needed').

- Install the self-confidence for simplicity.
- Install a simple early-awareness system to get as much lead-time as possible. This is more a matter of mindset than big formal systems and additional staff.

Reference

[1] For a more comprehensive and detailed description of the global car industry see the industry notes IMD-3-0911 by U. Steger, J. Kubes, W. Amann, and G. Raedler and IMD-6-0276 by R. Seifert, U. Steger, and W. Amann.

7

Managing Complexity with an Electronic Manufacturing Services Supplier

Wolfgang Amann, Carlos Cordon, Ralf W. Seifert, and Thomas E. Vollmann

Introduction

Companies across major industries have been struggling under the increased pressures of time, cost, and differentiation in recent years. Creating virtual supply chains and more dynamic value webs by means of outsourcing are tempting solutions for easing competitive pressures. The electronics industry is no exception, spawning a $100+ billion, global electronic manufacturing services (EMS) industry. After impressive growth in the late 1990s, and then severe consolidation and retrenchment between 2000 and 2003, there are signs of a sustainable recovery in the industry.[1] EMS companies nowadays provide a range of services to original equipment manufacturers (OEMs); they manufacture parts, subassemblies, and even entire products. Integrating vertically and horizontally and reaching a global scale, they have also assumed many repair and maintenance operations for these customers and are now providing logistics and considerable R&D services as well. Companies like Solectron, Flextronics, and Celestica may not be household names that can be found on the products they produce for the electronics industry, yet they – and other EMS providers – have become increasingly important in driving a reconfiguration of competences in this industry.[2] This rise of global EMS players has enabled an unprecedented interdependence of new value webs between OEMs and EMS providers, especially in this highly dynamic environment. However, navigating these changes is not an easy task.

The following case study illustrates a number of complexity challenges that arose over time when Hewlett-Packard (HP) created a virtual supply chain for its tape drive business unit by making use of EMS providers. The initial journey started with a simple one-off outsourcing decision to limit its future investment in its own manufacturing capacities in this area. As more and more products were being considered, however, it soon became apparent that incremental decision-making, the use of changing decision criteria over time, and the fact that the business was not always attractive to prospective and established partners inevitably led to an overly complex and highly fragmented supply chain back-end. In addition, the case acknowledges the dynamics of complex decision-making processes as well as the impact of uncertainty concerning future technology developments and cost assessments, which significantly added to HP's experience. At the end of the chapter, we outline some of the crucial learning that the reader can draw from this example.

Case study: HP's complexity dilemma[3]

Before HP's merger with Compaq in 2002, it was already a global provider of computing and imaging solutions and services for business and home, with sales of US$50 billion and an HR pool of around 90 000 people. HP's three main segments were imaging and printing systems (41 %), computing systems (42 %), and IT services (14 %); other business accounted for 3 %. HP's tape drive business unit employed 700 people and its headquarters were located in the United States (see Figure 7.1).

HP's tape drive business unit had three main areas: digital data storage (DDS), Ultrium, and storage solutions. In 2000 sales were just under $1 billion, with DDS generating most of this. Ultrium was the product of the future; it was based on an open standard – linear tape open (LTO) – developed together with IBM and Seagate.

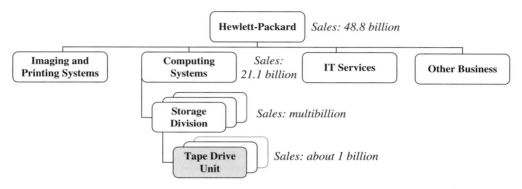

Figure 7.1 Tape drive business unit

Tape drive business

The tape drive business was part of the storage market. The storage market in general was expanding due to customers' business transformation. Customers were (1) taking advantage of opportunities on the internet, (2) increasing their demands and need for information, and (3) evolving IT to meet these unpredictable demands. Storage was a large market, reaching $46 billion in 2003.

Tapes were an economical way to store large volumes of digital data. Although the market had reached maturity and the time for major growth had passed, tapes were regularly 7 to 10 times better than disks in cost/gigabyte stored.

The type of tape drives most often used had also started to change and demand was increasingly for higher capacity, more complex equipment. The performance and quality of the product were qualifying criteria in the business. The key success factors were time-to-market and cost of the product. The cost was especially important in sales to original equipment manufacturers (OEMs). The lifecycle of a product was typically four years, which meant that getting the product to market as quickly as possible was critical for the company, to ensure the highest possible sales volumes and margins.

The business in transition

Tape technology was in a transitional phase. New technology – LTO and superdigital linear tape (SDLT) – had been introduced to upgrade from the traditional technologies of DDS and digital linear tape (DLT). Quantum was the major producer of DLT and was the overall market leader in the tape drive business, particularly the high-end segment. HP had kept its lead in the medium segment. DDS technology-based products were still a profitable product line. Table 7.1 gives the characteristics of tape drive products.

Table 7.1 Characteristics of tape drive products

Characteristics	Traditional technology		New technology
	Medium segment	High-end segment	
Competing products	DDS, AIT	DLT, AIT, Mammoth, 34XX	Super digital linear tape (SDLT), linear tape open (LTO)
Volume (per annum)	1.75 million	400 000	Low
Price comparison	$1000^a	$3\times$ to $5\times$	$7\times$ to $10\times$
Main producers (and market share)	HP (50–55%), Sony (30%), Seagate	Quantum (80%)	Quantum, IBM, HP, Seagate

^{a} Reference price.

HP's supply chain in the tape drive business

The supply chain consisted of four phases before final delivery to the customer (see Figure 7.2). HP sourced the main components from third parties who had special technology and expertise that HP did not have in-house.

The tape drives were sold to the end consumer either through OEMs or resellers. In volume terms the OEM channel was larger; in sales terms the reseller channel was larger and more profitable for HP than the OEM channel. OEMs tended to be demanding, but a successful delivery was a good reference.

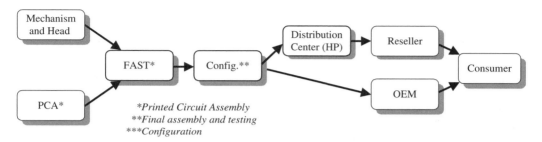

Figure 7.2 Supply chain for DDS products, showing the two channels to market (based on HP information)

HP delivered the product to its resellers through three regional warehouses – Asia-Pacific, Europe, and the US – which had varying degrees of performance. The OEM channel received the products directly from the factory, which worked well. HP had even won awards for being a good supplier.

Outsourcing of DDS products

In 1997 HP started to develop the LTO standard together with IBM and Seagate. This meant that the requirement for space and investment in the factory increased, but the manufacturing manager indicated there was no more space or investment for manufacturing. Outsourcing was the only option.

Between 1997 and 2000 HP outsourced all its models in the DDS product family, one by one. The organization did not have an overall strategy. The solutions were tailored to each individual situation. (see Table 7.2). HP always started the manufacturing in its own facilities in Bristol and transferred production to the contract manufacturer after the ramp-up had been done. OEM customers were ambivalent about outsourcing. On the one hand, they did not want to go through a new approval process of a new supplier for the product. On the other hand, their attitude to outsourcing was: 'Just make sure that this is invisible to us in terms of quality, delivery performance and cost.'

HP decided to outsource the final assembly and configuration of DDS2. It chose a contract manufacturer in Scotland to keep the risk of outsourcing low; the contract

Table 7.2 Evolution of the partners in the supply chain for the outsourcing assembly and configuration

		Players in the outsourced supply chain with different models of DDS			
Model	Start	Mechanism and Head	PCA	FAST	Configuration
DDS1	1990	Sony	CM A[a]	HP Bristol	HP Bristol
DDS2	1997	Mitsumi	CM A	CM A (Scotland)	CM A (Ireland)
DDS3	1998	Mitsumi	CM B	CM A (Scotland)	CM A (Ireland)
DDS4	1999	Mitsumi	CM A	Mitsumi	CM C (Ireland)

[a] CM = contract manufacturer.

manufacturer was close to HP, the engineering people liked it, and the price was competitive, although not the lowest.

Relatively soon after the deal, it became evident that the contract manufacturer could produce drives at a significantly lower cost than HP, largely because of overheads. HP had three or four people constantly in Scotland and the companies had regular team meetings. The core team consisted of people from the materials, finance, engineering, and logistics areas in the two companies. There was also a communications matrix through which HP people talked to their counterparts at the manufacturer.

HP also outsourced production of the DDS3 model to the same contract manufacturer based on capacity and cost, but wanted the contract manufacturer to have a new product introduction team for DDS3 since there was only one team to manage both DDS2 and DDS3. According to HP's procurement manager, 'The vendor management, inbound logistics and throughput suffered.'

Divisional finance involvement

In 1998 HP's divisional finance function became involved. It had been investigating opportunities for taking advantage of regional benefits that are now emerging at a faster and faster pace throughout the world. The tape drive unit assessed whether this would work for them and decided on a location in Ireland. This meant that configuration should move there. Legal issues complicated the matter since HP had to have the management of the operation in Ireland, so communication from Bristol went to the factory via the Irish office.

The regional benefits were so significant that the organization was willing to complicate matters operationally. Calculations showed that the financial advantages would be equal to double the normal returns from supply chain savings and efficiencies.

Worsening relations with the contract manufacturer

The relationship with the contract manufacturer deteriorated. Although HP intended to offer the company additional business, it no longer seemed motivated and could only envisage problems. Furthermore, it was not happy that HP wanted to consider a change of location in order to lower costs.

New outsourcing partner

For the DDS4 model, HP opted to work mainly with Mitsumi and another contract manufacturer. This arrangement was not ideal for the new contract manufacturer since it had to configure only one product. HP now had three major deals with different generations of DDS products. Since relations with the previous contract manufacturer were becoming difficult, HP had hoped to grow the business with the new one, but there were operational problems. Although the Mitsumi relationship was working well, the overhead to manage all the different relationships was high. Furthermore, heated debates were taking place between the functions (accountants, supply chain, and engineering) about the relative benefits of each outsourcing decision.

Launch of the new technology: Ultrium

Work on developing Ultrium started in 1997. HP partnered with IBM and Seagate to develop the standard, which was in competition with the Quantum one. Production of Ultrium began in late 2000. The supply chain looked similar to that for DDS products, with three main components: mechanism, PCA, and head (see Figure 7.3).

After six months' production of Ultrium, a reality check revealed that the supply chain clearly was not coordinated and cumulative volumes varied widely across the different

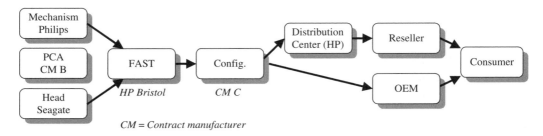

CM = Contract manufacturer

Figure 7.3 Supply chain for Ultrium (based on HP information)

stages. The lead-time across the supply chain was theoretically 90 days. The supply chain manager's ambition was to be able to deliver a tape drive to the customer in five days.

Alternatives

It was evident that HP needed to move towards virtual manufacturing and not produce any part of Ultrium. Four key issues were identified to determine the choice:

1. strategic alignment;
2. total cost of ownership;
3. partner choice;
4. cost of production.

The first two were the most important criteria. Strategic alignment included both supply chain and overall strategy of the storage division and meant that HP's investment would be low with quick returns. Many other companies in the industry had also moved towards outsourcing or virtual manufacturing. Outsourcing had seen the development of a new industry around contract manufacturers, the largest of which had global operations with high-level manufacturing and supply-chain management skills. During 1999 and 2000 the deals had become larger, reaching multibillion dollar levels in 2001.

HP had not been convinced of its contract manufacturers' capabilities in tape engineering. Fixed cost was not reducing as much as expected since HP had to do the engineering itself. It wanted to move away from its original practice of ramping-up the production in-house for six months and moving the production out after that. It wanted to change its manufacturing approach radically and get its partner involved from day one. To this end, HP outlined three main alternatives.

Alternative 1: path of least resistance – Philips

HP would give the final assembly and testing, configuration, and distribution to one of its suppliers, Philips. Philips had superb engineers who understood the tape business. However, it was a bit like HP, with high overheads, and the outsourcing deal did not seem to fit with Philips' overall strategy. The production would be done in Austria and Hungary with five or six HP people always on-site. In this case the accountants needed to be persuaded of the intangible benefits, since the apparent savings were lower. The key issue was: what would it take for Philips to take on this business and what would be left for HP?

Alternative 2: the ultimate supply chain – Mitsumi

This would involve designing the supply chain in the right way, from scratch. HP had talked with Mitsumi, which would ultimately have capabilities to manufacture both the head and mechanism and would also take care of the final assembly and testing, configuration, and – potentially – distribution. Mitsumi would emerge as a major tape drive manufacturer. The investment would be high, but the return would also be high. Ultimately this alternative would provide low cost and flexibility. At the moment Mitsumi did not have enough buying power and capabilities to produce the mechanism. HP would need to assist it with technology development for Ultrium. In the past, HP had had positive experiences working with Mitsumi. However, this time it would need to assist Mitsumi with technology development and was unsure about the implications of moving in this direction.

Alternative 3: consolidation – Seagate

This alternative included collaborating with a competitor. This approach would assume that consolidation was necessary in the industry and would concentrate on supply-chain efficiency rather than competition. This would be especially true as both companies would be competing against Quantum's standard. The main question was: should you help a competitor to survive? The relationship would be complex and troublesome.

Fast-forwarding one year

Twelve months passed with little or practically no action. The pending merger with Compaq further complicated the process for HP, but potential partners also made matters more complex.

In autumn 2001 HP decided on a variation of the Mitsumi option. The company believed that it was worth winning the battle for the tape drive business and thus wanted to create the ultimate supply chain, removing as many nodes as possible to improve efficiency. The idea behind the Mitsumi option was to move mechanism production, including equipment, technology, and tools, from Philips to Mitsumi.

HP discussed the decision with the Philips executive and reached agreement on the matter. Somewhat unexpectedly, however, his team resisted the transfer and through organizational play effectively made it impossible to proceed.

More time passed and eventually Philips came back with the alternative suggestion of using Flextronics as a contract manufacturer. Flextronics had an assembly plant in Hungary, a low-cost region close to where the Philips division was based. This was an attractive option, since it would provide the engineering expertise of Philips at lower manufacturing costs. The Philips and Flextronics executives were long-time business partners and this helped to establish the relationship. By then HP had finally said no to the Mitsumi option and negotiations with Seagate had gone cold. Shortly afterwards, HP learned about a management change at Philips. The new executive also subscribed to Philips strategy, but interpreted it slightly differently. It was no longer desirable for Philips to divest the mechanism manufacturing business to Flextronics as had previously been proposed. By that time HP had gone through all the options and in view of the significant loss of time had decided to go ahead with Flextronics anyway. The Flextronics option provided ample opportunity for supply-chain integration and was geographically close to Philips. It also provided low-cost manufacturing capability in its Hungarian facility.

The tape drive business continued to be a highly lucrative business for HP. The acquisition of Compaq strengthened HP's market-shaping capabilities. Customers were neither aware of nor worried about a 100% virtual supply chain, especially since the company continued to be highly innovative, with the speed of innovation picking up. Outsourcing eventually led to cost advantages; 30 % of fixed overhead was reduced and assets redeployed while this process and further gains were still ongoing. Inventories could also be reduced substantially, improving cost and profitability aspects, and quality issues were tackled much faster because of regional integration.

Learning points from the example
Managing complexity more effectively – the personal dimension

In highly complex situations with diverse, interdependent factors, clarifying the role, goals, and learning are essential tasks. HP's supply-chain manager for the tape drive business summarized his own learning:

1. **People buy from people**. Individuals make a difference and can alter decisions. A change of individuals will have a huge impact on potential deals.
2. **You get the vendor you deserve**. Vendor management and vendor development is extremely important. A partner who is constantly driven on cost is likely to cut resources to the point of poor performance. The vendor's performance often reflects the poorly developed vendor management practices of the customer, and indeed the other customers that the vendor works with.
3. **More accountants and lawyers are needed than engineers**. Regional benefits are extremely significant and can distort people's thinking. The supply chain should still be the primary driver of decisions but there is a great deal of opportunity to be taken through regional benefits.
4. **Like herding cats**. Large companies have difficulty organizing themselves. Bureaucracy and unclear accountability render decision making difficult. This applies to many multinationals and can be frustrating when two multinational companies try to work together.

Finally, it becomes obvious that HP's quest for optimizing such situations strongly benefits from simplifiers and an increased capability to cope with complexity. A crucial factor is teamwork. As HP's supply-chain manager put it, 'Any team halfway capable but focused could make any of the options work, as long as they want to make things happen and have shared values with the supplier. One should not underestimate the value of the right team and the right skills in making almost any option work.' Encountering complex decisions with capable teams as simplifiers could have saved HP a tremendous amount of time.

Managing complexity more effectively – the time dimension

HP originally aimed for simplification by outsourcing noncore competency-related activities. Freeing management capacity, tapping others' strengths, and time advantages were strong motives. However, because of the complexity in the decision-making process, 12 months passed, and then another 12 months, before actual products were available. While HP was lucky that Quantum was not too successful in establishing its standard and eventually lost a key client in Compaq, taking two years to come up with a decision is not good for profits and business prospects. This holds particularly true when the overall lifecycle of a product is rather short anyway.

At the same time, the 'miracle escape' rarely exists. Outsourcing decision making can become complex. It is tempting to go deeper and deeper into the issues, searching for the optimal solution, but this time may be better used during the actual implementation – for two reasons. First, not all uncertainty can be resolved and major assumptions are hard to verify in advance. Second, in times of ambiguous information and fast flux, any chosen option will require adaptation over time. Moreover, some options may only be available for a certain period and added learning will only be realized once the implementation is being progressed. HP waited too long and lost options. This indicates that fast flux can sometimes work in a company's favour but it can hardly be seen as a simplification and successful strategy!

Different phases of the lifecycle require different approaches and new collaborative efforts between the partners. Working with an outsourcing partner is an ever-changing situation. The products move from development to the ramp-up phase and in the end to ramp-down. Each of these phases requires a different set of skills and management collaboration between the outsourcing partners.[4] The baton of leadership and orchestration changes hands and both parties must adapt to the new situations – playing the proper role. However, the time required to develop the right working relationship is usually underestimated. It is therefore vital that as much coordination as possible is done internally instead of adding unnecessary tasks to the interfaces with suppliers.

Managing complexity more effectively – the cost dimension

The lower the level of the decision makers, the greater the need to ensure transparency about actual cost reality. They have to be aware of the risks of oversimplification due to a myopic view, e.g. by overemphasizing a 'manufacturing cost plus margins and tax' view versus the total cost of outsourcing, including the cost due to quality, supplier development, and potential deception. These costs are typically more difficult to assess but ultimately can outweigh the minor savings in material and labour costs. Likewise, companies still struggle today to quantify cost–benefit relations fully, due to more tightly integrated supply chains and because they do not necessarily work with a small and stable supplier base.

Managing complexity more effectively – the strategy dimension

Additional shaping factors in coping successfully with complexity are the locus and ownership of decision making, especially if the outsourcing decision deals with core competences (see Figure 7.4). All levels will be tempted by a decision that gives a home run, based on their individual view. Individual decisions may thereby have a perfectly valid business case when viewed in isolation. However, any lower-level execution of

		Top management attention	
		High	Low
Business activity	Perceived as core competence	Hopefully no longer-term problems	Relative risk to under-invest and slippage
	No longer seen as core competence	Management of business systems and industry structure	Hoping for 'miracle escape' through outsourcing

Figure 7.4 Relevance of outsourcing decision in relation to top management attention

decision making may be too tactical. There is substantial risk of underinvesting in the future or losing the opportunity to actually shape the future business systems and even industry structures. Whenever core competences are at stake, top management has to ensure ownership of the decision. Therefore, managing complexity starts with the proper assessment of the decision at stake.

In an attempt to simplify the back-end, HP added yet another partner to companies already in the network (see Table 7.3). It takes a non-negligible amount of time and attention to get any new partner in the 'loop' as the latter is likely to have some idiosyncrasies – even if EMS suppliers are becoming increasingly skilled and professional investments are significant.

Table 7.3 Development of supply-chain partners for HP tape drives over time

Players in the outsourced supply chain with different models of DDS					
Model	Start	Mechanism and head	PCA	FAST	Configuration
DDS1	1990	Sony	CM A	HP Bristol	HP Bristol
DDS2	1997	Mitsumi	CM A	CM A (Scotland)	CM A (Ireland)
DDS3	1998	Mitsumi	CM B	CM A (Scotland)	CM A (Ireland)
DDS4	1999	Mitsumi	CM A	Mitsumi	CM C (Ireland)
LTO1	2001	Philips and Seagate	CM B	HP Bristol and Flextronics	Flextronics
LTO2	2003	Philips and Seagate	Flextronics	Flextronics	Flextronics

This strongly relates to the perceived nature of the option space. The lower the level that actually carries out the decision making, the more statically people think. Higher levels perceive the option space as considerably more dynamic and shape industry structures in a more favourable way. Merely delegating the decision making to lower levels and thus turning a 'blind eye' to new and potentially better options clearly represents an unwise simplification strategy. Resulting isolated decisions can create a complex and fragmented supply chain. Furthermore, a series of these decisions can create a web of partners and a complex environment that requires significant management time.

This leads to the next dimension of managing complexity viewed from a strategic view, postulating two key aspects:

1. Accept complexity where it actually adds value to customers; (over-) simplify elsewhere to compensate.
2. Accept complexity where you can actually extract significant value, (over-) simplify elsewhere to compensate.

In the HP case, the profitability lies with the resellers, not necessarily with the OEMs on which HP allocates considerable attention to appease their worries. Designing the overall systems to increase the value to resellers represents a true alternative. HP could thus create positively the demand by resellers through better service, which in turn would lead to more business. In addition, HP has optimized the value chains for different products individually, but operates with a heterogeneous set of such individual supply chains. This may impede new product launches, because the time to set up a new value chain and to optimize interfaces anew is considerable. There are clear potentials for HP to do both – to add value to customers and extract returns by shifting complexity. Other areas in the supply chain – when consciously overcomplexified – promise better returns.

Outsourcing decisions may be easy in theory but are difficult in reality. Best practice in outsourcing is difficult to achieve and requires both firms to invest a lot of time. The partners' strategies may not always be aligned. Hence, the optimization must take place in value webs across traditional corporate boundaries. Hard work is required so that one can depend on the competences, processes, and infrastructure of others. The diversity of players and their agendas make it essential to find common denominators as simplifiers, reducing the repercussions of diversity.

Conclusion

EMS providers have seen their roles change in the last three decades by continuously increasing their weight in the industry. Many simplification tools have emerged, such as joint development teams, product champions, integrated process with suppliers, and attempts to establish a joint language. However, as the HP case has illustrated, putting everything together may continue to represent an overwhelming task, even for industry leaders. The diversity of options and players' agendas, the interdependence of decision variables, ambiguity about how solutions may work out, and ongoing changes in the business context often result in complex and fragmented supply chain configurations. When you outsource, you finally learn about all the things you actually knew, had improved over time, and won business for. Mastering the process of outsourcing requires new skills and new learning. It should not be considered as a panacea for dealing with problems – they will come back as cost. Tackling problems sooner rather than later frees critical energy reserves and prevents them from developing a life of their own when disregarded for too long.

Some illusions about outsourcing and virtual supply chains have been identified and ways of managing complexity in the EMS more successfully have been elaborated. However, even if the reader adopts the view of an industry insider or of someone who can learn from the experiences of other industries, it is of course important to adapt the learning to his or her specific case.

References

[1] http://www.electronics.ca/reports/electronics_manufacturing/.

[2] For a full review on the development of the industry see the industry note IMD-3-0863 by Petri Lehtivaara, Carlos Cordon, Ralf W. Seifert, and Thomas E. Vollmann.

[3] The case study is based on the EFMD award-winning case series IMD-6-0251 and IMD-6-0252 by Petri Lehtivaara, Carlos Cordon, Ralf W. Seifert, and Thomas E. Vollmann.

[4] For more details see C. Cordon and T. Vollmann, 'Outsourcing: The Need for a Strategic Focus', in *The Outsourcing Project*, Vol. 1, November 2002.

8
Managing Complexity in the Financial Services Industry

Arturo Bris

The most important factor driving complexity in the financial services (FS) industry is internationalization. In the last twenty years, we have witnessed a process that has changed the corporate landscape. This process entails two complementary phenomena: firms seeking capital abroad and investors looking for diversification opportunities in overseas markets. FS companies are playing an essential role in shaping both.

As firms grow bigger, the need for external funds has increased dramatically. Local markets cannot satisfy the needs of firms for external capital. In some emerging markets, illiquidity, a lack of investor protection and transparency, and unavailability of capital have forced firms to cross borders and seek financing in larger, more liquid markets, where capital is not scarce and where investors are willing to provide funds at a relatively low cost.

At the same time, as interactions among firms in a local market have increased, investors have realized that they can achieve a better trade-off between risk and return in markets overseas. Nowadays, companies in a local market co-move much more than they did just twenty years ago; hence, investors' desire for diversification potential is not found domestically. Not surprisingly, emerging markets have performed extremely well. The International Federation of Stock Exchanges reports that in 2005, countries like Colombia, Brazil, and the Czech Republic have returned almost 100% in a year in local currency. Not surprisingly, the total value of shares traded has increased by 386% in Colombia in the first quarter of 2006 relative to the same period in 2005. In Athens, where the market returned 32% in 2005, share trading has increased by 80% from January to June 2006. The *Financial Times* reported on 25 April 2006 that US investors allocated more than twice the amount to international mutual funds than they did to domestic funds.

What is the role of FS firms in this world? The World Trade Organization reports that international financing provided by financial institutions[1] is estimated at $6.4 trillion, of which $4.6 trillion is attributed to international lending. Total world banking assets amount to $20 trillion, insurance premiums are at $2 trillion, stock market capitalization is at over $10 trillion, and the market value of listed bonds is at around $10 trillion. In parallel with the increased internationalization of markets, FS firms

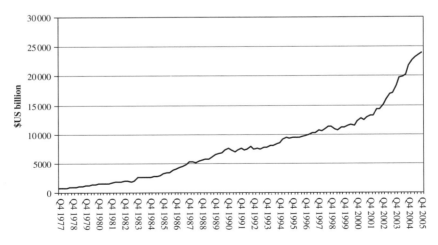

Figure 8.1 International positions of BIS banks
Source: Bank of International Settlements

have reached double-digit growth since 2002.[2] Today, the industry is worth around $560 billion in revenues per year. Europe and North America account for 48 % and 44 % respectively of the value generated by the industry, while Asia-Pacific represents 3.20 %.[3] FS firms bring firms and investors together; i.e. they bring the demand for funds together with the supply of funds. Complexity in this industry is thus driven by the complexity of the needs and characteristics of both parties. Figure 8.1 illustrates the process of internationalization of FS firms.

Complexity drivers in the FS industry
Diversity

The usual drivers of internal diversity are at play in the FS industry. The process of internationalization described above shapes the environment in which financial firms operate. The market requirements for personnel capable of responding to the demands of international investors have transformed global banks into small replicas of the United Nations. Management systems differ across firms and countries because historically banks have played different roles. In Germany and Japan, for example, the banking sector is an important player in the governance of corporations, while in the Anglo-Saxon system, the financial and real activities have generally been separated.

What distinguishes the internal diversity of FS from the typical bricks-and-mortar firm is the impact of macroeconomic factors on the balance sheet of FS firms. To illustrate this assertion, consider the case of a firm operating in the automobile industry. For such a company, the timing of cash flows is relevant to the extent that the business cycle determines the demand for automobiles in the near future. Once financing needs have been forecast and satisfied, the difference between selling a car today and selling a car five years from now is determined by the discount rate the firm uses – its cost of capital. Therefore, the uncertainty for the firm is cash flows, and hence the risk for the firm comes from the asset side of the balance sheet. It is true that there is financial uncertainty (for instance, uncertainty over interest rates), which makes the firm's liabilities risky. However, this source of risk is not firm-specific and can be alleviated if, for instance, the company is financed with long-term securities.

In banks, interest rates determine firm profits and also the financial costs. Banks essentially make money by borrowing funds from the public (deposits, debt, and equity) and lending it back to the market (loans). To the extent that the lending rate exceeds the borrowing cost, the bank is profitable, and profitability depends essentially on the ability of the bank to play with the yield curve. As interest rates vary, depending on the term of the loan, the timing of cash flows in financial firms is extremely important, and the time dimension is another specific factor of complexity for these firms. Playing with the time horizon of cash flows and financing costs is an important aspect of the banking activity. Indeed, banks essentially borrow short-term and lend long-term. The implication of this strategy is that shocks to interest rates affect bank profitability much more than in any other industry. We will analyse later how FS firms cope with this.

The second important determinant of internal diversity in FS firms is their growth strategy, based on acquisitions, especially cross-border acquisitions. For instance, Citigroup merged with KorAm of South Korea, Banamex from Mexico, and Computershare of Australia in recent years.[4] Also Grupo Santander acquired Abbey National Bank of the UK, Banco de Venezuela, and Banca Tota y Açores of Portugal. Consolidation results from the need to build larger businesses, to widen geographic scope, and to reach customers worldwide. More recently, financial firms are seeking entry into China and Russia, markets that were previously not accessible.

As a result of these cross-border acquisitions, five institutions account for 68 % of the assets of the globally diversified FS firms today: Citigroup (19 %), ING Group (15 %), Fortis (13 %), Instituto Finanziario Industriale (11 %), and JP Morgan Chase (10 %). More importantly, integration across borders brings about complexity: complexity in managerial cultures, complexity in the role of FS firms in the economy, and complexity as employees need to move between countries.

As with internal diversity, the sources of external diversity in FS firms are not specific: heterogeneous customer needs, differing cultural values, stakeholder interests that usually clash, competitors' differing strategies, and so on. The diversity that arises from heterogeneous customer needs is illustrated in Figure 8.2. This shows the percentage of assets held by the FS sector in 2004 in the US, by type of activity. FS firms provide different types of services, from pensions to banking, and cater to different groups of customers, from governments to individuals.

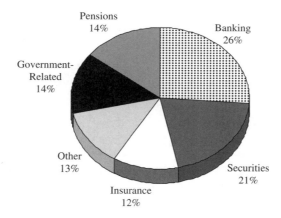

Figure 8.2   Assets of the financial services sector, 2004
Source: Board of Governors of the Federal Reserve System

There is, however, an incremental effect of the legal environment on financial firms. Today, a single financial transaction is subject to several legal regimes, depending on the nationality of the parties, the site of the transaction, and the location of the assets involved. The cost of compliance with multiple regulations becomes tangible as firms are required to report to different local authorities, forced to comply with sometimes contradictory provisions, and exposed to the possibility of a change in the law that makes previous attempts to comply useless. There is no way for FS firms to migrate to the most favourable legal system: their nature as financial intermediaries requires their presence in several countries, as has been discussed before.

The effect of regulation on the day-to-day operations of a financial firm is not the only issue. The financial sector is over-regulated in many countries in the world, and the entry strategy of FS firms in those countries is determined by legal issues. In China, foreign banks and insurance companies cannot directly own local financial intermediaries; therefore, foreign institutions participate in the Chinese financial system either through small stakes or through joint ventures with Chinese banks. In Europe, a series of merger attempts have recently been witnessed, not only in the financial sector, which have been blocked by national governments wanting to protect their 'national champions'. Banks belong in this category. Last year the press followed the scandal in Italy where the governor of the Central Bank, Antonio Fazio, favoured two Italian banks – Banca Popolare Italiana (BPI) and the insurance group, Unipol – which were targeting Banca Antonveneta and BNL, respectively. This defence was used as a means to avoid these two Italian banks ending up in foreign hands, as a Dutch (ABN AMRO) and a Spanish bank (Banco Bilbao Vizcaya Argentaria, BBVA) were after Banca Antonveneta.

Interdependence

FS firms are essentially intermediaries; hence, they connect and transfer risks across market players. This adds complexity to their activity, for a shock to either a supplier of funds or a creditor becomes a risk to the FS firm. Examples in recent years abound. The case that had the most impact was Long Term Capital Management, whose financial troubles started as several positions were unwound sequentially. The failures of Enron and Parmalat also resulted in severe financial troubles for Arthur Andersen, Citigroup, Bank of America, etc. The risk for FS firms is essentially systemic and the profitability of the sector is highly correlated with the performance of the market.

Ambiguity

It is thought that ambiguity in the FS sector is a natural consequence of the large scale at which these firms operate. HSBC, for instance, operates in several countries, several market segments, several customer segments, and under several regulatory regimes. In this setting, the information available is complex and always gives a distorted picture of the company. More importantly, such a large scale poses a challenge for management in the way that information flows from the bottom of the organization up and from regional managers to headquarters. In a similar vein, in large organizations, and especially in banks, it is of the utmost importance to be able to convey clear messages from top management to the bottom of the organization, especially when the organization operates on a large scale.

How do FS firms deal with complexity?

As FS firms operate in different countries, markets, customer segments, and under different legal regimes, the only way for them to survive in such a complex world is to *standardize* their activities and procedures. As seen below, in some cases standardization has resulted from the voluntary and proactive decisions of financial institutions and from the contributions of international organizations and regulators in other cases. In all cases, FS firms have simplified their reporting, risk policies, and management strategies. The main result of this trend has been *convergence*: FS firms are larger and fewer than only a few years ago, and they behave more and more alike. There is convergence in risk policies, legal regimes, sustainability policies, and performance indicators.

Standards in risk management

The Basel Committee is the pioneer in the standardization of Bank Risk Policies. The Basel I system of 1988 established a procedure for banks to manage their risks by forcing them to maintain a certain percentage of their assets as capital. This well-known system has created more problems than it has solved because it did not give clear guidelines on the risk characteristics of certain bank instruments, it did not take into account the diversification potential of other instruments, and it created, in some cases, the wrong incentives by inducing banks to take excessively low risk levels.[5]

In the Basel II system, the objective was to align required capital more closely to a bank's own risk estimates. The finalized Basel II Accord was released in June 2004, and it is expected to be fully implemented by the end of 2007. Basel II is based on three pillars:

- minimum capital requirements;
- supervisory review;
- market discipline.

Banks are required to assess three types of risk: credit risk, market risk, and operational risk, and they are obliged to hold at least 8 % of the weighted risk as capital. As with the previous system of 1996, banks are allowed to value credit and market risk using a proprietary system, which must be approved by the regulator. For credit risk, banks can opt into one of three systems:

- A standardized approach similar to the old system. The bank allocates a risk weight to each of its assets and off-balance-sheet positions and produces a sum of risk-weighted asset values. A risk weight of 100% means that an exposure is included in the calculation of risk-weighted assets at its full value.

- A foundation internal rating-based (IRB) approach. Under the IRB approach, banks will be allowed to use their internal estimates of borrower creditworthiness to assess credit risk in their portfolios, subject to strict methodological and disclosure standards. Distinct analytical frameworks will be provided for different types of loan exposures, e.g. corporate and retail lending where the loss characteristics are different.[6]
- An advanced IRB approach. Lenders with the most advanced risk management and risk modelling skills will be able to move to the advanced IRB approach, under which the banks will estimate their probability of default (PD), the expected loss given default (LGD), exposure at default (EAD), and maturity of the loan (M). In the foundation IRB approach, LGD, EAD, and M cannot be estimated by the bank – they are explicitly determined by the regulator.

For operational risk, banks can also opt into one of three different systems. Under the basic indicator approach, a supervisory factor (called 'alpha') is applied to the total gross income to deliver the capital requirement. Under the standardized approach, the gross income is split over eight different business lines, namely corporate finance, trading and sales, retail banking, commercial banking, payment and settlement, agency services, asset management, and retail brokerage. A different factor (called 'beta') is applied to each different business line. The most advanced option for determining regulatory capital for operational risk consists of a class of approaches referred to as the advanced measurement approaches (AMA). Under the AMA, the regulatory capital requirement is calculated on the basis of the banks' internal operational risk measurement systems.[7]

The internal systems developed by FS firms to calculate their required capital are called economic capital (EC) methodologies. Economic capital is primarily used by financial institutions to support decisions about what business lines or transactions to pursue. A firm defines its economic capital as owners' equity, retained earnings, and subordinated debt. Then the approach consists of identifying within the firm those business lines that offer the best use for capital in terms of risk. In order to make such an assessment, banks employ risk-adjusted performance metrics like return on risk-adjusted capital (RORAC) and risk-adjusted return on capital (RAROC).

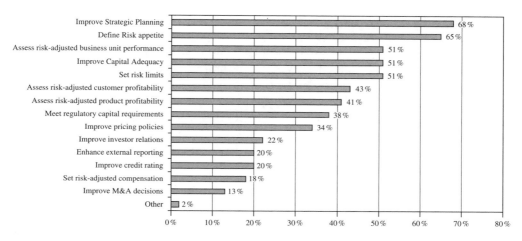

Figure 8.3   Reasons to adopt an economic capital system
Source: PricewaterhouseCoopers

In 2005, PricewaterhouseCoopers surveyed industry participants in their use of economic capital (EC) systems.[8] Figure 8.3 illustrates the effectiveness of EC systems in eliminating complexity in the FS industry. Most of the respondents (50–60%) report that their objective for implementing EC is to improve strategic planning, assess performance, and set risk limits.

A final point should be made on corporate risk management. One important trend in past years is that the pricing and management of credit risk has become more market oriented. The adoption of economic capital systems is just one example. The development of derivative markets is an important consequence of such a trend, which by itself affects financial firms as well as firms in the real sector. The market approach has increased financial stability and reduced complexity in transactions, because pricing is more transparent and efficient. In this setting, a large group of rational market participants sets prices, and new products are created as demand arises. Of course, increased complexity in the transactions calls for a new role for financial regulation, which is aimed at creating new standards of practice.

Standards in regulation

To simplify financial transactions, countries and legal systems are converging towards a unique legal financial system. What are the principles driving this convergence? Above all, investor protection is paramount. The objective of financial regulation must ultimately be to protect shareholders against the egoistic behaviour of directors who seek to benefit themselves rather than maximize the value of the company. Some supranational institutions, like the World Bank, have been pioneers in the effort to standardize the rules protecting investors because, as the Bank recognizes, 'The improvement of corporate governance contributes to the development of capital markets, both private and public.'[9]

A good example is listing standards. In the last few years, especially following the passing of the Sarbanes Oxley Act, non-US firms have started reviewing the costs and benefits of having their stock listed on US markets. ITV, Britain's largest commercial TV broadcaster, decided to deregister its stock in 2005, arguing that the reporting obligations imposed by the US SEC (Securities and Exchange Commission) were 'very costly'. ITV estimated that they were saving $13 million over two years as a result of this decision. Multinational firms like BMW and Samsung have long refused to list in the US. A number of European companies are considering whether to terminate their listings, arguing that the costs outweigh the benefits, and they are actually claiming that there may be no benefit at all. In Europe, new markets with very strict listing requirements have failed to attract companies and investors.[10]

The convergence of the norms of good governance, in short, starts by assuming that certain systems are better than others, independent of the particular circumstances of a country or a company. The systems that work are, apparently, those of the more developed countries, i.e. the United States and the United Kingdom. Several proposals for corporate reform in Europe – including those in France, Germany and Spain – establish certain recommendations based on the international studies available. What do these fundamentally academic studies suggest? What is known nowadays is that the value of companies in countries with better governance systems is, other things being equal, higher; those companies invest more efficiently, the allocation of resources is therefore more efficient, and, finally, growth rates are greater. It is also known that in Anglo-Saxon countries, there is more transparency and shareholders are better protected.

There are two fundamental problems with all these statements that make the tendency to copy what works in other markets dangerous. First of all, the 'international studies' referred to above are based on comparing countries. Indeed, in the United Kingdom, the shareholders are better protected than in Venezuela. In comparing both countries, the stock exchange capitalization in the United Kingdom represented 137 % of the average GDP between 2001 and 2003; in Venezuela, it represented only 4.5 % of the GDP. Also, the British economy grew 2 % annually between 2001 and 2003, whereas the Venezuelan economy grew at a negative annual rate of 5 %. It is tempting to admit that the World Bank is right and that a causal relation exists between the transparency of the markets and economic growth. Nevertheless, the GDP per capita in the United Kingdom is eight times greater than in Venezuela and it is probably certain that the least developed countries have worries other than the relationship between directors and shareholders. This explains why their corporate governance systems are weaker. In other words, it is not known what was first – the egg or the hen.

The second problem is that, to date, there is not a conclusive study that demonstrates that the improvements in corporate governance in a country help the development of financial markets. The conclusion of the studies made in some Eastern European countries that have carried out deep legislative reforms based on the American model is discouraging. Russia is a good example. One could borrow from Katherina Pistor, a legal scholar from Columbia University, and say that in all transplants there are sometimes rejections.[11]

Why do I think that we must be cautious when we assume that it is best for a company to have a small board of directors and that there must be fluid communication between the institutional investors and the firm, or that, when a company goes bankrupt, it is better to leave the control in the hands of the directors and not of the creditors? (These are, by the way, some of the axioms that companies are importing and legislators are trying to impose.) There are several reasons:

- In the first place, the Anglo-Saxon model of corporate governance considers maximizing shareholder value as the only objective of the director. With this objective in mind, there is no room for the employees, the current and potential customers of the company, or even the firm's creditors. Allen and Gale challenge in a recent article the view that this system is socially optimal, especially when markets are not perfect.[12] For them, an alternative system of 'interest groups' (the *stakeholder system*) that prevails in Germany and Japan, and in which workers participate in the governance of the company, produces better results in the long term. The simple reason is that the directors have shorter-term objectives than those of employees. With virtually no investor protection, the profits of Toyota have increased 8% per year from 1999 to 2005. In the same period, the profits of General Motors – a poster-child of good governance – have fallen 23% per year.

- The second reason why convergence is dangerous is that the Anglo-Saxon system works in markets in which the ownership of the company is dispersed and where there is no concentration of significant share blocks. Therefore, the conflict of interest to avoid is the one that exists between the directors and the shareholders. In the ten largest US companies, the three majority shareholders have on average 20% of the capital. In countries as different as Spain and Venezuela, this number is 51%. In Greece, on average 60% of the shares in the largest 50 companies are held by shareholders who own at least a 5% block. The relevant conflict of interests in Greece, Venezuela, and Spain is not, therefore, the one that exists between directors and shareholders, but between majority shareholders and minority stockholders.

  What can be worrisome is that the new legal codes in Europe and Asia ignore this feature of the financial markets. With regard to the recommendation that companies be fluid in their communication with institutional investors, the Spanish code of good governance declares that '[...] we did not ignore that this legal initiative always involves the risk of access to sensitive information [...]. These are, however, smaller risks that can always be alleviated with the formulation of some norms of conduct.'

- Finally, good governance systems are effective only when there is a supervisory agency that is independent from the political power. The reason is that governments also have their objectives, depending on their political sign. The example of the Italian banking system described above is a good illustration.

In sum, the process of convergence towards a unique system of financial regulations seems natural. The important question to ask ourselves is 'Which system is that?' If we do not take into account the specifics of every country and every legal system, we will create more problems than solutions. Regulators need to consider the importance of ownership concentration in corporations, the role of institutional investors, the long-term objectives of the society as a whole, and the degree of intervention by the government in the financial system.

Finally, it is not clear that a system of protection for minority shareholders is desirable at all. One of the best-performing companies in the US, Wal-Mart, recognizes as its immediate goal the well-being of the consumers, not of the shareholders, and it is well known that Enron and WorldCom were exemplary companies in terms of good governance.

Standards in corporate sustainability: the equator principles

In the last decade, corporations around the world have become especially concerned about sustainability, i.e. the willingness to preserve the long-term welfare of a firm's shareholders by guaranteeing the preservation of the corporate assets. As financial intermediaries, corporate sustainability is especially important for FS firms. They are providers of financing and, therefore, they promote certain investments at the expense of others. Sustainability has become one of the key issues in project selection, and the standardization process described above has also included this aspect in the activity of FS firms. In 2005, the financial industry agreed on some basic principles called the Equator Principles, which are an industry benchmark for determining, assessing, and managing social and environmental risk in project financing. In the preamble of the principles it states:

> The Equator Principles Financial Institutions (EPFIs) have consequently adopted these Principles in order to ensure that the projects we finance are developed in a manner that is socially responsible and reflect sound environmental management practices. By doing so, negative impacts on project-affected ecosystems and communities should be avoided where possible, and if these impacts are unavoidable, they should be reduced, mitigated and/or compensated for appropriately. We believe that adoption

of and adherence to these Principles offers significant benefits to ourselves, our borrowers and local stakeholders through our borrowers' engagement with locally affected communities. We therefore recognise that our role as financiers affords us opportunities to promote responsible environmental stewardship and socially responsible development. As such, EPFIs will consider reviewing these Principles from time-to-time based on implementation experience, and in order to reflect ongoing learning and emerging good practice.[13]

What are the main implications of standards of sustainability? First of all, they indirectly affect the entire corporate sector, whether it be financial firms or not, since the Principles dictate who gets financing and who does not. Second, within the industry, the Equator Principles act as both a factor of convergence and as a motor of competition. As the Principles are adopted voluntarily by banks and financial institutions, they all end up applying the same policies. As sustainability becomes an intangible asset priced by the market, FS firms compete on their implementation. The *Financial Times* is now publishing an annual ranking of 'Sustainable Banks'. In the annual reports, banks, especially in Europe, compete for the best image in sustainability. The Equator Principles are one of the best examples of how FS firms are coping with the complexity involved in their businesses.

Standards in objectives: key performance indicators in the financial services industry

One consequence of the enlargement of the financial sector is that determining objectives at the firm level has certainly become complicated. Firms now operate in several countries and, as shown above, in many different activities. Should the objective of an FS firm be to maximize growth? Increase revenues or size? Maximize customer satisfaction? Maximize stock returns? More importantly, how can certain objectives empower employees to achieve their goals? In financial firms, this is extremely difficult, since it may be hard for a loan officer in a bank to assess the impact on the profitability of the firm. Top managers in financial firms have become more and more concerned about a clear definition of their key performance indicators (KPIs).

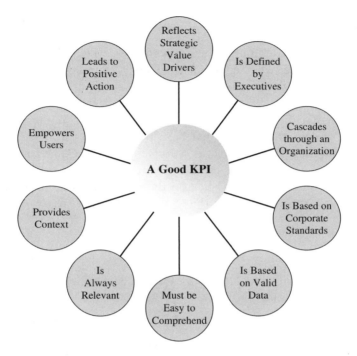

Figure 8.4   Definition of a good key performance indicator
Source: TDWI

Figure 8.4 describes the criteria that a good KPI must satisfy. These criteria apply to financial service firms in particular. Because KPIs are dictated top-down, but are implemented and reported bottom-up, they standardize the corporate activity within the firm and reduce complexity by focusing on information that is most relevant and on the firm's activities that really matter. Moreover, because there is also convergence in KPIs across financial firms, they reduce market uncertainty and, therefore, reduce complexity in the industry.

To summarize, KPI definitions are among the best strategies that financial firms have envisaged to reduce complexity. They help investors and employees and they contribute to more efficient competition among firms.

Conclusion

This chapter focused on the financial services industry. The particular challenges that financial service firms face when coping with diversity, interdependence, and ambiguity have been stressed and it was found that, given their role as financial intermediaries, complexity in this industry generally has broader implications. It was argued that the main instrument that the industry has found to deal with complexity is standardization. In the last decade, the industry has been transformed through a process of standardization in risk management practices, convergence in regulation, standardization in performance measures, and the establishment of common principles of corporate sustainability. Some light has been shed on the impact that these practices have had in financial service firms and also on the corporate sector at large.

References

[1] Includes only banks reporting to the Bank for International Settlements.

[2] Source: Datamonitor report.

[3] Source: Datamonitor report.

[4] Source: Datamonitor report.

[5] See A. Bris and S. Cantale, 'Bank Capital Requirements and Managerial Self-Interest', *Quarterly Review of Economics and Finance*, 2004, **44**(1), 77–101.

[6] Source: Bank of International Settlements.

[7] Source: European Central Bank.

[8] See PriceWaterhouseCoopers, 'Effective Capital Management: Economic Capital as an Industry Standard?', 2005.

[9] Lubrano, M., 'Why Corporate Governance?', *WorldBank: Development Outreach*, March 2003.

[10] See *The Financial Times*, Mastering Series, May 2006.

[11] Pistor, K., 'Patterns of Legal Change: Shareholder and Creditor Rights in Transition Economies', EBRD working paper No. 49, 2000.

[12] Allen, F. and Gale, D., 'A Theory of Comparative Corporate Governance', working paper, 2001.

[13] Source: http://www.equator-principles.com/principles.shtml.

Part III

Solutions for Managing Complexity on the Functional Level

9
Breaking Down Complexity Management to the Functional Level

Wolfgang Amann and Ulrich Steger

I n our quest to understand complexity and master it, this part of the book sheds light on why the different parts of the value chain deserve a differentiated look at their special complexity challenges. The usual complexity drivers recur not only at the macro and industry levels but also at the traditional functional level.

The diversity of tasks performed in each function often requires and leads to different subcultures within a function. Varying compensation and incentive systems foster such centrifugal forces. It is by no means certain that all functions will necessarily adopt a global view in a homogeneous way. There are conditions that may foster either a centralized or local approach to procurement, manufacturing, IT, or marketing – independent of other functions. It is demanding to find the right balance of sufficient localization and internal integration, while these parts of the organizations and their environments remain in constant flux. Different units, products, and services sometimes require an even more differentiated approach, thus entailing further complexity.

The interdependence of factors, processes, and behaviours is reaching new levels as corporate boundaries become increasingly open and fluid, with practically all modules of functions substituting the traditional value chain with value webs, achieving far-reaching integration with external players. Complementors are often critical if products and services are to achieve exponential growth. As our colleague Adrian Ryans notes, companies do not necessarily wait until complementary products and services are offered by other players.[1] Instead, they promote complete solutions to direct and indirect customers. They may even encourage more competition between complementors to drive up quality and lower prices.

Designing and implementing successful strategies has never been more challenging than it is now. The diversity of markets served – which pushes complexity down the organization through global mandates for business units and shorter lifecycles for products, technologies, and industries – and truly new types of competitors from emerging countries make strategists work hard for their money. The increasing number of cumulative choices in each phase of the strategizing process underlines the basic tenet that global companies are complexity incarnate. As our colleague Jean-Pierre Jeannet outlines in his chapter, four levels stand out: (1) multiple global drivers or logics affecting companies and markets; (2) multiple pathways to develop a business globally; (3) many strategic options around generic global strategies; and (4) multiple resource games allowing companies to connect to an ever-widening choice of resources.

R&D is the function that matters most in a variety of industries. Without a pipeline packed with breakthrough innovations or at least continuous improvements, the chances of shareholder value creation in the future grow dim. In his chapter, our colleague Georges Haour presents the concept of distributed innovation to address complexity challenges, while simultaneously calling for the ability to lead such highly complex projects. Managing complexity thus requires simplification of some aspects of the organization and functions, but simultaneously for the skills honed to cope with this simplification. The alternative is a predictable performance downturn.

Breaking down silos between functions, and thus acknowledging the true potential hidden in a greater degree of interdependence, often leads to two challenges. On the one hand, managers need to be able to understand and cope with this increasing interdependence. On the other, cross-functional, cross-lateral, and cross-company teams put an unprecedented diversity of people into the same project team and meeting room. While there is obvious value in diversity, there are also non-negligible downsides. Adapting to complexity as a result of diversity, however, goes beyond human resources management as a function. It calls for the right leadership from the top, as the chapter on diversity from our colleagues Martha Maznevski and Karsten Jonsen illustrates.

Some companies are better at dealing with complexity than others. Our colleagues Donald Marchand and Amy Hykes describe how a company's ability to manage and use information effectively is a key factor in determining how well the company can deal with complexity. This is not merely a question of implementing expensive IT solutions that may soon become outdated. It is a broader issue and starts with encouraging proactive information behaviours and values among all employees. It involves developing information-processing practices linked to business strategies and investing in smart IT for management support. This information capability-centred approach, which goes beyond mere IT, is described as a way forward.

Closely linked to this subject is the emerging field of knowledge management, which is increasingly resulting in the creation of a post of chief knowledge officer within companies. Our colleague Kazuo Ichijo outlines how companies in complex, global environments gain, maintain, and enhance competitive advantage with this increasingly crucial 'function'.

Marketing and supply-chain management are further areas where complexity may rear its ugly head. The chapter by our colleague Ralf Seifert and also Wolfgang Amann explores the potential hidden in mass customization, a concept that may help in addressing the increasing diversity of fragmented segments. Interdependence starts to matter when companies add mass customization to their existing operational set-up and product line-up. Uncertainty increases the complexity here, as innovation often has to start in a small way, leaving management with the dilemma of how much or little to invest; their decisions will in turn heavily impact on the future success of the initiative.

The chapters in this part of the book will outline the function-specific complexity dilemmas further and suggest ways forward.

Reference

[1] Ryans, Adrian, 'How You Can Build More Profitable Markets', in *Perspectives for Managers*, No. 115, IMD, 2005.

10
Complexity in Global Business Strategies: The Cumulative Impact of the Crisis of Choices

Jean-Pierre Jeannet

Causes of complexity in global business strategies[1]

A wave of overhauling business unit strategies has occurred at many international companies. Increasingly, corporations ask individual business units to pursue global strategic goals, assigning them a *global mandate*. Firms prefer to own businesses that command a leading strategic position in world markets. Under a global mandate, a corporation assigns responsibility for the entire world market to a single business unit, no longer subdividing market responsibility by country or region. Companies such as Philips, Siemens, ABB, Novartis, and GE have all experienced this debate. With business unit managers facing new global mandates, the question of how to deal with the added complexity becomes the major issue.

Even for firms operating in a single market, strategies and strategy development can be a complex process. This complexity is typically created by ever-increasing levels of technology, markets where segments multiply, internal and external supply chains meshed intricately with other businesses, and a volatile economic and political environment. These factors are compounded when developing business strategies on a global scale. For the purpose of this chapter, we would like to explore the reasons for the incremental complexity caused by the global dimension, understand its drivers, and appreciate how the never-ending race for superior resources contributes to this complexity. Finally, we need to appreciate approaches businesses can deploy to reduce complexity, or how to arrive at the realization that managing it rather than eliminating it might be the only way forward.

Increasing options at several stages contribute to complexity. The absence of choice, or of options, reduces complexity. On a global level, choices and options are multiplied and compounded, giving that special texture of all-encompassing or interwoven pathways that make the running of a business so much more intricate. Each layer of choices multiplies with the next layer, compounding into ever more complex situations.

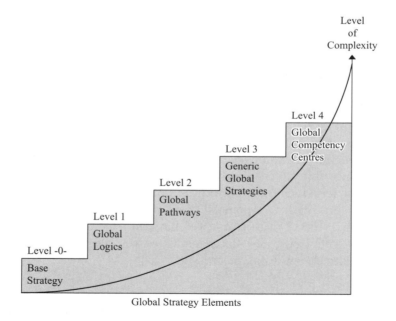

Figure 10.1 Levels of complexity in global business strategies

Four levels stand out (see Figure 10.1): (1) multiple global drivers or logics affecting companies and markets, (2) multiple pathways to develop a business globally, (3) many strategic options around generic global strategies, and (4) multiple resource games allowing companies to connect to an ever-widening choice of resources. How to deal with these choices will be the major focus of this chapter.

Complexity level 1: accommodating competing global logics[2]

As a company begins to look at its business globally, one of the first concepts to be dealt with is the extent of global pressure experienced by any participant company in a given industry sector. Given the added complexity of developing a business globally, it would not be recommended to 'go global' unless there was a substantial imperative to do so. The strength of that force, or the extent of *global logic*, will have to be assessed by the industry sector. Only companies active in industries with significant global logic would need to deal with the extra complexity of globalizing all or parts of their strategy.

Unfortunately, global logic forces emanate from different directions, and there are several sources that might add global logic in a given industry sector. As the response to globalizing a business strategy greatly depends on the extent and origin of these forces, a full appreciation of the possible global logic forces is imperative.

Research and experience has allowed seven major global logic forces to be defined. The sections below both describe specific global logics and their possible implications in terms of global business strategies. Any firm neglecting to accommodate significant global logic forces in its industry would do so at the risk of its competitiveness.

Accommodating global customer logic

There is evidence of strong global customer logic when customers would penalize a firm if it did not pursue a global strategy. This may result when there is similar demand across countries for products or services or there is a global need present across many countries. More complex is the functionality required, or the benefits sought. Global customer logic is present if only one of the three elements may be verified and is very strong if all three exist. The different levels of global customer logic drive the generic global strategy required. In particular, strong global customer logic indicates an opportunity to adopt a global marketing strategy.

A company facing significant global customer logic would naturally adopt global product, global benefit, and global segment strategies. A global segment strategy would be indicated by a similarity of customers and requirements across country markets. Global product strategy would offer similar product configurations around the world. Global customer logic tends to drive highly visible globalization, as decisions affecting products or benefits, and thus communications, are strategy elements with high market visibility. What is significant, however, is that global customer logic is not the only driver for globalizing business strategies and is not even a necessary requirement. Other logics are equally important.

Accommodating global purchasing logic

While the logic above deals with customers' requirements, global purchasing logic deals with their purchasing practices. A company must assess to what extent its customers purchase locally, nationally, regionally, or even globally. In some industries, as with many consumer products, end-users purchase locally from easily available sources. In business-to-business situations, customers have begun to coordinate purchases regionally, e.g. across Europe or globally through global purchasing contracts. Some companies may find direct customers such as retailers or wholesalers purchasing globally whereas end-users buy locally. If a global purchasing logic is present, companies must consider this and adjust their business and marketing strategy accordingly.

The presence of global purchasing logic indicates that customers have moved from local to regional and global purchasing. This move may occur at several levels, such as end-users, retailers, distributors, or wholesalers. Global purchasing logic may not drive all purchasers with equal force. However, implications for the choice of generic global strategy are similar.

A company facing strong global purchasing logic will want to reach customers with either global account management strategies or focused global customer strategies.

These generic strategies capture a wide purchasing range and can accommodate companies that coordinate purchasing globally and need to show a uniform approach. Equally important are global pricing strategies. Global distribution policies are often required to deal with global purchasing logic, coordinating logistics, and distribution involving wholesalers, distributors, or retailers.

Accommodating global information logic

Customer acquisition of information, such as approaches used to learn about products or services and media sources consulted, determine the extent of global information logic. When customers scan the world for product information, global information logic prevails. This also applies to products purchased by customers who travel extensively, either for business or privately. When customers consult only local media, the information logic would be entirely local.

The global search by customers and users, and the fact that they 'search the purchasing space extensively', presents the opportunity for global branding. Global branding driven by global information logic is differentiated from the global customer logic described earlier. When customers scour the globe for products or services, it is critical to be present worldwide with the same brand to assist customer identification. For luxury products, initial learning about the brand may take place in Hong Kong, but the purchase may take place in London, Dubai, or New York. Customers who have become moving targets signal the benefit of global branding.

For a global event such as a sporting event watched by large audiences from many countries, the benefit of using a global branding strategy is clear. At the soccer world championship watched by millions in dozens of countries, for example, companies can become sponsors with their names displayed around the stadium. Only companies with global branding strategies will benefit from this type of sponsorship.

The above three global logics – customer, information, and purchasing – represent global logic forces that stem from the customer base. Equally important, however, are the forces that stem from a given industry sector and competitors. They are now described next.

Accommodating global competitive logic

Global competitive logic is present if a firm consistently runs into the same competitors, possibly with a similar strategy. This may indicate a single global competitive theatre where market share can best be measured globally, not on a country-by-country basis. Alternatively, competitive theatres may be regional, such as pan-European, or local, when there is little opportunity to leverage a competitive position from one country to another. A strong global competitive logic exists in many professional service sectors, in the automotive industry, and in many electronics industries.

Companies facing global competitive logic must coordinate their business strategy worldwide. The capability to play 'tic-tac-toe' on the global chessboard and to retaliate against competition, e.g. in the UK with counter-action in Germany or Japan, places special demands on any business.

Accommodating global industry logic

A company must determine whether global industry logic is present, based on similarity of industry key success factors (KSFs). The industry logic for a business and the KSFs for a given country form a 'code' for success. Management needs to determine whether this code applies only to one country or is relevant for other countries. Industries with strong global industry logic are those wherein the way to succeed is similar around the world. Such similarity opens avenues to leverage the operation of the firm, independent of customers. Many industries with different customer requirements (global customer logic) operate under a high degree of global industry logic, e.g. brewery, cement, and telecommunications operations.

When global industry logic is strong, there is enormous benefit for a company to leverage its operations into other geographic areas. Leverage would primarily take place around operational areas, often resulting in 'invisible' globalization. Not engaging in such leverage would result in negative competitive circumstances, or 'leaving money on the table' as the Americans would say.

Accommodating global size logic

Global size logic is present when investment requirements are not driven by the number of countries entered. The pharmaceutical industry is an example, where the development and launch of a new drug can exceed $750 million. The bulk of the expense incurred is for testing and launching in the initial regulatory environment, with successive introductions costing less. Given the need for most pharmaceutical companies to keep R&D costs below 20 % of sales, the volume required from a new drug exceeds $3.5 billion over its lifetime on the market. Similar step-up expenditures exist in other industries. Few single markets can ensure such volume, thus driving firms into multiple markets for sufficient coverage. Such forces signal global size logic.

Global size logic forces companies to choose a broader global market to write off commitments, be they research or operational, against a growing market territory. The typical outcome is a global reach strategy to maximize market coverage. This strategy needs to target the most important markets – the 'must-win' markets – and be driven by a sophisticated understanding of the global opportunity.

The global reach imperative can supersede weaker global logics such as customer or purchasing. The need to push for global coverage must be balanced against differentiated demand. Companies may need to reduce the global offering to a modular design and be judicious in determining which elements to use subject to global reach. In machinery, it may be only one component, while other components are driven by local demand. In pharmaceuticals, the core element may be the initial molecule, with different forms of the product (liquid, pills, patch) required to fit local market demand.

Accommodating global regulatory logic

Global regulatory logic, determined by the nature of the regulatory environment, prevails in industries where governments play a major regulatory role. Telecommunications, banking, insurance, and healthcare are examples. Where regulatory roles are locally executed and the environment differs among markets, little global regulatory logic can be detected. In circumstances where the regulatory logic becomes increasingly homogeneous, as in the pharmaceutical industry with its pan-European approval pattern, a strong global regulatory logic can emerge. When the regulatory environment is similar, companies have more reason to enter other markets at only an incremental extra investment. In contrast, companies operating in industries with multiple, fragmented regulatory environments can restrict themselves to a given set of markets where they may meet the requirements.

Interpreting global logic patterns

Strategic guidance requires combining global logic assessments into a single mosaic. Elements of global logic may be pictured as individual rays emanating from a centre, with global pressure shown with the extreme points indicating a high degree of global logic. Connecting points of the logic rays creates a picture of a spider web, with the large area covered by the web indicating high overall global pressure.[3] A large footprint

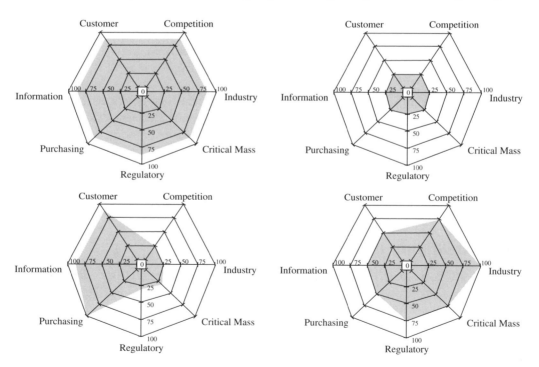

Figure 10.2   Widely differing global logic patterns

indicates strong global logic pressure, whereas a small footprint indicates weaker global logic pressure. What is important, however, is to locate the extreme points, or the global logic where the pressure is strongest. Varying global logic pressures suggest different generic global strategies. This will be the focus of the next section (see Figure 10.2).

Complexity level 2: adopting different pathways to global engagements[4]

When the debate on global business strategies first took off some time ago, there was the usual confusion as to what could be called a global strategy. Ever since the seminal work of Vijay Jolly, it became apparent that there were several different pathways companies could pursue, and yet, in some way, they could all be called global strategies.[5] Companies can consider either globalizing their asset base or their market coverage, as well as globalizing their source of ideas.

Global market strategies are based on maximizing global market coverage. As a result, a company might be looking to pursue opportunities in key markets and attempt to cover as much of the global opportunity as is relevant to the business mission. Global asset strategies occur when firms spread their assets, either in the form of production, supply, or research assets, globally across key markets. Contrasting these two globalization pathways, firms might thus be pursuing a global market strategy from a single production asset, or factory, by exporting. Alternatively, another firm might pursue a global asset strategy by sourcing globally and yet selling in one single (domestic) market. Although this is the classic role of the importer, it is the reverse side of exporting and still operates on a global scale. The combination of pathways, namely global asset and market strategies, was the traditional way of operating global firms. As already seen, that is but one of several global pathways.

Finally, there exists what can be called the 'third dimension' in the form of idea sourcing. Some firms depend entirely on their local market for new ideas, related to products or business processes. By contrast, other firms pursue the best from wherever they can get it. That would be a global idea strategy. Clearly, for sustainability, companies need to borrow the best ideas from wherever they arise and thus need to

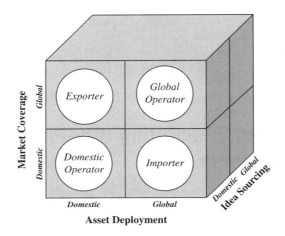

Figure 10.3   Multiple pathways to 'go global'

pursue at least a global idea strategy. What this discussion demonstrates is the fact that companies face very different pathways to 'go global' (see Figure 10.3), enlarging the set of options and thus adding to complexity. Though this is only the first fork in a long series of choices, it does not make it any easier.

Complexity level 3: dealing with multiple generic global strategies

At the outset of the globalization debate, companies believed they had to choose between either a global or a multidomestic strategy. A global strategy typically included standardized product offerings and functions, in particular the marketing function. Such global standardization is now understood as limiting. In reality, companies face strategy choices, which permit selective globalization with varying degrees of integration. Furthermore, some strategy elements may need to be globalized, while it may be better for others to remain localized. For most firms, the globalization conversation has become an issue of choosing from among a number of different generic global business strategies, a more complex situation than the previously accepted simplistic choice of global versus nonglobal.

Searching for generic global business strategies[6]

The following section examines some of these generic global strategies. It is intended to give an idea of some of the prototype patterns available, recognizing that in actuality businesses face a large number of possible permutations, ranging from going completely global to multidomestic. The partially global strategies reign supreme in this debate. Large firms consisting of several different businesses must make choices for each business (see Figure 10.4).

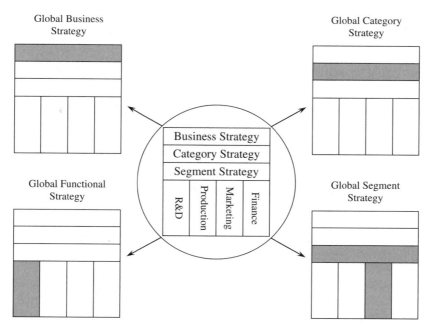

Figure 10.4   Multiple options for generic global strategies

When considering an integrated global business strategy, a company subjects most functions, processes, products, and strategies to full globalization. Underlying this strategy is the assumption that markets and customers are similar and that a company may unfold its business strategy along similar paths in most countries. Coca-Cola is frequently cited in this category. Reality indicates that such situations are not the norm and completely integrated global business strategies remain the exception. The previous section on global logic forces should certainly have signalled that different patterns emerge for different industries, thus generating a large number of semi-global strategies.

Several generic global strategies are identified for illustrative purposes. The generic global strategies outlined below demonstrate partial or selective globalization with some elements globalized and others adapted to the local environment.

Companies pursuing a global category strategy adopt a shallow form of globalization. The company limits the freedom of operating units by requiring each to stay within the same line of business. Advantages of this strategy are operational efficiency and learning across many markets in the same field. This strategy does not globalize products, communications, or segment choice. It is the least invasive generic global strategy.

Under a global segment strategy, the firm pursues a customer or application worldwide. The segment strategy is more restrictive than the category strategy, as it leverages a common segment experience with a certain customer group across the world. Homogeneous segments in all key markets drive this approach.

Some companies build global customer strategies around specific customers for worldwide service or delivery. This strategy is often adopted by global financial service firms (Citibank for global corporate customers, Deloitte for audit and tax clients) in response to customers who want seamless global service in multiple locations. It is one of the most rapidly growing generic global strategies today.

As industry KSFs become more specific to function, a company may adopt a global functional strategy, concentrating leverage on a critical function. For an industry where KSFs are heavily oriented towards marketing, the marketing operation would be subject to global leverage. Such leverage, or global function strategy, may not include brand names, positioning, and other specific marketing outputs. Instead, it may address the general approach to marketing and leverage the operational and process experience. The food industry, with its many country-based differences, comes to mind. Firms such as Nestle give operating managers considerable freedom regarding marketing decisions, including branding, advertising, positioning, and pricing. However, Nestle and others have a common marketing process that can be transferred from one operating unit to another. Experience is transferable even when customers are different and no visible global strategy exists. With a global functional strategy the company globalizes an entire business function, such as marketing, production, or R&D. Globalized R&D at most pharmaceutical companies exemplifies this strategy, with the entire function organized to run globally. Other functions that can be globalized include the finance function, IT, or accounting.

Using the marketing function as an illustrative example, a company can select from a series of generic global marketing strategies such as product, branding, advertising, and audience, as described below. A global product strategy offers a product with a high degree of standardization worldwide, emphasizing physical properties, service, and similarity in function. Cameras, automobile tyres, and batteries for electronic devices are examples of global products. A global branding strategy uses the same brand name or logo across world markets. For example, Coca-Cola and DaimlerChrysler use a global branding strategy for Coke and Mercedes-Benz respectively. Financial service firms such as ING, CitiGroup, HSBC, and AXA have also adopted this strategy. A global advertising strategy uses similar advertising or communications around the world. This strategy may accompany a global branding strategy, or it may focus on different brands. Intel is an example. A global audience strategy addresses a clearly defined audience globally, e.g. consumers or industrial end-users. The audience may be scattered around the world but feature similar interest groups, e.g. scientists, medical professionals, or a large number of consumers from many countries gathered for an event such as the Olympics.

Matching global generic strategies with global logic patterns

One of the major managerial choices when building a global business is to select a generic global strategy. This selection determines the business elements a company is willing to subject to globalization. The choice to use a generic global strategy needs to be made against a background of understanding the global logic forces that affect

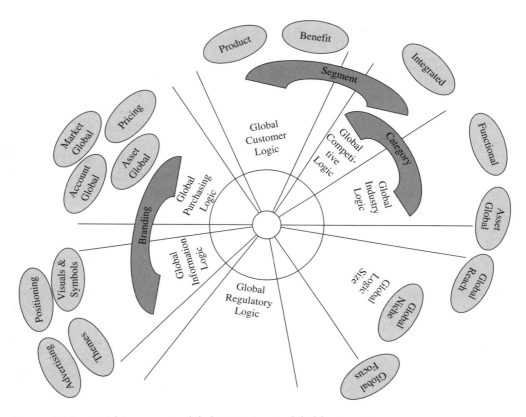

Figure 10.5   Matching generic global strategies to global logic patterns

a business. Global logics vary by industry and apply to all players in the competitive space. Disregarding global logic forces can influence long-term survival as competitors drive towards globalization (see Figure 10.5).

Complexity level 4: tapping resources from dispersed global competency centres

The final 'complexity multiplier' addresses the resource base of a company embarking in the direction of a global business strategy. At the outset of a firm's development, the resources for business development are typically in a single market. New firms develop contacts with local talent and typically hire locally. The financing is based on local resources. Technology is often local as well, as is market access. It is the combination of these best local resources that drives the development capacity of a business.

However, remaining plugged into local resources means that a business might be limited by the amount, quality, and sophistication of these local resources. Many firms today, particularly those looking to develop their businesses globally, cannot be satisfied doing just that. How then can a firm hitch its development speed to a higher trajectory if the local resource base is a limitation?

This can be illustrated with a recent example from sports. Many readers will be familiar with the incredible feat accomplished by the Swiss-based Alinghi team when they competed against the venerable teams from New Zealand and the United States to win the famous sailing trophy, the America's Cup.[7] Even though the Alinghi team did not have previous Cup experience (as a team), Alinghi managed to overcome a number of handicaps with regard to funding, technology, and talent. Alinghi hired its team sailing talent from anywhere, Swiss or not, and it was able to combine the best technologies for a competitive boat, regardless of origin. In doing so, it was able to overcome the handicap of having its base 'land-locked' in Switzerland. Alinghi could combine several sponsors from different countries to create a sufficient funding base. Essentially, by 'unplugging' itself from its local market base (Switzerland) and by re-plugging itself into a richer and more intense global resource base, a higher level of competitiveness was achieved. In fact, globalizing the resource base allowed Alinghi to compete effectively despite a small funding base. Rather than requiring additional funds, the globalizing of its resources saved funds.

We have seen this development in other sports businesses as well. The examples among European football clubs are indicative of this new trend.[8] Clubs that were able to expand their resource base beyond their home town, such as Manchester United, were able to acquire more resources that they could in turn invest in better sporting talent. This often led to superior outcomes, which resulted in more resources. The resources to be globalized were a fan base that spanned far beyond the team's home town stadium, the means to communicate the football experience into all corners of the world, and the ability to recruit the best sporting talent from anywhere. Becoming a global attraction

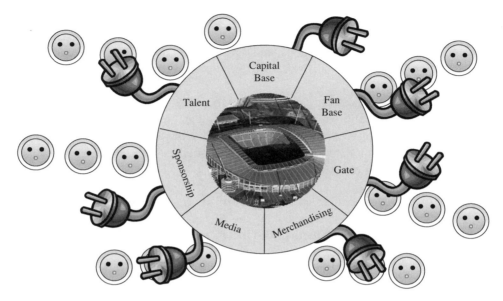

Figure 10.6 Manchester United re-plugged into powerful global sockets

resulted in more spending by sponsors who could justify higher amounts for a 'globally recognized' club (see Figure 10.6).

The lessons that are valid for Alinghi or Manchester United also equally apply to many firms, and particularly those who have to fulfil a global mandate. Just as Alinghi did, such businesses need to 'unplug' themselves from their local resource base and 're-plug' themselves into higher energy 'sockets' for superior results. The search for better and more potent resources may lead anywhere in the world. While this is increasingly accepted for markets and human resources, it is less accepted for technology and financial resources. Many firms have found it necessary to find stronger, freer, and more flexible financial markets and thus 'select' London or New York as the funding base even though they are based in a different country. Equally, with technology flowing quickly from one part of the world to another, companies need to chase the best, be it in Silicon Valley, Bangalore, or Shanghai.

The globalization of a firm's resource base means that not all of its 'plugs' will be plugged into the same country or market. Instead, a firm will invariably find that the relevant lead markets for its operation are dispersed, with the best possible R&D base or technology talent located in a different country than the best financing base. The same applies for lead customers or hiring the best talent for its operation. This dispersion of the firm's resource base across multiple geographies will add considerably to the complexity of running a business as collocation of all activities will become ever less likely, or advisable. While the sudden burst in technological communication capabilities has enabled the business community to link more dispersed operations, the sheer challenge of having to bridge distance and time zone gaps and link with different mindsets of staff will increase managerial complexity exponentially.

Reducing the complexity of global business strategies

The previous sections, outlining the four levels of complexity involved in global business strategies, point out that complexity grows exponentially and is cumulative. Each level compounds the complexity of the previous one(s). The thought of adding ever more complexity to the strategy process should invariably lead to the idea of reducing complexity. If so, how and at what stage can reduction be achieved?

If the previous section has a common thread, then it is the inevitability with which this is affecting businesses. The power of global logic is increasing, not decreasing, as is strongly in evidence in recent publications by Thomas Friedman, a leading US-based journalist with a keen understanding of the globalization process, both politically and economically.[9] If global logic is present, it will become a requirement for all members of a given industry, regardless of where they are located, to comply and accommodate it. Once a business is on the way to accommodating global logic, the compounding of complexity is inevitable. Approaches to reduce complexity will have to be sought. Two approaches stand out: a firm can either reduce complexity through a focus strategy or through the adoption of a global mindset that will help manage the centrifugal forces otherwise present in rampant, uncontrolled globalization.

A focus strategy implies going back to the underlying business strategy and reviewing the scope of a firm's business. There is already considerable complexity stemming from a firm's chosen markets, segments, technologies, business systems, and business models, regardless of any global strategy that might be applied to this underlying business strategy (see Figure 10.7). This focus might take many forms. A company might choose to limit its business to a restricted customer group or a clearly defined segment. The company might opt for a limitation of the product range and a reduced set of technology options offered. Furthermore, the company can decide to reduce the scope by centring in on core manufacturing processes, out- or insourcing others if relevant. Any of these moves will mean that the firm will be involved in fewer activities, which will invariably result in reducing the complexity of its business. While there may be imperatives that will dictate most segments and most markets, the opportunity to reduce choice and complexity at the basic business strategy level are greater and will invariably allow the firm to pursue a more aggressive global stance.

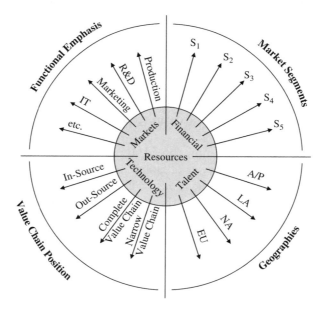

Figure 10.7   Resource trade-off dilemmas

There are several examples of recent strategy successes stemming from firms who reduced business complexity while pursing aggressive globalization. Both Nokia of Finland and Alcon Laboratories of the US stand out in this respect. Nokia, possibly the better known firm of the two, was a traditional conglomerate some 20 years ago, engaging in businesses as basic as paper and chemicals, all the way to electronics and telecommunications. When the firm reached a critical impasse in the late 1980s, Nokia, over the period of about 10 years, divested itself of everything but its mobile telecommunication business, which included both handsets and infrastructure. This focus strategy unleashed the necessary energy to develop the mobile business globally, eventually leading to global leadership.[10]

Another company that demonstrates the power of focus is Alcon Laboratories, a Texas-based firm dominating the ophthalmology field. Alcon, a company that had, for decades, stayed away from marketing anything other than products related to ophthalmology, has built a global franchise for its pharmaceuticals, its surgical products, and eye lens care. The company has grown from humble beginnings over the last 25 years into a $4 billion juggernaut, despite the fact that its business scope remains one of the narrowest of any major firm – it is focused on a single customer group that is global in reach.

References

[1] This is a revised and expanded version of a previously published article, 'Strategists in the Spider's Web, Mastering Globalization', *The Financial Times*, 1999. Similar concepts have been published in *Global Marketing Strategies*, 6th edn (Houghton Mifflin, 2004) and *Global Account Management* (John Wiley & Sons, Ltd, 2003) with David H. Hennessey, *Managing with a Global Mindset* (*The Financial Times*, Prentice-Hall, 2000); and 'Creating Global Businesses: A Conceptual–Strategic Approach', *Nanyang Business Review*, 2002, 1(1).

[2] Adapted from Jean-Pierre Jeannet and H. David Hennessey, *Global Marketing Strategies*, 6th edn, Boston: Houghton Mifflin, 2004, Chapter 7.

[3] Jeannet, Jean-Pierre, *Managing with a Global Mindset*, London: *The Financial Times*, Prentice-Hall, 2000, Chapter 6.

[4] Jeannet, Jean-Pierre and Hennessey, H. David, *Global Marketing Strategies*, 6th edn, Boston: Houghton Mifflin, 2004, Chapter 8, pp. 257–261.

[5] Jolly, Vijay, 'Competitive Global Strategies', *Strategy, Organizational Design, and Human Resource Management* (ed. Charles C. Snow), Greenwich, Connecticut: JAI Press, 1989, pp. 55–110.

[6] Adapted from Jean-Pierre Jeannet and H. David Hennessey *Global Marketing Strategies*, 6th edn, Boston: Houghton Mifflin, 2004, Chapter 8.

[7] Jeannet, Jean-Pierre and Lanning, Martha, 'Alinghi and the 2003 America's Cup: Strategy to Win', IMD case no. IMD-3-1450, 2004.

[8] Jeannet, Jean-Pierre, Collins', Robert C. and Schuepbach, Mwezi. IMD Football Case Series: 'Manchester United PLC' (IMD-3-1319, 2003), 'Real Madrid Club de Futbol' (IMD-3-1321, 2003), 'Juventus Football Club' (IMD-3-1320, 2003), and 'Football Club Ajax' (IMD-3-1323, 2003).

[9] Friedmann, Thomas L., *The World is Flat: A Brief History of the 21st Century*, New York: Farar, Straus & Giroux, 2005.

[10] Steinbock, Dan, *The Nokia Revolution*, New York: Amacom, 2001.

11
Various Dimensions of Complexity in Effectively Managing the Innovation Process – The Role of China

Georges Haour

Introduction

Technological innovation is a key engine for value creation. The hypercompetitive world, however, requires novel approaches for the innovation process to be more effective. Distributed innovation is such an approach. It requires an ability to lead highly complex projects, which increasingly bring together different actors, each contributing a piece of the technology required to develop 'high-impact offerings', as the firm becomes a true architect of innovation.

Furthermore, it is a high priority that the firm has one of its technical innovation centres in China, in order to be close to this large and fast-growing market. Effectively integrating this presence into the global innovation activity of the firm induces yet another level of complexity.

A 'Hypercompetitive' world

Our interdependent world creates compelling challenges for firms to change and adapt in a timely way, in order to create and maintain competitive positions. A powerful way to achieve this is for a technology company to effectively manage its innovation process more effectively than its competitors.

In industrial sectors such as pharmaceuticals or ICT (information and communication technologies), companies are defined as generating technical knowledge, in contrast with service companies (e.g. airlines, banks), which are primarily users of technology. In the former case, a particularly complex challenge is to turn long-to-acquire technical knowledge into cash by developing and launching effective innovations on the market.

The accelerating pace of the competition dynamics may be illustrated by the fact that the price of DVD players has diminished by half within two years, whereas this price-halving took six years for video-recording machines in the 1990s. The best response to this relentless dynamic of price erosion is to create higher value for customers by identifying and developing 'high-impact offerings', using the novel approach described below.

The novel response of distributed innovation

Innovation is about effectiveness. The recent book *Resolving the Innovation Paradox*[1] offers a powerful new approach for making the innovation process more effective in larger companies. In the first step of this approach, the top management mobilizes the considerable talent of the firm's staff, to identify 'high-impact offerings' to be launched that will 'make a difference' in the market. This process must be based on the firm's considerable intimacy with the market, including competitors, as well as the regulatory agencies in the case of the pharmaceutical industry.

The selected offerings are then developed by the company by extensively drawing on external technologies, so as not to be constrained by internal capabilities. This process truly acts on the implication of the banal phrase: 'There are many more developments going on outside the firm than inside.' It takes an entrepreneurial perspective, since a fully market-oriented firm first identifies the opportunity and then marshals resources to address that opportunity.

Not only are the resulting innovation projects multifunctional but they must also proactively integrate inputs from different actors: government laboratories, start-ups, other large companies, small firms, different countries, each bringing a technical piece to the complete puzzle required to develop the targeted offerings effectively.

Such a market-oriented, entrepreneurial, outward perspective, which draws on external resources, is needed to stimulate the currently excessively internal innovation process. Both types of processes must go side by side, with the distributed innovation approach occasionally mobilizing the firm and injecting into it a strong outward outlook. Companies must move along that path to secure more options for their pipeline of innovations.

Certain firms practise elements of this approach in a piecemeal way. For example, pharmaceutical companies frequently complement their own, often failing, portfolio of drug developments by purchasing new molecules from innovative start-up firms.

Distributed innovation implies that a firm must learn to be an effective architect of innovation. This involves a major increase in complexity, as it requires mobilizing the staff, in order to proactively identify opportunities in the market and lead multi-actor innovation projects. Such an entrepreneurial perspective is indeed quite different from the current ad hoc, piecemeal, and uncoordinated practices of 'outsourcing' innovation.

The global innovation system: cost-driven or talent-driven?

Technology companies have a worldwide array of R&D units, inherited, in a large part, through successive acquisitions and mergers. Often, some time after the merger, the acquiring company 'discovers' unknown R&D units 'buried' somewhere in the purchased firm. Such a system is thus not the result of a carefully crafted innovation strategy. It often presents considerable duplication of efforts. Indeed, upon merging, companies such as Glaxo and SmithKline, Hoechst and Rhone-Poulenc, or Sanofi and Aventis used the opportunity to close doubling-up of activities and reduce the R&D headcount. Such mergers also provide a rare opportunity to substantially re-orient and re-energize their development activities.

Streamlining this innovation system requires a sustained effort. Global electrical equipment manufacturer Schneider Electric, which has made a number of acquisitions in recent years, recently completed such a restructuring phase, closing and merging several sites to concentrate development efforts in three large centres in North America, Europe, and Asia.

Technology companies are increasingly open to the idea of complementing their own activities by partnering with external suppliers of technology or development. In the 1990s, ICT companies extensively purchased software work from firms in India because such labour-intensive technical services were available at a considerably less expensive rate.[2] At that time, Indian firms also hired out large numbers of software engineers to companies in the US at a rate much below that of their American counterparts. Since then, the salaries of Indian software engineers have essentially caught up with those in the most industrialized countries, rising at a rate of roughly 25 % per year.

Bangalore, in Southern India, is home to a yearly multibillion dollar business in 'offshoring'. In that region, key actors, such as Infosys or Wipro, grow at a rate of 30 % per year, making a tremendous business by taking over large parts of the IT activities of multinational companies, such as Nokia in the case of Infosys.

IBM, in India since 1992, currently has 43 000 employees in that country and plans to invest $3 billion until 2010. For its business services, IBM-Europe draws on teams of 30 to 50 engineers, located in Bangalore, in order to develop solutions for large Western clients. The Bangalore team spends several intensive weeks in Europe, in order to get acquainted with the client's specific requirements, as well as with IBM's way of doing business. Back in Bangalore, the team often requires an underestimated amount of management time, in order to ensure a smooth connection between the work carried out in Bangalore and the expectations of IBM's client. As a result, IBM retains a substantial fraction of the value-added, while the lower overall cost makes it possible to provide better cost–benefit services to its clients.

If 'offshoring' of software-based services has been essentially motivated by lower costs, it is a very different matter when it comes to innovation activities. When a firm decides to invest in a new technical development unit, the choice of the location is not motivated by lower costs. In 1992, Motorola, the first Western company to start an R&D unit in China, did so, not for cost reasons, but because China's mobile telephony was a potentially very large, dynamic, and highly competitive market. As the saying goes: 'You just had to be there.'

Similarly, in the 1980s, firms did not establish R&D centres in Japan because of lower costs. The move was not justified by the need to tap into local talent either. At that time, the motivation was that Japan was a large, growing market that was extremely demanding on product quality. By competing in such a market, firms concluded that they would learn lessons, which would be transferable to the company as a whole. For example, Tetra Pak had a unit in Japan that was scouting for specific, innovative packaging solutions in that country in order to get inspiration on new approaches, which it could then spread all over the world.

By its size and dynamism, China's market represents a compelling attraction to Western companies. As a result, China must be included in the global system in an effective way.

Including China in a Western-centric system

As indicated above, Western firms in the ICT industry have been present in China for many years along each element of the value chain: sales, manufacturing, and R&D. In the latter case, product adaptation is first carried out for the local markets; then, product innovations emerge. In some cases, China is poised to see the development of new home-grown devices that will conquer the world market. This dynamic market is fast becoming a source of innovations for the worldwide market in that industry. Motorola currently has 1300 R&D staff in China. Alcatel has the largest presence in this arena, with 2000 staff working in its Chinese R&D.

In the healthcare industry, which includes pharmaceutical and biotechnology companies, as well as medical technology firms, a similar movement is underway: AstraZeneca, Bayer, Eli Lily, GlaxoSmithKline, Merck, Novartis, Novo, Pfizer, Roche, and Servier all have R&D initiatives in China. Indeed, the size and the formula chosen vary considerably: Novo has a unit embedded in Tsinghua University, in Beijing, while Garnier has a joint venture. Most others have a wholly owned laboratory.

The newcomer Roche set up a centre in Shanghai in 2004, with plans to reach 250 staff in 2008. With generous tax holidays and infrastructure projects, Shanghai competes with other Chinese cities in order to attract laboratories, as these provide high-value, desirable jobs. Shanghai's municipal government has the ambition of making this city a world centre for pharmaceuticals and biotechnology.

China has the compelling appeal of a large, fast-growing pharmaceutical market, as this country is expected to be the fifth largest health market in the world by 2010. The statistics show impressive numbers of graduates coming from Chinese Universities each year. Very few, however, are true candidates for jobs in Western companies. These companies tend to rely fairly heavily on Chinese expatriates returning from stays in highly industrialized countries.

In the coastal regions, the infrastructure is generally better than that of India. Visitors to the sprawling 'industrial park' of Suzhou, a 2500-year-old city east of Shanghai, indeed often exclaim: 'This certainly is not the scene I expected in an emerging-economy country!' Like elsewhere, the Chinese government strongly encourages Western firms to set up an R&D unit in their country. High-value job creation and a 'high tech' image are sought, as well as 'rapidly learning from Western practices'.

Finally, a specific asset is China's centuries-old knowledge of and experience in traditional medicine. Several firms focus a large part of their work in this area. China also presents several specific challenges: substantial cultural and language gaps (Western companies had experience with this in Japan in the early 1980s), issues around intellectual property (IP), and a growing difficulty recruiting the appropriate workforce.

Clearly, the challenges of the language and of the cultural gap add to the difficulty for Western companies to manage effectively their innovation process globally. At present, the managers of their local units are generally non-Chinese, who do not speak Mandarin. In addition, they usually have very little experience in managing in the high context culture of China, where nonverbal messages and assumptions have to be picked up with tact. The Chinese staff, on the other hand, usually represents a diversity of individuals, some returning from abroad, people from Greater China (Hong Kong, Macao, Taiwan), and staff from China's various provinces. Differences between these populations are usually not well understood and are underestimated by Western management.[3]

Concerning the IP situation, which is crucial for pharmaceutical companies in particular, the international standards of a legal infrastructure have been introduced as a result of China joining the WTO (World Trade Organization) in 2001.[4] However, the actual practices of patent litigation are recent and somewhat erratic, depending on the court. An appeal to the Beijing courts is indeed possible, but it is likely that it will be a few years before the scene is stabilized. Many consider that China's IP system is generally performing at least as well as that of India.

Retaining staff is difficult as Chinese employees practice job hopping as soon as they have been trained by a Western company (the 'train and go' syndrome), similar to what was practised in Silicon Valley during its heyday. This high turnover of staff is indeed particularly detrimental in technical development activities, since specialized knowledge, which is difficult to secure, walks out the door with the employee.

In addition to the particular challenges posed by a country's specific characteristics, emerging economies often require Western companies to help put in place the framework, which is a prerequisite for the markets to develop. This is the case of the regulatory environment for drug development and qualification, illustrated below.

The complexity of doing business in emerging markets: developing stakeholders

Under the general assumption that countries must follow Western practices, the following example illustrates that sometimes Western companies must develop specific elements required for operating in the emerging country. It concerns the need for pharmaceutical companies to operate in a stable regulatory environment, with agencies such as the FDA (Federal Drug authority) in the US, EMEA (European agency in the Evaluation of Medicinal Products) in Europe, and the Ministry of Health in Japan.

In 1994, China did not have any concept of what clinical trials for new drugs were. Novartis, then present in China for marketing and sales, introduced an identical study protocol to the one Germany applies to its clinical trials for the Chinese authorities. Later Dr Zhao of Novartis wrote a book in Chinese on GCP (good clinical practice) for medical doctors – the first Chinese text on Western standards for carrying out clinical trials. Then, in 1999, China's Ministry of Health spun off the SDA (State Drug administration) and, today, the SFDA (State Food and Drug Administration), which has close to 300 staff, is fully independent and has the same status as a ministry.

As a result of a trusting relationship between China's government and the Western pharmaceutical companies, China was able to rapidly set up a regulatory environment, which allowed the introduction of drug regulations similar to those in the West. This system is now generally considered to be superior to that of Japan and the best in Asia. Indeed, the quality and rigour of the process for qualifying drugs is widely accepted. This allows pharmaceutical companies to conduct clinical trials in China and to have access to a large population of patients, which represents a considerable advantage at a time when access to patients often constitutes a bottleneck in Europe or the US. Novartis currently has ten new compounds being tested in China with more than 5000 patients. Depending upon the therapeutic indication, time between the start of a trial and the final study report may vary between a few months and eight years.

In the particular case of Novartis, Dr Zhao acted as an effective bridge between China's authorities and Sandoz, where she started her career, before it merged with Ciba-Geigy. This trusting relationship that Dr Zhao developed with the authorities over the years now results in substantial goodwill in favour of Novartis in China, where the market for pharmaceuticals is expected to continue to grow at a double-digit rate annually.

Orchestrating a truly global innovation process

By and large, technology firms still manage their various development sites as separate entities. The 'psychological distance' between a site and headquarters further fragments the system into disconnected units, in spite of electronic communications and numerous management meetings.

In developing technical innovations, the challenge is particularly acute, because of 'knowledge inertia'. According to this, it takes a long time for a firm to develop a competence in a leading-edge technical area and that firm will long resist terminating an area in which so much has been invested. Second, the relative aloofness of specialized individual professionals results in the 'expert syndrome'. Because of their somewhat self-centred attitude, there are barriers to collaboration – each expert has to be 'seduced' into working with another expert in order to collaborate on a challenging project.

In carrying out clinical studies, pharmaceutical companies try to coordinate their efforts globally as much as possible, in an attempt to introduce a new drug in several countries within a short period of time. Such companies also have the resources to connect the various units involved worldwide and to organize meetings for team members based in various continents. By and large, however, firms continue to be poor at leveraging the combined horsepower of their technical development capabilities spanning the world: globalizing the innovation process is far from being complete.

A major bottleneck in this area is the scarcity of high-performing managers of innovation projects. Such individuals must be able to deal effectively with a host of diverse issues in the business, technical, people, and cultural differences arenas. This job is particularly complex when it comes to distributed innovation, where, as described earlier, the contributions of different actors, in various locations, must be brought together to develop new offerings in a timely way. Leaders of such innovation projects must have a truly general management outlook. For this reason, they will be called 'mini CEOs'. The future profits of the firm often rest on their shoulders. Companies must make a much more concentrated effort to develop managers of complex projects.

In order to foster the globalization of innovation, it will be most useful to have the tools to manage in the electronic space. This includes e-mail contacts, management software, and computer-supported synchronous meetings involving team members located in different time-zones. In addition, face-to-face meetings must take place, as they alone allow the exploration of fledgling new ideas for offerings or services as well as help to build a trusting rapport among employees.

The crucial human factor

In managing the complexity of distributed innovation projects, it is crucial that appropriate persons engage in productive conversations. They need to develop trust and to form a collective judgement on the best routes to develop the market-oriented offerings that have been identified. In particular, this may be fostered by two mechanisms: (1) well-organized forums and (2) internships, as discussed below.

When a new technology-intensive business development opportunity appears, evaluating its potential may be a very good reason to convene a 'forum' involving a relatively small (20 persons or so) group of employees coming from different functions and locations within the firm. These persons must provide the right mix of competencies to identify, discuss, and evaluate the opportunities. Management has to make sure that carefully prepared and articulated presentations offer the various perspectives on business, market/brand, competitor analysis, and technical areas, all aligned with the business objectives at hand, but pitched in such a way as to keep the options open. Indeed, presenters have to be coached and prepared for effective discussions. Such a forum may sound expensive, but it is better to invest in discussions in the 'upstream' stage of the innovation process, rather than going ahead with a project that will have to be aborted for reasons that would have surfaced in early discussions. In the course of the innovation process, it is important to 'pick the winners' and have 'early failures' for the 'bad' projects.

The value of internships is well recognized for students or apprentices. Firms seem to forget this for their permanent employees. As it is difficult and expensive to move people permanently (dual careers, benefits for expatriates, etc.), in some cases the best 'ersatz' solution is to have 'short-term expatriates'. This means that a manager would spend a well-prepared stay in a different part of the firm. Thoughtful planning must go into the purpose and conditions of the internship; in particular, the intern's manager as well as the management on the 'receiving' side should both be convinced about the value of the specific internship and agree on the way to go about it, in order to maximize the learning for the intern, as well as for her or his entourage.

In dealing with the complexity of today's innovation projects, management must have a 'coaching', positive, and contributing attitude towards the managers of such projects. Management must be eager to contribute knowledge, experience, and judgement. This aims at both accelerating the individual's development and enhancing the effectiveness of the project. A 'walking around manager' style is very much what is needed. In this way, the manager keeps in close contact with the project leaders – encouraging them, guiding them, and making suggestions. It is up to managers to 'make time' for this important coaching role.

Conclusion

The complexity of managing the innovation process in a technical context is escalating and firms do not give enough attention to providing managers with the proper mindsets and skills. A particular challenge is represented by the novel approach of distributed innovation, which aims at effectively fusing external elements with the firm's internal elements. Furthermore, this approach requires true innovation leadership on the part of top management, which is rarely encountered, since current short-term financial considerations have the top priority.

China offers a challenging arena for technology-intensive firms. This is particularly true for firms in the healthcare industry. The question is not only when and where to invest, or further invest, in technical development activities; it is also how to carefully select new hires and provide appropriate incentives and management development. A sustained innovation strategy must also position these activities in such a way that, in the relatively near future, they become a source of ideas, knowledge, and innovation, not only for the Chinese market but also for Asia and the global markets. No doubt, Chinese companies, such as the 20-year-old telecommunications company Huawei, which invests 10% of sales in R&D each year, will seize the opportunities offered by the global markets just as well. These firms will devise their own strategies and their specific approaches in order to conquer the world markets.

In our 'hypercompetitive' world, the novel approach of distributed innovation brings more entrepreneurial, proactive energy into the innovation process of technology firms. The latter must do much more to develop effective leaders of innovation projects. Yet another step in complexity is the challenge of effectively integrating emerging sources of technology such as China and India. These large, fast-growing giants are indeed quickly becoming fountainheads of innovation for world markets.

References

[1] Haour, Georges, *Resolving the Innovation Paradox-Enhancing Growth in Technology Companies*, London: Palgrave, 2004 (see the book website www.innovationparadox.com).

[2] Carmel, Erran and Tijia, Paul, *Offshoring Information Technology*, Cambridge University Press, 2005.

[3] Gassmann, Oliver and Hua, Zheng, 'Motivations and Barriers of Foreign R&D Activities in China', *R&D Management*, 2004, **34**(4), 423–436. See also the *Journal for Technology Management in China*, Emerald (see:www.emeraldinsight.com).

[4] Haour, Georges, 'How should Technology Firms pace their R&D Investments in China?', *Perspectives for Managers*, 117 (IMD, April 2005).

12
Managing Complexity with Diversity Management

Martha Maznevski and Karsten Jonsen

Diversity is part of the solution, not the problem

On 11 September 2001 the perspective of globalization as complexity was reaffirmed – a characteristic that is likely to endure. As Prime Minister Tony Blair said, 'We are all internationalists now, whether we like it or not.'[1] Executives need to embrace this perspective more than ever, understand more fully the complexity with which they are dealing, and learn to cope more effectively with it.

Tightly coupled, complex global organizations operating in tightly coupled, global environments become more vulnerable as their potential for interdependence increases.[2] The increase in complexity leads to a decrease in buffers, slack resources, and autonomy of units. There is also less time to contemplate corrective action. Ambiguity makes problem diagnosis and action planning difficult and managerial control is decreased. Problems appear and must be resolved. 'Now' has become the primary unit of time in the world of global managers.

If customers, governments, interest groups, competitors, and the physical environment were passive, a corporation could manage the complexity by simply adding more managers, computers, and operations. That would be an increase in detail complexity.[3]

However, globalization is characterized by dynamic complexity.[3] There is simultaneously an increase in the scale of operations and an increase in the interconnectedness among the diversity of players who have differing agendas, motives, and goals. Subsystems are interconnected in such a way that cause and effect are no longer easy to determine. The effect of diversity is a greater issue because it is accompanied by an increase in interdependence. The increase in interdependence and diversity leads to more ambiguity. Ambiguity makes understanding diversity difficult, and so on. Such a scenario can create messy situations for executives, but global managers must deal with these situations.[4]

The most natural reaction to complexity is to try to limit it. However, what if you cannot control it any more? Adaptation is a large part of the answer!

Complexity increases uncertainty, which makes the results of actions unpredictable, and that makes planning and managing tough, especially for executives who have built their careers on simplifying things well enough to get the right results. Complex organizational structures are created and intricate budgeting and quarterly financial reporting exercises are employed. However, internal complex systems and processes may not always be the right response to a rapidly changing and unpredictable environment.

There seems to be two straightforward alternatives for dealing with increased complexity: elimination of input variety or amplification of decision makers. Elimination of variety is the reduction of input variety,[5] achieved by not being able or willing to see and understand the complexity in the environment impinging on the company, or by seeking or creating situations of certainty that executives think can be controlled, and thereby ignoring potentially high impact external conditions, situations, and behaviours. Such ostrich-like behaviour is not likely to bring success.

Amplification[6] means increasing the number of decision makers. Generally speaking, more decision makers, or team members, leads to more variety. Yet mere amplification will not necessarily work. If, for example, executives operating out of a corporate headquarters in Norwich, Connecticut, cannot generate the requisite variety in their decisions to match the variety existing in a global marketplace, simply increasing the size of the team may not work. If multiple decision makers are highly homogeneous, with similar outlooks, a similar vested interest in the outcome and reliance on the same selected sources for their information, their 'sensory input' will be fooled; i.e. they will think they are facing less variety than they actually are.[7]

When the environment delivers high levels of complexity, it is time to stop trying to control everything and to start adapting. Adaptability is the capacity for internal change in response to external conditions. According to Ashby's 'law of requisite variety', an organization can adapt if its internal variety matches the variety of its environment. This simply means that a flexible system with many options is better able to cope with change, which ultimately increases long-term survival chances in less predictable markets. Workforce and management diversity provide a renewable source of internal variety. The more complexity an organization faces, the more diversity can potentially help it adapt. The word *potentially* is used because diversity must be managed well, and that takes certain skills and a different approach to management. This is an approach whereby diversity is accepted, acknowledged, and appreciated in a working environment where people feel 'safe' and encouraged to express different views.

Managing complexity requires a new way of thinking. The fundamental shift is to 'simply' embrace diversity as an essential key to the solution of how to deal with complexity, and not just as a cause of it.

Face complexity with workforce diversity

Diversity provides adaptive capacity in two ways.[4] First, it gives access to a broader scope of perspectives to help understand and clarify the complexity. In a complex and ever-changing world, it is hard enough to find the right information and even tougher to make sense of what it all means. When most people in the organization see things the same way, things may seem to run smoothly, but there is a greater chance of missing and misinterpreting information. People with different backgrounds and training tend to be linked to different networks inside and outside the organization. This means they hear different things and can test ideas and actions in a broad variety of ways. They also bring different filters to the information – they see the same thing differently and together can build a more complete picture, whether looking at labour market issues or consumer purchases. Individuals may continue to experience uncertainty and complexity, but collectively they cope by sharing perspectives and creating a more comprehensive picture of what is going on.

Second, diversity helps companies adapt by combining perspectives in new ways. When facing complexity and increased uncertainty, yesterday's solutions will not address tomorrow's challenges – innovative solutions are needed. Diverse teams are simply more creative and innovative. The source of this creativity goes beyond scanning the broader set of ideas and selecting the best ones. In a team where members are similar, the team often arrives at a solution quickly and alignment is strong. In a diverse team the process is more difficult. However, when team members ask each other the question 'Why would you think that solution could work?' they end up confronting their own assumptions and questioning them. Seemingly contradictory perspectives are compared with each other and then combined, developing new ones that are more comprehensive and thoroughly tested. This leads to higher quality decisions and even the creation of brand new approaches. Diverse teams have been seen to produce results way beyond anyone's expectations. A diverse team from a manufacturing firm had a target of cutting US$800 million from its annual cost base and the team found creative ways to cut US$1.6 billion and invest the savings in research for a new product stream for the future. A global account team with diverse membership increased its accounts' performance by 85 % in one year, compared with an average of 30 % for the less diverse teams. Diversity helps just as much at lower levels in the organization, and this is *not* just restricted to R&D departments. A multicultural team of men and women – a highly diverse back-office bank team in a cosmopolitan city – increased its efficiency fourfold and secured the bank's position against competitors in a brand new market in that city. In all of these cases, the teams and workforces were able to use the different perspectives effectively to adapt to changing situations in innovative ways.

To respond to today's global complexity, organizations must shift the focus of response. Instead of structures and policies, the appropriate response to complexity today focuses on processes and people: the right people to decipher the informational content in the environment and appropriate organizational processes for managing the complexity and executing action plans. As Weick and Van Orden state: 'globalization requires people to make sense of turbulence in order to create processes that keep resources moving to locations of competitive advantage'.[8]

Increase diversity without chaos

Differences among people exist. They are inherent to human nature. The differences will remain even if an attempt is made to try and mask them – which is often done. However, there is extensive evidence that similarity leads to attraction. Cognitively, people feel more attracted to similar than dissimilar others, e.g. when it comes to physical characteristics, personality, attitudes, and values. They gravitate towards those who provide verification and drift away from those who do not. People naturally emphasize the qualities they share with a group and de-emphasize their uniqueness. The great challenge in human life, as well as organizational, is to verify people's unique attributes and perspectives so that they can offer their ideas and creativity for the benefit of the whole.[9] This leads the way for the *potential* variation becoming *realized* variation, and is essential when using diversity to manage complexity.

Managing diversity can be compared to creating laser light and white light. You align people with a laser, then let diversity shine with the white light. Laser light is a beam of light in which all the photons are moving in the same direction, at the same speed and wavelength. It accomplishes a specific purpose. A company's laser is the answer to the question: what do we *not* want different perspectives on? There should be a very clear definition of what performance means in the company, separating it from what people often assume it means. The laser could include the company values and direction. In the continuing 'war on talent', the laser light and clear definitions of what there must be alignment on often allow organizations to look beyond the typical 'pool of similarity' and tap into a broader variety of potential workforce – even if it means loosening up or revising traditional job descriptions. The laser also provides alignment while allowing diversity to work for the organization, rather than against it.

White light is about creating a broad spectrum of ideas and perspectives on other issues. It answers the question: what should we have diversity on? Which different views and values can and should thrive in the organization without destroying the laser? The toughest part to answering this question is separating real performance criteria from assumed ones. Many multinational firms, for example, have a policy that 'everyone who is to be considered for a senior management position must have both line and international experience'. This is a good example of a laser: it identifies an important set of experiential criteria that are related to judgement needed to run the company. However, in many companies there is an unwritten rule that potential senior managers must have both line and international experience before they turn forty – after that time they are considered 'too old' to gain the required experience. This unwritten rule inadvertently enforces homogeneity: most people who have both line and international experience early in their careers define career and ambition in the same way, and tend to focus on similar aspects of performance. Diversity on these perspectives, which could help the company manage complexity, is reduced for the sake of simplicity in the career management system.

How can diversity be managed?

The pressure is on how diversity is valued and utilized rather than just contained. The laser light/white light is the backbone of the organization! When this condition has been firmly established through dialogue, people will be increasingly self-managed, provided the right climate, processes, and skills are in place:

1. **Creating the right climate**. The first approach is to create an environment that encourages debate and open dialogue. An inclusive culture is one that encourages different views on certain things (the white light) and where there is a high degree of trust, respect, empowerment, and acceptance and verification of differences. In this work environment there is a high tolerance for debate and conflict, as long as these are primarily rooted in task-related matters. At the same time, there is a low tolerance for discrimination and a hard stand on harassment. Diverse views on complexity arise and are considered.

   An internal Shell investigation revealed at least part of the reason behind the success or failure of mixed teams.[10] The diversity of the 56 teams investigated was measured by non-work-related factors (gender, age) and work-related factors (number of years in the company, function). It showed that diverse teams had low performance if they also had a a low level of inclusiveness – the extent to which the members of a group feel connected to each other in one team. However, diverse teams had high performance if they also had a high level of inclusiveness. In other words, inclusiveness is the determining factor for the effect of diversity on outcomes such as learning, participation, and communication, as well as performance.

In organizations with an inclusive climate, the networks of informal influence are also diverse on demographic and other characteristics. There is no 'old boys' club' with only one segment of the population; nor are others compelled to 'mimic' the demographic group in power. In fact, the power/dominance dynamics are not ignored. To increase inclusiveness, some organizations provide formal networks where no informal ones exist, e.g. creating a network for women or for international (nonheadquarters company) employees. Another common approach to building inclusiveness is to create mentoring programmes, ensuring that members of nondominant groups are brought into the informal networks through mentors. In this way, the diversity of perspectives is available throughout the organization, not just through the hierarchy in formal ways, and can address complexity wherever it is found.

2. **People management systems**. The second approach to managing diversity effectively is to make sure that the management systems are supporting the laser performance and that individuals feel part of them. The vision of diversity only becomes real when the processes and systems in the organization support the official statements of equal opportunities. One example is the reward systems. Performance appraisal and reward systems must reinforce the importance of effective diversity management. For example, if there are no measures or metrics that can reward managers for hiring a diverse group of managers, or at least making sure that they consider hiring a diverse group, it is less likely to happen. Many organizations give priority to recruitment in their diversity efforts. However, hiring is not enough. Retention is equally important. Many organizations with stellar records of recruiting managers from non-dominant groups, such as women or people from nonheadquarters countries, find that the higher the level of the organization the less diversity there is. People from nondominant groups often exit the organization. Many leaders who feel excluded from the norms of their organization because of their gender or country of origin, and they often leave their positions or company because the environment is not inclusive and the systems and processes are not supportive of their career and advancement. To counter this, it is helpful to look at retention rates, both to keep that valuable diversity and also because retention rates are good indicators for measuring the extent to which the climate is inclusive. A large global construction firm, for example, has recently instituted individual performance measures for managers, based on the proportion of women retained in their business units.

Other important systems for creating 'full structural integration'[11] include:

- *Education efforts*. Ensuring that skills and education levels are evenly distributed throughout the organization, so there is no correlation between a person's identity group and the job status.
- *Career development*. Ensuring that there are special career development efforts for members of nondominant groups. This can also help create a healthy talent funnel for objective and fair promotion processes.
- *Flexible work schedules and benefits*. Ensuring that there is structural flexibility in the workplace, policies, and benefits that enable women, single parents, dual-career couples, and minorities to carry out their 'multiple commitment roles'.

3. **Skilful communications and interactions**. The third approach to harnessing diversity for managing complexity ensures that managers are skilled at bridging across differences for effective communication and leadership. Bridging is the ability to communicate effectively across differences, taking differences into account – transmitting meaning as it was intended. Bridging requires practising three sets of communication skills: positive attitudes, decentring, and recentring. The positive attitudes are motivation to understand others from their own point of view and confidence that this will help performance. Decentring is speaking and listening from the others' point of view (seeing white light). Recentring is creating common ground (laser light) and building on it.

   Bridging is part of the MBI approach (map, bridge, and integrate differences).[12] Mapping is the ability to understand the relevant differences in a management situation, while integrating is the ability to bring the differences together, combining and building on them in a synergy. This means that differences have to be acknowledged, respected, and communicated in order to make them productive. Although integrating leads directly to performance, especially on complex and strategically important tasks, it is bridging that enables the performance. With good bridging, integrating happens almost automatically. With poor bridging, integrating cannot happen.

When all this is put together and practised as often as it is preached, organizations can reach the highest level of diversity perspective, the 'integration-and-learning perspective',[13] which can provide the rationale and guidance needed to achieve sustained benefits from diversity in complex environments.

Leadership from the top

The dialogues that lead to a definition of white light/laser light are not held by the top management alone; it is important that people from all levels and parts of the organization contribute to ensure inclusivity and alignment (all members in the organization discuss these issues anyway, in corridors, at picnics, in the coffee corners, etc.). It is, however, the responsibility of the strategic level to facilitate and organize dialogues so that organizational members can learn from them and use them in a coherent way, especially in the face of complexity.

As with any major initiative related to shaping the mindset of all employees, top management's support and genuine commitment to diversity is crucial. However, it is astonishingly easy to find good arguments for not taking action:

> I believe that placing arbitrary national or gender quotas on management teams is fundamentally wrong. It should be performance that counts.

> Choosing managers based on nationality or gender is a lousy way to run a company.

These are the views about diversity that are heard frequently. They are not even wrong – of course performance is more important than particular demographic characteristics! But so often the systems reinforce homogeneity and a particular, simple easy-to-measure definition of performance and how to get there. This creates performance that is not adaptable to a complex and dynamic environment. In the long run the attitudes behind these statements decrease long-term performance in complexity, rather than increase it.

Top management must provide the human, financial, and technical resources to influence the environment, systems, and skilful interactions; they must also set out a vision for diversity and exemplify it ('walk the talk'). When a CEO, for example, articulates values but does not follow through in actions, people will develop scepticism, cynicism, mistrust, and low commitment to action. This is particularly important when it comes to the many middle and line managers who feel threatened by diversity initiatives and therefore resist.

Overcoming extreme resistance in a single CEO or in a few top managers is often close to impossible. In this case, the best advice is to warn the company that it will lose many of its best people (it may also lose contracts!) and another company will see the performance gains in the long run. Leaders who do step forward and genuinely support diversity with their actions will achieve higher performance from this, and model it for others. This is the single most powerful way to change a company culture.

Adapting to complexity with diversity

Workforce and management diversity can be the company's greatest natural resource in a complex environment. Most companies already have diverse workforces and relatively diverse management teams. The key function is to let this diversity actually work for the company, rather than be suppressed in a set of norms and expectations that equalize everyone. After engaging in dialogues to create laser light, managers can shine white light on to the complexity by creating an inclusive environment, adapting performance management systems, and facilitating skilful communication and interactions.

References

[1] Nussbaum, Bruce, 'Building a New Multilateral World', *BusinessWeek*, 21 April 2003, p. 43.

[2] Weick, Karl E. and Van Orden, Paul 'Organizing on a Global Scale: A Research and Teaching Agenda', *Human Resource Management*, Spring 1990, **29**(1), 49–61.

[3] Senge, Peter, *The Fifth Discipline*, Doubleday, 1990.

[4] Maznevski, Martha and Jonsen, Karsten, The value of different perspectives, *The Financial Times*, 24 March 2006.

[5] Harnden, R. and Leonard, A. (eds), *How many grapes went into the Wine. Stafford Beer on the Art and Science of Holistic Management*, Chichester, West Sussex: John Wiley & Sons, Ltd, 1994, p. 135.

[6] Harnden, R. and Leonard, A. (eds), *How many grapes went into the Wine. Stafford Beer on the Art and Science of Holistic Management*, Chichester, West Sussex: John Wiley & Sons, Ltd, 1994, p. 16.

[7] Beer, S., *Brain of the Firm: The Managerial Cybernetics of Organization*, 2nd edn, Chichester, New York, Brisbane, Toronto: John Wiley & Sons, Ltd, 1981, p. 356.

[8] Weick, Karl E. and Van Orden, Paul, 'Organizing on a global scale: A Research and Teaching agenda', *Human Resource Management*, Spring 1990, **29**(1), 49.

[9] Swann Jr, William B., Polzer, Jeffrey T., Seyle, Daniel Conor, and Ko, Sei Jin, 'Finding Value in Diversity: Verification of Personal and Social Self-views in Diverse Groups', *Academy of Management Review*, 2004, **29**(1), 9–27.

[10] Bredero, Jet, de Bruin, Leontien, van Doveren, Lida, ten Hove, Lotte, and van der Vegt, Gerben, *Team Diversity Research*, Groningen/Assen: University of Groningen/Shell, 2003.

[11] Cox, Taylor, The multicultural organization, *Academy of Management Executive*, 1991, **5**(2), 34–47.

[12] DiStefano, Joseph J. and Maznevski, Martha L., 'Creating value with diverse teams in global management', *Organizational Dynamics*, 2000, **29**(1), 45–63.

[13] Ely, Robin J. and Thomas, David A., 'Cultural Diversity at Work: The Effects of Diversity Perspectives on Work Group Processes and Outcomes', *Administrative Science Quarterly*, 2001, **46**(2), 229–273.

13
The Role of Information in Creating Value Efficiently

Donald Marchand and Amy Hykes

Abstract

Why are some companies better at dealing with complexity than others? A company's ability to manage and use information effectively is a key factor in determining how well a company can deal with complexity. Effective information management requires a company to encourage proactive information behaviours and values among all employees, develop information-processing practices linked to business strategies, and invest in IT for management support. High-performing companies have systematically developed and matured these information management capabilities over time and understand how to use them efficiently to create business value. They use information to identify areas where they can reduce costs and add value, enabling them to achieve superior results in their industries. Leading companies, such as Dell and CEMEX, have developed mature information capabilities and understand how to effectively leverage those information capabilities (IC) to optimize all areas of their businesses – the organizational structure, people, processes, customers, suppliers, and financial management. This is called the IC optimization effect. By using information effectively, companies can optimize all areas of their business, enabling them to operate more efficiently and effectively and more easily to manage and respond to complexity.

Why do some companies deal with complexity better than others?

Every company is confronted with growing complexity. Externally, relationships with competitors, customers, and suppliers are becoming more complicated and involved. Internally, many companies have complex processes, diverse business units, layers of management, and a diverse employee base. Why therefore are some companies able to deal with this complexity better than others and outperform the competition?

A company's ability to manage and use information effectively is a key factor in determining how well a company can deal with complexity. Every company manages information at some level, but the companies that outperform the competition are the ones that have developed mature information management capabilities. Effective information management requires a company to encourage proactive information behaviours and values among all employees, develop information-processing practices linked to business strategies, and invest in IT for management support. High-performing companies have systematically developed these information management capabilities throughout their company over time.

Once a company has achieved a mature level of information management, it can use information about customers, products, operations, and performance to optimize other business capabilities. By having the right quality and quantity of information, knowing how to use it appropriately, and operating more efficiently and effectively than the competition, these companies are able to successfully sense, manage, and proactively react to any complex situation that confronts them. It is the companies with immature information capabilities that find it difficult to deal with complexity and achieve good results. Without the right information, these companies do not know how to react appropriately to internal or external events. As a result, they require more resources and time to get things done and are, thus, less efficient and effective. The difference in how companies are able to deal with complexity is directly related to how well they can manage and use their information.

What is effective information management?

Unfortunately, over the last several decades, the majority of managers have focused on the management of information, mainly within the context of their company's information technology. Many companies continue to subscribe to a 'technology-centric' mindset – IT is seen as the 'silver bullet' to solve all of their information problems.

Managing information is a more challenging and complicated task than just implementing a technical solution. Companies that use information effectively understand how to leverage information, people, and IT practices systematically to improve business results.

To help managers identify and map those business practices critical to creating effective information use in their companies, a management framework called 'information orientation' (IO) has been developed. IO is made up of the following three capabilities, which are collectively called 'information capabilities' (IC).

* **Information behaviours and values (IBV)** are the capabilities of a company to instil and promote behaviours and values, such as integrity, control, transparency, sharing, and proactiveness, in its people for the effective use of information and IT.
* **Information management practices (IMP)** are the capabilities of a company to manage information effectively over its lifecycle, which includes sensing, collecting, organizing, processing, and maintaining information.
* **Information technology practices (ITP)** are the capabilities of a company to manage appropriate IT applications and infrastructure effectively to support operations, business processes, innovation in products and services, and management information and business intelligence.

Being good at just one information capability does not lead to effective information management. Managers must continually invest in and effectively implement all three information capabilities across all the people and processes in the company. This holistic, integrative, and ongoing approach is difficult for some companies to replicate, thus providing a competitive advantage for those that can.

INFORMATION MANAGEMENT
Refers the capabilities of a company to build:
– information behaviours and values
– information management practices
– information technology practices

ORGANIZATIONAL STRUCTURE
Refers to the hierarchical and network relationships in organizations, including:
– spans of control
– allocation of decision rights
– degrees of job enlargement

PROCESSES
Refer to the sets of logically related tasks which are performed to achieve a defined business outcome. Processes can be:
– business processes (production, product innovation, delivery)
– management processes (strategy development)

PEOPLE
Refers to the investment in human capital and the mix of shared values and behavioural norms exhibited by people over time in an organization, including:
– competencies (knowledge and skills)
– motivation rewards
– communication networks

EXTERNAL RELATIONSHIPS
Refers to a company's activities to build competencies and capabilities outside organizational boundaries, including:
– mergers and acquisitions
– joint ventures and alliances
– customer relationships and supplier

FINANCIAL MANAGEMENT
Refers to the effective use of an organization's assets and can include the management of:
– investments
– balance sheet
– accounts receivable and payable
– cash flow

Figure 13.1 The six key business capabilities

The advantage of developing mature information management capabilities is that a company can then use information to manage other business capabilities efficiently and effectively, as noted in Figure 13.1.[1] Since information capabilities can significantly impact all other business capabilities, they are the most influential business capabilities. This can be called the IC optimization effect – information's ability to make other business capabilities more efficient and effective. It is the companies that take advantage of the IC optimization effect that can achieve superior business results and successfully deal with complexity. In the next section, the IC optimization effect will be discussed in detail.

The real power of information – the IC optimization effect

Today, with the ability to represent information digitally and access information from almost everywhere, many companies have started to substitute information for the movement of people, paper, and products across geographical areas, time zones, markets, and organizational boundaries. They have replaced physical processes with electronic ones and the need for rigid organizational structures with more flexible virtual networks of people.

The real power of information capabilities is not just in the replication and automation of work processes, but also in their unique ability to manage other business capabilities better. Some companies have started to realize that an investment in information capabilities can directly impact the productivity and performance of other business capabilities, such as people, process, and organizational structure. For instance, companies who develop mature information capabilities can reduce the number of people required to perform a specific task, thus resulting in cost savings and efficiencies.

A simple example of how IC can make a business capability more efficient can be seen in the customer ordering process. By using information capabilities to set up an online store, companies can easily and quickly provide customers with a wealth of information about the company and their products. Customers do not have to go to a retail store to compare products, call a customer representative to answer a question, or mail in an order form to purchase a product. As a result, the process is more efficient and the company is able to realize cost savings in retail space, sales force, and printing/mailing of product information. Amazon is a good example of a company that has used technology to reach its customers efficiently. The only way customers can order from them is online – they have no retail locations.

What many companies have not realized is that by leveraging information capabilities they can simultaneously make business capabilities both more efficient as well as effective. Once a business capability is made more efficient, the freed-up resources could be focused on adding value and identifying new opportunities.

The IC optimization effect happens when a company uses information capabilities not only to eliminate inefficiencies and provide cost savings but to go a step further and add value. Returning to the ordering process example, a company could use IC to capture customer information and preferences based on what a customer has previously looked at, requested, or ordered from an online site. The company could then use that information to create new product offerings, marketing campaigns, or product information targeted at specific customer needs. For instance, when you sign in at Amazon.com the company presents you with a customized website that is tailored to your specific interests or needs. The site lists books or products that you might be interested in based on your previous purchases. Amazon uses its information capabilities to sense what the customers want and to present product information to each individual customer, thereby making the process more efficient and effective.

Figure 13.2 outlines scenarios in which IC can influence the five other business capabilities.[1] For instance, companies can use information capabilities to create a flatter organizational structure, thus making the communication, approval, or reporting structure more efficient. By decreasing the necessary layers of management, information capabilities allow companies to make decisions faster and increase a company's flexibility and ability to react to market changes. Information capabilities can also influence external relationships, by making it easier and more efficient to communicate and coordinate with partners or suppliers. IC can also add value by enabling companies to share more information with partners or suppliers about inventory needs or customer requirements. This can result in more effective inventory management and improved customer service.

In the next section, we will discuss how two companies have capitalized on the IC optimization effect and are using information to efficiently create value, deal with complexity, and outperform the competition.

IC	Organizational Structure (OS)	Processes (P)	People (PL)	External Relationships (ES)	Financial Management (FM)
SAVES (creates efficiencies)	• Increases local decision making • Improves monitoring • Flattens the OS • Lowers communication/coordination costs	• Simplifies processes • Standardizes processes • Reduces the number of required processes • Improves cycle time	• Allows for more efficient use of time • Increases output • Reduces the amount of direct management required to track performance • Decreases headcount	• Provides direct relationships with customers • Creates more focused supply relationships • Decreases the interface overhead • Lowers coordination costs	• Improves cash management • Speeds up collection • Improves cash conversion • Frees up assets for other investments
ADDS VALUE (increases effectiveness)	• Enables virtual teams • Increases the OS's flexibility and adaptability to change • Places more value in each layer/node • Delegates authority • Extends the communication networks	• Allows 'make-to-order' production or 'just-in-time' delivery • Permits tight internal and external links with other groups • Creates reconfigurable processes	• Improved decision making • People have more time for value-added activities • Employees can easily measure their performance and impact	• Improves servicing • Facilitates customer contact • Empowers customers • Increases communication • Tightens relationships	• Provides assets for new business opportunities • Permits new investments • Improves risk management

Figure 13.2 The IC optimization effect. (adapted and modified from D. Marchand, W. Kettinger, and J. Rollins, *Making the Invisible Visible*, Chichester, West Sussex: John Wiley & Sons, Ltd, 2001, p. 215)

The IC optimization effect at work

To illustrate the IC optimization effect, we looked at two companies in two very different industries – Dell, in the information technology industry, and CEMEX, in the cement industry. Both companies have developed mature information capabilities over time and have learned how to manage people, technology, and processes to achieve superior business results. Both understand the power of information, and they have been able to capitalize on the IC optimization effect.

Dell began as an entrepreneurial exploit out of Michael Dell's college dorm room in the early 1980s. It was originally capitalized with $1000, but is now worth more than $100 billion. It operates in 80 countries and has over 53 000 employees. It is famous for the direct model and build-to-order production – selling customized computers directly to the customer, building it to the customer's order, and delivering the highest quality product most quickly at the lowest cost. However, Dell's success or competitive advantage is not just a result of an innovative business model or the use of technology to drive efficiencies. It is Dell's ability to create and maintain a culture with high expectations, discipline, consistent execution, and the flexibility needed to compete in a rapidly changing industry.[2] The company clearly understands the importance of information and its ability to create value in an organization. Dell hires people who can and would share information, remain flexible in a rapidly changing environment, and can deal with complex situations. Their employees effectively use information to measure their own performance, satisfy customers' needs, lower prices, speed up cash conversion, strengthen supplier relationships, expand into new product markets, and grow geographically.[3]

In CEMEX's case, the company started in 1906 as a local cement producer in Mexico. It was only in the early 1990s that CEMEX aggressively started to expand its operations globally through acquisitions. Within a decade, it became the third largest cement producer in the world and now operates in over 50 countries. The company has become famous for its 'information-centric' culture, which has enabled the company to integrate acquisitions quickly, improve their understanding of the customers, and standardize 'best-practice' processes globally while continuing to innovate locally. In order to develop such a culture, CEMEX made the necessary investment in cultivating employee attitudes and behaviours towards knowledge sharing and effective information practices. The company has also led its industry with respect to its management and use of information technology.[4] CEMEX's focus on information capabilities has clearly paid off. Over the last 15 years, they have increased revenue and EBITDA at compound growth rates in excess of 18%. During the same time, they have produced average EBITDA margins of 31%, making them the most efficient global cement company.[5]

Although Dell and CEMEX are in different markets and use different business models, they exhibit similar characteristics of effective information use. Let us look at each of the five business capabilities and discuss examples of how Dell and CEMEX have used their information capabilities to optimize people, organizational structure, processes, external relationships, and financial management.

Organizational structure

Today, most large companies regularly restructure in order to create a 'flatter' organization that improves the reporting or responsibility within the company. Information capabilities can play an integral role in eliminating redundancy or unnecessary layers in an organizational structure. By streamlining processes, minimizing layers, facilitating communication, and improving monitoring, information capabilities have helped create more agile and flexible organizational structures.

Let us look at some specific examples of how the IC optimization effect can impact an organizational structure. First, information capabilities allow for greater decentralization of decision authority by decreasing the cost of knowledge transmission and allowing companies to take better advantage of local information while maintaining overall corporate control. This can reduce the burden of 'information overload' on centralized decision makers and facilitate the decision-making process. By opening up lines of communication and facilitating decision making, companies no longer need to operate in a vertical hierarchal structure and are able to save time and money by reducing headcount and response time.

Second, IC can also enhance an organizational structure and make it more effective. With the freeing of the structural boundaries and the decreased need for vertical integration, a company can form more virtual networks and virtual communities that leverage different people's perspectives and encourage innovation. Companies that encourage the sharing and development of ideas between different groups and management functions are more likely to enhance innovation, creativity, and product development.[1]

CEMEX's organizational structure is aimed at improving business results through standardizing effective processes around best practices. The company splits its organization into regional groups that are responsible for the business results in each region. They have identified key processes that cross all regions, such as commercial, ready mix, or operations. For each key process, the company has created groups that are sponsored by senior executives and are responsible for that process globally. The groups consist of experts from different areas of the organization and representatives from IT and human resources. This matrixed organizational structure allows the company easily to identify best practices or innovations in various geographies or process groups and then implement those ideas globally.

CEMEX's organizational structure allows for open communication and the sharing of best practices across the entire company. CEMEX's use of technology enables it to share information quickly and consistently with its employee base. CEMEX executives have real-time access to colleagues across the globe, by using push technology that automatically delivers information via the internet to employees' computers. CEMEX uses proprietary software programs that lets divisions create virtual communities through which they can identify, share, and improve upon the company's best practices. These communities assist the company in its efforts to further streamline business activities globally.[4]

Dell has a flat organizational structure that is organized functionally and by customer segments, so each customer segment has its own product engineering, marketing, sales, and service team. This organizational structure enables Dell to focus on and support each customer segment's unique needs. It also allows the company to share both successes and failures freely within the organization, since their functional areas communicate across the customer segments instead of acting as silos hoarding information.[6]

At Dell, openness and sharing is an important part of the culture. The company openly communicates its performance with all employees. Since Dell's business performance is so transparent, no one is able to hide performance issues. The executive team is made aware of all significant performance issues and it is typical for the executives to e-mail an employee several organizational layers down asking for information on what happened. The company culture expects people to address any performance issues with a fast and direct response. For instance, Dell employees are given the freedom to make key operational decisions to ensure that no opportunities for meeting customer expectations are lost due to hierarchical constraints. Dell's direct communication and quick response are not the norm in many organizations, where response time is slow because communication with senior management must be filtered through layers of reviews and approvals. One of Dell's core competencies is its ability to disseminate and react to information directly.[7]

Processes

Processes are a collection of related business activities that are undertaken in pursuit of a common goal. Some typical processes in an organization include manufacturing products, processing orders, delivering products, customer servicing, and creating new products, as well as back-office processes, such as accounts receivable, payroll, expense reporting, and recruiting. Companies are continually looking at ways to redesign processes to make them more efficient and ultimately effective. Electronic data interchange (EDI), radio frequency identification (RFID), efficient customer response (ECR), and continuous product replenishment (CPR) systems are just a few examples of ways companies can use IC to improve the efficiency and effectiveness of its processes.

The most obvious impact that information capabilities have on business processes is their ability to reduce costs, by streamlining processes and replacing physical processes with electronic ones. Information capabilities can also boost operational effectiveness by coordinating similar process tasks across functions and disparate channels, so that everyone in a company is working together towards a common goal – such as serving the customer. Information capabilities can make process improvements that lower defect rates in the manufacturing process, improve information relevance in the marketing process, and speed the time to market in the distribution or sales process.

Dell has improved its business processes over many years by using information capabilities effectively. By selling directly to the customer online, Dell has eliminated the middleman and the associated markup and call centre sales costs. Thereby, Dell has been able to save millions of dollars in the sales process. Dell processes customer orders in real time. When customers call to place an order with Dell, the order is immediately disseminated throughout the company, scheduled through the assembly line, and sent to suppliers and partners. This is critical, since suppliers hold the only inventory in warehouses or 'hubs' and wait for orders to be processed by Dell. When Dell receives an order, it triggers a flow of components from their suppliers, through the warehouses and then to Dell's assembly sites. Once the order is complete at the assembly site it is loaded directly on to trucks for delivery. The computers are typically delivered to the customer's door within days.

Dell developed information systems and processes to ensure efficient delivery. First, the company set up an internet connection with shipping companies to arrange pick-ups. Second, Dell stopped carrying computer monitors. Instead, when a machine is ready to be shipped from any of its factories, Dell sends an e-mail to the shipper, who obtains a monitor directly from a supplier's stock and schedules it to arrive with the PC. This process saves time as well as inventory carrying and delivery costs.

For companies like Dell, each day's success in responding to customer orders is based on the real-time synchronization of all the suppliers and delivery companies to make sure that every order is built to unique customer needs and delivered on time. Seamlessly linking the IT systems of Dell's partners to fulfil an order from placement to delivery enables Dell to make its direct model work.[6]

Through its global process standardization programme, 'the CEMEX Way', CEMEX has gained significant efficiencies and cost savings of $150 million per year. This programme is aimed at documenting best practices and sharing them across the global organization. It is a push for explicit knowledge that is formalized, codified, and transparent about core business processes.

The CEMEX Way has facilitated rapid learning and has reduced the time it takes CEMEX to integrate an acquired company. For example, the time needed to integrate the Southdown acquisition in the US in 2000 was only 4 months and the Puerto Rican Cement Company in 2003 was only 2 months, as opposed to 18 months for the first acquisition in Spain in 1992. To leverage previous integration experience and to ensure the integration of people's mindsets and information practices, a multinational post-merger integration team, consisting of people-oriented experts and managers from different countries and functions, is sent to each acquired entity.

The CEMEX Way enables the company to launch initiatives quickly to increase customer satisfaction. For example, CEMEX launches a new electronic storefront in different countries as often as every two months, and is even able to customize the online sites to local requirements, making them more effective. Most importantly, the CEMEX Way has further refined the company's disciplined approach to documenting and sharing knowledge developed within CEMEX.[4]

People

People are a critical resource – they are the ones who capture, manage, and use information. It is the people who are ultimately responsible for executing the company's business plan. There are many ways that managers might invest in their 'people' resources. They might hire people during a period of growth, train employees to improve their skills and expertise, or provide motivational tools (monetary and nonmonetary). Since an organization's culture can influence how employees execute their tasks, managers can also instil corporate values and behavioural norms to develop a culture that contributes to the company's success.

Companies can also optimize people resources by investing in information capabilities. With the right people, technology, and processes, companies are able to reduce the number of people needed to achieve the same desired business results. In addition, information capabilities make information processing less costly by creating common 'social conventions' and standardizing ways of collecting and communicating information that allow for more efficient management of projects and control of functional tasks. Companies with mature information capabilities are able to monitor people and performance more closely in real time, which decreases the required number of direct managers. An investment in information capabilities can reduce human capital costs and increase people's efficiency.

Being able to use people efficiently is just one part of the equation. Information capabilities can also enhance people's jobs by increasing communication, coordination, and access to information and knowledge. For instance, information capabilities can provide improved skills training by standardizing information across the company, making it easily accessible via the web and helping develop a learning culture. By providing tools for continuous training, a company is improving people's performance and their understanding of the business. It can help to create a culture where people work together to learn from mistakes and leverage the expertise of fellow employees.[1]

By using information capabilities effectively, Dell is able to provide its employees with the information they need to perform their jobs successfully, as well as culture and behavioural norms that value and act on that information. Dell employees know how their jobs influence the company's performance, are able to focus their time and efforts in areas where they have the most impact, and can quickly identify problems and proactively come up with solutions to minimize the impact.

Dell uses information capabilities to ensure that all employees understand how they impact the business and take responsibility for their performance. They have created a shared language and shared culture with clearly defined metrics that are tracked and communicated daily to employees. This enables employees to identify any potential problems or areas of poor performance quickly. The company's top leadership team expects every Dell manager to know and be able to present current, detailed performance figures at a moment's notice. He or she must be able to respond quickly to questions about performance problems. As a result, Dell managers update, check, analyse, and report operational numbers 24 hours a day, seven days a week.[7]

If employees are not meeting specific targets, they are expected to make a change proactively in order to minimize or avoid any down time. For example, if the people in the consumer business notice that they are not getting enough calls in the morning, they can then immediately start running a promotion on the web, change their pricing, or run more ads. Dell has created a sense of constant urgency in its organization, and employees realize they must be proactive in dealing with issues. They understand that they cannot wait for the next day to address an issue, because by then it is usually too late and the damage is already done.[6]

The CEMEX Way has enabled CEMEX to develop an internal worldwide benchmarking database for procurement, production, and sales that managers and employees can access. As information in these acquired entities had generally been reserved only for senior management, the new database has created an openness, which helps remove the skepticism of some employees within newly acquired business units and encourages them to share information and learn from mistakes. By clearly communicating their standard global processes, CEMEX helps employees quickly become efficient in their jobs and coordinate with each other based on the company's shared language and standard way of doing things.

The company motivates employees to innovate and share process improvements by agreeing to share any realized savings with employee(s) whose proposed process improvements are successfully implemented. The company has also introduced a balanced scorecard to help employees understand CEMEX's strategies and motivate them to execute the strategies by developing and sharing better practices. CEMEX employees clearly understand how they can efficiently add value to the organization.[4]

External relationships

Most companies have several types of external relationships – they can include customers, partners, suppliers, joint ventures, and/or alliances. These external relationships have increasingly become important in creating a competitive advantage and being able to reach global markets. Information capabilities can play an integral part in improving communication and coordination between an organization and external parties.

With the supplier relationship, IC can lower supplier coordination costs by forging a close and transparent relationship. For instance, suppliers can be alerted to any demand changes in real time and be given the opportunity to reduce or increase the production of parts. This can help decrease the costs related to overproduction or underproduction of parts, thus making the supplier more efficient. Forming a close supplier relationship is critical in the retail world where out-of-stock occurrences can severely damage margins and profits. Companies want to ensure that suppliers are aware of and can meet the changing consumer demands.

Dell's virtual integration of the entire supply chain has created operational efficiencies for itself as well as its suppliers. The company has very collaborative and transparent relationships with its suppliers. Dell's systems are linked with its suppliers' planning and execution activities, enabling them to gather real-time information about inventory levels at various points in the supply chain. The suppliers are also expected to share information such as capacity outlooks and new technology drivers. In return, Dell provides direct signals of customer demand to suppliers and shares current and projected market shifts and sourcing strategies. In addition, Dell is often the first to communicate a component quality problem because it ships typically within five days of assembly and can get reports of issues in the field directly from customers. This visibility up and down the supply chain enhances the collaboration and commitment by suppliers and allows Dell to manage demand in real time.[6]

In exchange for building partnerships and sharing information, Dell expects its suppliers to meet lofty performance goals. The suppliers that live up to Dell's expectations not only get access to large volumes of business but also receive training and development in improving their processes. Once every quarter, Dell meets with each supplier to provide direct feedback on performance and future expectations. The supplier is given a scorecard, which compares the supplier against its industry peers on cost, quality, reliability, and continuity of supply.[7]

Information capabilities can also play a key role with the customer relationship. Companies with mature IC are able to collect and analyse customer data efficiently. These companies are also able to act on that information effectively, by providing customers with tailored information, products, or services – thus adding value. Companies that are able to provide a more personalized interaction with customers generally have higher customer satisfaction and retention rates.

With the development of their IC, CEMEX has been able to improve customer satisfaction. Customers are guaranteed ready-mix cement deliveries within 20 minutes of schedule within designated geographic markets, regardless of weather conditions, and even in Mexico City's chaotic traffic. If there are delays, customers receive discounts of approximately 5 %. These guarantees have been made possible through a net-based logistics system for truck dispatch and use of a global positioning system (GPS) to speed deliveries to customers. This system has increased truck productivity by 35 % and eliminated costly delays.[4]

Financial management

When financial management is discussed, we are not talking about calculating or reporting financial numbers, but a company's ability to manage its money (cash flow and working capital) efficiently and effectively. Finance is all about numbers and data, so it makes sense that companies who effectively manage information are most often the ones that evaluate investment risks, achieve optimal returns, leverage their global wealth, and manage the balance sheet better than the competition. By making operations more efficient, companies can liberate liquidity that has been tied up in inefficient resources and use it to create value and invest in new opportunities.

Two areas of financial management that information capabilities are impacting include cash and risk management. First, companies are starting to understand the importance of cash management and the impact it can have on the bottom line. Many companies have started to review their payment periods, timing of supplier payments, inventory levels, reconciliation processes, and management of receivables and payables, all in an effort to improve the inflow and outflow of cash. The more efficient they are at collecting cash or at avoiding excess inventory the more cash they can generate. One example is consignment inventory – when a company does not pay a supplier for its inventory until it sells it and is able to free up cash that had previously been tied up in inventory management. Companies with the right information about their cash flow can focus on how to increase the efficiency of their cash management and can ultimately increase the bottom line.

Second, information capabilities can help companies minimize the risks involved in operating in today's complex and global business world. A company's financial risks can include credit and market and operational risks. These risks exist due to market volatility, commodity price fluctuations, interest rate changes, tax liabilities, and foreign exchange rate adjustments. It is important for companies to determine the appropriate level of risk within their organization and then to evaluate projects or clients across the organization on a risk versus reward basis, not just as an individual client or project risk. A company needs to be able to look at the entire risk portfolio of an organization before it can make a more informed and accurate decision on whether to move forward with a specific activity, project, or client. This requires that they have the right information available for accurate analysis. Surprisingly, many companies are not able to look at their risk portfolio with a holistic view or do not have accurate enough information to make an informed decision.

Any company in the financial industry should understand the importance of effective financial management and specifically risk management. For example, by using consumer credit information, banks or credit card companies are able to determine the appropriate line of credit for customers. Also, many commercial banks use various credit-scoring methodologies to evaluate the financial strength or performance of clients. In both situations, these organizations are using information to limit their financial risk.

Most importantly, successful financial management requires a company to be able to track and monitor its performance. Companies need to be able to create metrics and help their employees understand those metrics so that they realize the financial impact of their actions or decisions. Information capabilities can help a company capture the data and metrics required for efficient and effective financial management. With the right tools, a company can easily determine its risk profile, days of outstanding sales, cash conversion cycle, etc. Without this type of information, a company cannot measure its improvement efforts, let alone determine what areas they need to improve.

Dell provides several good examples of using information capabilities to improve financial management. In late 1995, Dell implemented a cash management initiative. It motivated all employees – and even suppliers and customers – to concentrate on converting what the company sold into cash as quickly as possible. Dell developed a set of easy-to-understand performance metrics to measure liquidity – day's sales outstanding, day's sales in inventory, day's payables outstanding, and cash conversion cycle – that they clearly communicated and tracked for their employees. As a result, Dell successfully improved its cash conversion cycle from an industry-acceptable 40 days to a phenomenal negative 5 days in a year.

Dell's asset management team has also made frequent presentations to educate employees about the importance of liquidity management and how to interpret metrics information. The team made the liquidity improvement initiative a bottom-up approach by asking employees to generate ideas on how they could all contribute to fixing the problem. For example, a single employee could improve the company's liquidity if he or she simply reduced the number of errors made in the processing of sales orders and, thus, the number of merchandise returns. The finance team has been the facilitator of this process, but everyone in the company supports it.[6]

When a Dell employee takes an order from a customer, they access a system that is directly linked to suppliers. The system monitors inventory and estimates how a specific component might impact the build time as well as the profitability of that specific machine. The sales people can also see how the profitability changes with any change the customer makes to the order. This system has provided the sales people with the information they need to be able to understand and impact the company's profitability.[8]

The direct model has allowed Dell to avoid advance payment of credit to distributors, since it deals with customers directly. In addition, Dell has a special relationship with its suppliers – it does not pay its suppliers until it receives payment from the customer first. This provides Dell with negative working capital.

CEMEX has also successfully managed its finances. It has been able to deal with the variability in demand for cement by creating a trading arm that buys and sells cement. The trading arm owns a fleet of ships for specific shipping routes, and by having global plants, it permits CEMEX to sell excess cement to nearby countries to minimize shipping costs and delivery time. This enables all plants to run at full capacity and minimizes CEMEX's risk to market fluctuations and demand variability.[4]

Mature information capabilities enable companies to create value efficiently and deal with complexity successfully

The differences in how companies react to complexity are directly related to how mature they are at managing information. Companies such as Dell and CEMEX understand the value of information, and they have focused on developing and maturing their information capabilities – people, information, and processes – throughout their organization over time. Their investment in information capabilities has allowed them to leverage the IC optimization effect and, thus, to operate their businesses efficiently and effectively. As a result, they are able to deal with complexity and outperform the competition.

As already discussed, information management is not just the implementation or deployment of technology but the combined development and use of technology, management practices, and people's behaviours and values. It is the combined development and maturation of these information capabilities over time that enables a company to optimize other business resources. Companies such as Dell and CEMEX, who have the right information and use that information appropriately, are the ones that can most effectively make sense of and respond to complexities and efficiently create value within their organization.

Key take-aways

- Companies with effective information management capabilities not only have the right information but they also understand how to use that information to reduce costs, add value, and operate more efficiently and effectively than the competition.
- Companies that outperform the competition, such as Dell and CEMEX, systematically develop information management capabilities over time. They continually focus on encouraging information behaviours and values among all employees, linking their information-processing practices to strategy and investing in IT that supports management decision making.
- The IC optimization effect explains how a company with mature information capabilities can leverage their information, people, and processes to make other resources – organizational structure, processes, people, external relationships, and financial management – more efficient and effective.
- Once a company has developed mature information capabilities throughout their organization, they are able to use that information to optimize other resources and operate more efficiently. A company needs to have the right information and the ability to use that information to operate efficiently in order to deal effectively with and respond to complexity.

References

[1] Marchand, D., Kettinger, W., and Rollins, J., *Making the Invisible Visible*, Chichester, West Sussex: John Wiley & Sons, Ltd, 2001.

[2] Stewart, T. and O'Brien, L., 'Execution without Excuses', *Harvard Business Review*, March 2005, **83**(3), 102–111.

[3] Marchand, D. and Kettinger, W., 'Dell's Direct Model: Everything to Do with Information', IMD Case Study IMD-3-1149, 2003.

[4] Chung, R., Marchand, D., and Kettinger, W., 'The CEMEX Way: The Right Balance between Local Business Flexibility and Global Standardization', IMD Case Study IMD-3-1341, 2005.

[5] Zambrano, L., 'CEMEX Building the Future 2004 Speech at CEMEX's Annual Analyst and Investor Meeting', http://www.cemex.com/pdf/ir/am2004/LHZ-transcript.pdf.

[6] Marchand, D. and Boynton, A., 'Direct in Europe: Delighting the Customer with Every Order', IMD Case Study IMD-3-0785, 1999.

[7] Fugate, B. and Mentzer, J., 'Dell's Supply Chain DNA', *Supply Chain Management Review*, October 2004, **8**(7), 20–24.

[8] Murphy, C., 'Imagining What's Possible; Dell Is Proud and Protective of the Business Processes It Uses to Take Advantage of Technology', *Information Week*, 8 September 2003.

14
Dealing with Complexity by Managing the Knowledge-Based Competence of the Organization

Kazuo Ichijo

Knowledge as Competitive Advantage in the Age of Increasing Globalization

In this phase of globalization, much manufacturing and back-office work is being transferred beyond geographical boundaries, often to countries with newly developing technological capabilities. At the same time, many firms are moving operations to the more developed world to create and offer knowledge and knowledge-based services that, at least at the present time, can only be done in these countries. This emphasis on change in the global environment puts knowledge management at the heart of what organizations need to do to cope with today's fast changing environment. Therefore, the success of a company in the twenty-first century will be determined by the extent to which its leaders can develop intellectual capital through knowledge creation and sharing on a global basis. Knowledge constitutes a competitive advantage in this age. Knowledge creation and imagination have never been more important than in this age of globalization since, in a flat world, so many of the inputs and tools for collaboration are becoming commodities available to everybody.[1]

To compete successfully, companies must hire, develop, and retain excellent managers who accumulate valuable knowledge assets. Attracting smart, talented people and raising their level of intellectual capabilities is a core competency. In addition, the unique feature of knowledge as a resource lies in the fact that it can become obsolete in the future. Therefore, new knowledge has to be created continuously. At the same time, companies should encourage proficient managers to share the knowledge they develop across geographical and functional boundaries in an effective, efficient, and fast manner. In other words, to win in the competitive environment, companies need to be able to manage knowledge strategically. That means management of knowledge should also constitute a core competency.

Despite the growing interest in knowledge management and the initiatives many organizations have taken to manage it, few companies have actually succeeded in creating a knowledge-based competence to gain and sustain a competitive advantage. According to McKinsey, a global consulting company which itself has an excellent system for global knowledge management, there are only four companies that employ more than 200 000 people while also delivering consistent profits per employee of $25 000 or more. They are General Electric (GE), IBM, Toyota, and Citigroup.[2] This fact suggests that very few companies have been able to combine massive scale and complexity with consistently high profits.

In order to reduce complexity and make the most of size for competitive advantage, knowledge management is a must, especially in the case of global companies. Sharing best practices across regions, functions, and businesses will help global companies increase profitability by reducing inefficient overlap of work and moving effectively and efficiently. For example, at GE and Toyota, knowledge management plays a strategically important role in gaining and sustaining their competitive advantage in a global market. Toyota widely articulated its crucial knowledge programme for practising *Kaizen* (continuous improvement) so that people working in different Toyota subsidiaries can produce high-quality cars consistently. Their knowledge was summarized as the

'Toyota Way 2001', and was transferred beyond functional and regional boundaries. At GE, knowledge about best practices is actively shared through its famous operating mechanisms. Various meetings that constitute GE's operating mechanisms, such as global leadership meetings, corporate executive councils, and corporate officer meetings, are utilized for sharing knowledge. These operating mechanisms are based on GE's unique social architecture, which is enabled by GE values, 'work-outs', and the boundaryless behaviours of GE employees. Knowledge sharing is enabled by this social architecture. Given the small number of global companies that manage complexity effectively, it could be said that knowledge management is still not easy to execute. Before the reasons for this are discussed, it would be useful to know something about the development of knowledge creation and management and the contributions of some of its important thinkers.

The development of knowledge creation and management

Interest in knowledge as the source of a corporation's competitive advantage has a long history in several disciplines. For example, in the discipline of economics, Adam Smith noted that workers learned from experience in *The Wealth of Nations* and Victorian economist Alfred Marshall later highlighted knowledge as a productive resource. The Nobel Prize winning economist Kenneth Arrow gave this phenomenon further expression in his 1962 article, 'Learning by Doing'. They argued that if organizations can become better at learning by transferring what workers know, then they can become more efficient. Developing these learning strategies became an important theme of knowledge management.

In the field of management, as early as in 1959, Peter Drucker used the term 'knowledge worker' for the first time in his book *Landmarks of Tomorrow*. Knowledge workers include those in the information technology fields, such as programmers, systems analysts, technical writers, academic professionals, researchers, and so forth. More recently, in this discipline, management of knowledge became a hot topic beginning in the 1990s. Thomas A. Stewart introduced *Fortune* magazine readers to knowledge management and intellectual capital in an article, 'Brainpower' (3 June 1991). Stewart described early projects undertaken by knowledge management practitioners and later went on to write two books on the subject. Ikujiro Nonaka and Hirotaka Takeuchi wrote about the use of knowledge by Japanese companies in their well-known 1995 book, *The Knowledge-Creating Company: How Japanese Companies Create the Dynamics of Innovation*. This book is one of the most cited in the knowledge management literature.[3] In the same year, Dorothy Leonard-Barton published *Wellsprings of Knowledge: Building and Sustaining the Sources of Innovation*. Her description of Chaparral Steel was one of the earliest case studies showing how an entire company reinvented itself around knowledge. In 1998, Tom Davenport and Larry Prusak published *Working Knowledge*, sharing lessons from knowledge management practices in over fifty firms. By the end of the 1990s, articles on knowledge management were proliferating in the *Harvard Business Review, Sloan Management Review*, and *California Management Review* as well as more academic journals.

Like other management movements, the issue of managing the knowledge-based competence of a corporation was in response to perceived changes in the larger economic environment. Changes are taking place in the external environment across a wide variety of dimensions at an accelerated pace. These include strategic alliances, open innovation, globalization of markets and of supply chains, technological breakthroughs, emergence of new industries, demographic trends, changes in the workforce, and geopolitical power games, to name a few. Such endemic change in the external environment demands continuous and rapid change within the organization. Of all these changes, it is the drastic changes caused by globalization and the advancement of information technology that are the key driving forces for growing corporate interests in knowledge as a source of competitive advantage. Because of globalization and by means of effective information technologies, big corporations are now free to manufacture and sell their products in almost any country they want, with very few rare exceptions. As Thomas L. Friedman pointed out in 1999:

> While there are a lot of similarities in kind between the previous era of globalization and the one we are now in, what is new today is the degree and intensity with which the world is being tied together into a single globalized marketplace and village. What is also new is the sheer number of people and countries able to partake of today's globalized economy and information networks, and to be affected by them.[4]

Globalization has been evolving since then, especially due to the integration of emerging markets such as India and China into the global economy and the global diffusion of productive knowledge that allows these and other developing nations, symbolically called BRICs (Brazil, Russia, India, and China), to compete with more developed nations because of much lower labour costs and by means of information technology. Computers have become cheaper and are dispersed all over the world, and there has been an explosion of software–e-mail, search engines like Google, and proprietary software that can chop up any piece of work and send one part to the US, one part to India and one part to China, making it easy for anyone to do remote development. As a result of these changes, a new corporate global platform has been created 'where intellectual work, intellectual capital could be delivered from anywhere'.[5] Again, according to Thomas L. Friedman, we are now entering the phase of Globalization 3.0. The dynamic force in Globalization 1.0, which lasted from 1492 when Columbus set sail, opening a battle between the Old World and the New World, until around 1800, was the beginning of countries in global competition. Globalization 2.0, which lasted roughly from 1800 to 2000, interrupted by the Great Depression and World Wars I and II, was companies in global competition. Globalization 3.0, which started around 2000, is the new-found power for individuals to collaborate and compete globally. In this phase, work has become global knowledge work.[6]

It would be a serious mistake, however, to conclude that knowledge creation and management are important only to globally organized firms. Domestic firms, no matter what competitive environment they are in, can build a competitive advantage by developing and sharing knowledge within their organizations.

We return now to examining why knowledge management is so difficult to execute in practice.

Knowledge management: difficulty in execution

It has been found that there are two main reasons for the difficulties firms experience in developing effective knowledge creation and management programmes. First, the traditional disciplines of management do not lend themselves to knowledge management and should be revised so that the knowledge-based competence of a corporation can be managed effectively and efficiently. Traditional notions about strategy, human resource management, finance, and marketing should be re-examined and revised to manage knowledge for competitive advantage creatively, effectively, and efficiently. Knowledge is tacit as well as explicit. Tacit knowledge involves human processes in knowledge management – creativity, conversation, judgement, teaching, learning – and it is difficult to quantify and, therefore, it is difficult to manage in the traditional disciplines, which are more quantitative rather qualitative. Management of knowledge should rely on a new sense of emotional knowledge and care in the organization, one that highlights how people treat each other and that encourages creativity – even playfulness. It throws out new challenges to traditional disciplines.

Second, the business impact of the practical application of the knowledge management theoretical framework in actual business settings remains vague. This is partly due to the fact that there are too few research initiatives that analyse how knowledge management can specifically contribute to overcoming the important management issues corporate leaders are facing now. As a result, managers tend to discuss knowledge management per se, without applying it to actual business issues. This has had the effect of information technology being overemphasized. As a consequence, they fail to learn how knowledge management can actually contribute to solving important business issues such as globalization, corporate governance, and corporate change management. Knowledge management ends up on the agenda for IT managers, not on the agenda for top management.

In order to overcome these difficulties and manage the knowledge-based competence of organizations strategically, there must be a better understanding of the role of knowledge for gaining and sustaining competitive advantage.

Strategic role of knowledge

In a business context, knowledge can be separated into two broad categories: unique knowledge held exclusively by the firm and public knowledge held by several competitors. For unique knowledge to be a source of sustainable competitive advantages, it has to satisfy three more criteria: it must be valuable, difficult for competitors to imitate, and difficult to substitute.[7]

Unique firm knowledge is valuable if it can successfully be applied to value-creating tasks (competence) and if it can be used to capitalize on existing business opportunities. Since competitors, in developing their own strategies, are likely to benchmark themselves against the industry leader to bring their performance up to the leader, knowledge must also be difficult to imitate. In order to make it difficult to imitate, companies should devise and execute various initiatives for protecting knowledge. What first comes to mind in this regard is knowledge in the form of patents. Interestingly, the only processes or products that can be patented are based on explicit knowledge. Filing a patent is a time-consuming and costly process, but more important for the strategic role of knowledge, patent rights are difficult to enforce. An ever-increasing number of patent engineers in various industries complain that manufacturers at distant locations – especially in developing countries – eagerly imitate their technologies. In some instances, patents can be circumvented by making incremental alterations in the basic technology, thereby even enhancing the value of a final product for the customer.

Tacit social or individual knowledge, however, is typically more difficult to imitate than explicit knowledge captured in documents and manuals. Either the knowledge is actually impossible to replicate or the imitation process is so costly that it deprives the imitator of the cost parity it set out to achieve. In 1980, a US government study showed that Japanese manufacturers, on average, had a competitive cost advantage of $2200 per car manufactured in the subcompact class, which was primarily based on better inventory control, personnel management and quality control.[8] This created a strong effort among American car manufacturers like Ford, General Motors, and Chrysler at the time to tap the manufacturing knowledge of Japanese automotive companies. Numerous fact-finding missions were undertaken, several consulting assignments initiated, and numerous books written, but the source of the cost advantage proved tremendously difficult to imitate.

In fact, much of the knowledge in Japanese car manufacturing remains tacit;[9] it is tied to personal relations, shared habits, and intuition, all of which are not easily documented. For example, quality problems in supplies are resolved by intense face-to-face interactions with supplier representatives, not just by exchanging manufacturing procedures or transferring engineering documents and product specifications. This is possible because of the close physical proximity of suppliers and manufacturers. The average distance of suppliers from Toyota, for instance, is 30 miles; as a consequence, the company clocks 10 635 person days of face-to-face contact with its suppliers. This is difficult for Toyota's American counterparts to match. General Motors, for example, is located an average distance of 427 miles from its suppliers, and the resulting face-to-face contacts with them amount to 1107 person days.[10] Moreover, better personnel management involves job-rotation programmes and on-the-job training, which are either poorly documented at Japanese companies or difficult for an external observer to comprehend. Even in terms of inventory management, tacit knowledge plays an important role. Suppliers to Japanese car manufacturers are invited to share tacit manufacturing knowledge by working as guests during a company's manufacturing process, especially at the initial stages.

Tacit knowledge at such companies has another essential dimension: it is social, not just individual. It is deeply embedded in the social capital of a corporation. Although it may be hard to document such knowledge in a manual or computer programme, it is shared by all relevant organizational members, as well as other stakeholders like suppliers. The competitive advantage of Japanese car companies, based as it is on tacit social knowledge, allows for a better understanding of how supplied parts affect final product quality, especially when the bottlenecks are located in the manufacturing process, the storage conditions for and usage of supplied parts, just-in-time manufacturing schedules, and so on. Suppliers are also integrated into the improvement of the car manufacturing process itself, continuously creating new knowledge that is difficult, if not impossible, for competitors to imitate.

It is not appropriate, however, to emphasize the merit of unique tacit corporate knowledge too much. It has indeed potential disadvantages. As long as it remains tacit, it takes time and requires considerable efforts to share it beyond functions, businesses, and geographical regions. For example, Toyota, the best automotive company in the world in terms of its market capitalization, sends its Japanese coordinators to Toyota's overseas operations to let its local affiliates share unique tacit corporate knowledge developed at Toyota in Japan face-to-face. As described above, most of Toyota's unique knowledge is tacit and shared among its Japanese employees face-to-face. Toyota has been steadily developing its business globally and has faced the challenge of letting non-Japanese employees share Toyota's unique corporate knowledge. Although their business domain was expanded beyond Japan, Toyota did not change the way of letting Toyota employees share its knowledge face-to-face. Coordinators have been sent to every business function such as manufacturing, sales and marketing, accounting, and HR. The coordinator system has worked very well and, as a result, Toyota has been growing fast outside Japan. This fast growth, however, has made it very difficult for Toyota to continue to use this coordinator system. It has become very clear to Toyota that it cannot continue to send a sufficient number of coordinators to communicate Toyota's unique knowledge. The number of coordinators required would be well above the actual number of coordinators. In addition, Toyota wants to be able to grow fast as the interest in Toyota's energy-efficient hybrid engines grows. The face-to-face coordinator system would constrain potential growth.

Facing this challenge, Toyota announced the 'Toyota Way 2001'. With the geographic expansion of Toyota's businesses and the widening of its business domain, people with diverse perceptions have come to be part of the global Toyota team. While recognizing the importance of diversity, Toyota has also realized an urgent need to articulate clearly and implement a set of common values, beliefs, and business methods, some of which are tacit and shared face-to-face to support and guide the continuing evolution of its worldwide operations. Known as the 'Toyota Way', these approaches – which until now had been implicit in Toyota's corporate tradition – were compiled into a brochure that was distributed worldwide. Despite their effort to articulate unique tacit knowledge, Toyota believes that some of it will not be articulated. Due to the nature of knowledge, it is impossible to articulate precious corporate knowledge completely. Certain tacit knowledge will remain, and this point is very important to protect its competitive advantage. Companies must be careful about what must be articulated and what must not. Toyota's experience teaches that a company might have to change its strategy for managing knowledge as it grows its business globally.

Finally, in order for knowledge to be a source of sustainable competitive advantage, it must be difficult for competitors to achieve the same level of costs or differentiation by substituting it with other knowledge. Efficiency in current operations, as well as innovation, can be enhanced by transferring and leveraging unique individual and social knowledge and by sharing investments and costs across products, markets, and businesses. Some tacit knowledge can almost never be substituted because of what is called the 'hegemonic effect'. One or a group of companies (A) with the only source of tacit knowledge engages in knowledge sharing with another company (B) based on expected returns, but when those returns are satisfactory for (A), future transactions with other companies (C) to achieve similar returns are avoided. This typically happens when suppliers work closely with customers, tapping their tacit knowledge in order to provide future solutions to customers' problems. Once a company has successfully shared tacit knowledge with a given supplier, however, it is unlikely to continue such exchanges with other firms.

Given that a firm's unique knowledge often adds such value, can public knowledge ever allow a company to achieve a sustainable competitive advantage? Based on the above discussion, the answer would seem to be no. Typically, public knowledge is the technical sort shared in research reports, engineering drawings, conference publications, textbooks, consulting manuals, and classrooms; often it represents general technical solutions that are freely available on the market. It is predominantly social explicit knowledge or individual tacit knowledge with the potential of becoming social in easily documented forms. Some public knowledge is of a narrative kind,[11] in which managers tell, hear, and re-tell stories about the industry, their competitors, the company, and themselves. Narrative knowledge often takes the form of, 'Did you hear that company A tested out the new XC 3400 machine with excellent results?' In this way, narratives give substance and life to technical knowledge and may catch the interest of the listener enough for him or her to investigate further.

While public knowledge may not be as obvious a source of competitive advantage as unique knowledge, it is proposed that the process matters more than the content; in other words, what the company eventually does with its knowledge in terms of applying it to value-creating tasks matters more than the public availability of the content. The ability to transfer generic knowledge to various areas of a business may play a key role in a company's success, and the process itself may be unique, valuable, difficult to imitate, and difficult to substitute. Shared public knowledge across organizational units in different products, markets, or businesses can improve innovation and ultimately secure the sources of competitive advantage. For example, Buckman Laboratories, a US-based producer of specialty chemicals, built an electronic communications system to encourage relationships among its employees and to allow for the effective transfer of knowledge, both public and unique, throughout its worldwide network of companies. Buckman's success lies more in the commitment of employees to using the electronic means of communication than in the sophistication of the systems. In fact, the information technology itself can be imitated. However, recreating Buckman's culture of communication, in which organizational members actively use the system to solve their local problems, is a very difficult task.[12]

Four-core knowledge activities for strategic management of knowledge-based competence of a corporation

In the past, discussions about the strategic management of the knowledge assets of a corporation tended to focus on creation and sharing activities for managing knowledge-based competence of a corporation. However, in order to gain and sustain in the increasingly complex environment, a more holistic view over them is required. Holistic knowledge management consists of four main activities: creating, sharing, protecting, and discarding.

Companies should be knowledge-creating companies, trying to generate new knowledge well ahead of competitors.[13] After successfully creating new knowledge within a company, this knowledge has to be shared among organizational members across regions, businesses, and functions. Protection is literally about protecting knowledge assets from competitors. Preventing knowledge from being imitated is all about activities that increase 'complexity', 'tacitness', and 'specialty' of products or services. Furthermore, companies should reflect on whether or not their knowledge is outdated. In some cases, it may be necessary to discard the existing knowledge and promote new knowledge creation. Figure 14.1 illustrates this progression.

It should be kept in mind that the maintenance of enabling conditions is indispensable for facilitating these activities. Sharing a mission and vision throughout an organization, a unique strategy to attain them, an organizational culture that promotes knowledge creation and sharing, and leadership to initiate building up strong competitiveness are all considered to be the necessary enabling conditions. Such activities, building blocks of knowledge management, not only need to coexist but they should also be linked with each other. In short, it is very important to make them influence one another to allow knowledge assets to reach their full potential.

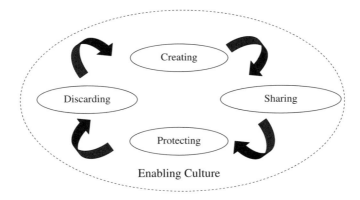

Figure 14.1 Strategic management of the knowledge-based competence of a firm

Conclusion

In order to utilize the knowledge-based competence of a corporation best, the conventional theories and business practices must be challenged from the viewpoint of seeing explicit and tacit knowledge as the most important source of competitive advantage. The time has come to realize holistic strategic management of the knowledge-based competence of a corporation and gain sustainable competitiveness. Those who intend to 'gain' and 'sustain' in the rapidly moving environment must pay more attention to the importance of creating, sharing, protecting, and discarding knowledge and consistently facilitate these activities consistently. These four activities are important for companies to improve their intellectual assets consistently. In the complex environment, the increasing performance of organizations will be accomplished by managing knowledge-based competence of corporations effectively, efficiently, and creatively.

References

[1] Friedman, T., *The World Is Flat: A Brief History of the Twenty-First Century*, New York: Farrar, Straus & Giroux, 2005, p. 443.
[2] *The Financial Times*, Wednesday, 2 November 2005, p. 8.

[3] Wei Choo, Ch. and Bontis, N., 'Knowledge, Intellectual Capital, and Strategy', in *The Strategic Management of Intellectual Capital and Organizational Knowledge*, New York: Oxford University Press, 2002, p. 11.

[4] Friedman, T., *The Lexus and the Olive Tree*, New York: First Anchor Books Edition, 2000, p. xvii.

[5] Friedman, T., *The World is Flat: A Brief History of the Twenty-First Century*, 2005, pp. 6–7.

[6] Friedman, T., *The World is Flat: A Brief History of the Twenty-First Century*, 2005, p. 11.

[7] Barney, J. B., 'Firm Resources and Sustained Competitive Advantage', *Journal of Management*, 1991, **17**(1), 99–120.

[8] See documents from the Grace Commission (1980–1984).

[9] Spear, S. and Bowen, K., 'Decoding the DNA of the Toyota Production System', *Harvard Business Review*, September–October 1999, pp. 97–106.

[10] Dyer, J. H., 'Specialized Supplier Networks as a Source of Competitive Advantage: Evidence from the Auto Industry', *Strategic Management Journal*, 1996, **17**(4), 271–293.

[11] For more on 'narrative knowledge', see J.-F. Lyotard, *The Postmodern Condition: A Report on Knowledge* (translated by Geoff Bennington and Brian Massumi), Minneapolis: University of Minnesota Press, 1984.

[12] This example is based on Knowledge Inc. (1997) and a 1997 presentation by Buckman Laboratories.

[13] Nonaka, I. and Takeuchi, H., *The Knowledge-Creating Company: How Japanese Companies Create the Dynamics of Innovation*, New York: Oxford University Press, 1995.

15
Managing Complexity in Marketing and Supply Chains

Ralf W. Seifert and Wolfgang Amann

Introduction

Over the last three decades, product variety has increased substantially in most industries, by 2% in cars, 4% in PC screen sizes, 5% in bicycles, 14% in contact lenses, and 16% in sneakers, every year.[1] Volkswagen, for example, had more than 40 segments by 2005 – with lifestyle being the main differentiator – up from only nine segments 20 years earlier.[2] Such a diversity of customer groups and corresponding offers represents a new complexity challenge, not only for marketing but also supply chain operation. Many companies are exploring mass customization (MC) as a way to demonstrate market leadership and capture price premiums, and with a view possibly to adapting their own supply chain set-up in turn. In this chapter, we will illustrate how this trend challenges organizations with an existing operational set-up to handle the complexities associated with this type of requirement. If not managed properly, substantial integration problems can arise given the variety of issues that result from blending both mass production and mass customization operations. Indeed, the operational implications of such a move can easily curtail any marketing-driven ambitions to respond to consumer individualism with increased product variety and custom ordering.

Clarifying the concept of MC represents a necessary first step. MC moves beyond the traditional logic of trade-off between variety and volume. MC, as an ideal and as coined in the five As of Nissan's Year 2000 vision,[3] refers to a business strategy for profitably providing anybody, anything, anytime, any volume, anywhere! In practice, MC refers to a customer co-design process of products and services, which meet the needs of each individual customer with regard to certain product features. All operations are performed within a fixed solution space, characterized by stable but still flexible and responsive processes. As a result, the costs associated with customization allow for a price level that does not imply a switch to an upper market segment.[4]

This chapter presents and examines Adidas's 'mi adidas' initiative, aimed at delivering customized athletic footwear to retail customers. It discusses the practical implications of complexity associated with expanding the initiative from a small pilot to a wider operation with a permanent retail presence. Along the way, the situation at Adidas illustrates a set of interlinked issues, starting from a marketing innovation with retailer selection and information management, production and supplier management, distribution, project management, and strategic fit for Adidas. Taking these issues into consideration, Adidas's management had to decide on the best route forward. At the end of this chapter the lessons learned for managing complexity are outlined by putting this example into perspective.

A case in point – the complexity challenge of the 'mi adidas' mass customization initiative[5]

In October 2001 Rolf Reinschmidt, head of the Forever Sport Division of Adidas-Salomon AG, was reviewing Adidas's mass customization (MC) initiative, 'mi adidas':

We all talk a lot about experiences these days – experiences that consumers and retailers expect to have with brands like ours [adidas]. Well, here is an experience our

> brand is uniquely able to offer, differentiating us significantly from the competition and building an incredible image for the Forever Sport Division.

Reinschmidt had been sponsoring mi adidas for some time to create a customization experience. The journey had started many years earlier, with the company providing tailor-made shoes for top athletes. Now, customized shoes had been made available on a much broader scale. Competitors also tested the market, and a trend towards MC was visible in other industries, from PCs to made-to-measure jeans. The time had come to make specific recommendations on the best course of action for mi adidas. Reinschmidt had three alternative routes to choose from, all of them with pros and cons:

- **Withdraw**. Celebrate the success and PR effect accomplished to date but quietly withdraw from MC in order to focus on adidas's core business.
- **Maintain**. Maintain the developed capabilities and selectively run mi adidas fairs and planned retail tours following top events such as the soccer World Cup and world marathon series.
- **Expand**. Expand mi adidas to multiple product categories and permanent retail installations. Elevate it to brand concept status while further building volume and process expertise.

Mi adidas had gained substantial momentum – it needed direction.

The Global Footwear Market[6]

In 2001 the global footwear market was worth $16.4 billion.[7] North America accounted for 48%, Europe 32%, and Asia/Pacific 12% of the market. The degree of concentration in the footwear segment was relatively high, with the three largest companies controlling roughly 60% of the market: Nike commanded 35%, adidas 15%, and Reebok 10% market share. Nike was particularly strong in the US market, with a 42% market share in footwear, but also led in Europe with 31%; adidas was significantly stronger in the European footwear market, holding a 24% market share compared with its 11% market share in US footwear.

adidas-Salomon AG

For over 80 years adidas had been part of the world of sports on every level, delivering state-of-the-art sports footwear, apparel, and accessories. 2005 was a key year in restructuring adidas-Salomon. First, Salomon, the winter sports equipment wing, was sold to the Finnish rival Amer for about €485 million in mid-2005. The adidas-Salomon link-up was originally supposed to balance the highly cyclical and seasonal sales of both companies, but failed to satisfy the expectations. In order to focus even more on the emerging core strength in the athletic footwear and apparel market, adidas subsequently bought Reebok International Ltd for €3.1 billion. This considerably strengthened its position as the world's second-largest sporting goods maker. However, back in 2001, the time of the early days of the complexity dilemma, adidas-Salomon AG's total net sales reached €6.1 billion and net income amounted to €208 million. Its main brands were adidas with a 79% share of sales, Salomon with 12%, and TaylorMade-adidas Golf with 9%. The company employed 14 000 people and commanded an estimated 15% share of the world market for sporting goods. Headquartered in Herzogenaurach, Germany, it was a global leader in the sporting goods industry, offering its products in almost every country of the world: Europe accounted for 50%, North America for 30%, Asia for 17%, and Latin America for 3% of total sales. Then adidas was reorganized into three consumer-oriented product divisions: Forever Sport, Originals, and Equipment.[8] Forever Sport was the largest division with products 'engineered to perform'. Technological innovation and a commitment to product leadership were the cornerstones of this division. Sales fell into a few major categories: running 32%, soccer 16%, basketball 11%, tennis 9%, and others 32%.[9] Reinschmidt was the head of the division. He reported directly to Erich Stamminger, head of global marketing for adidas-Salomon AG.

'Mi adidas'

'Mi adidas' was envisaged as an image tool and a centre of competence for the Forever Sport Division. Christoph Berger, director MC, was responsible for mi adidas and led a small but dedicated team. Berger came from an old shoemaking family and followed a traditional apprenticeship as a shoemaker himself. Having earned an Executive Master of Business Administration (EMBA), he started working for adidas in 1995. The pilot was sponsored directly by Reinschmidt and Stamminger. Without formal line authority,

Project Management	Product Development	Product Configurator/Design Tool	Marketing → Event → Communication	Information Management	Production	Logistics/Shipment	Service/Fulfilment	Payment Tracking
• project organization • tracking • budgeting/payment • project kick-off • project evaluation • meetings & presentations • handle critical situations	• product development • pattern engineering • foot bed • fit test • sample production • budget	• layout • image to transport • configuration principle • handling • general architecture • potential for future • other categories • eCommerce • intelligence • data flow interfaces • budget	**Product Configuration** • colour variations • positioning/layout of all decorations • clarify: stiching or printing of deco's • cosmetics **Event** • concept • message we want to bring across • PR-image we want to create • communication strategy (name of programme/product!) • pre-event • event organization • post-event • cooperation with regions • conceptualization of product Configurator • budget	• general IT structure • data tracking • handling • storage • research • speed • intelligence • future plans • budget	• data reception • creation of bills of material • planning • operation • production on demand • QC on demand • preparation for shipment • packaging • interfaces to systems and projects (e.g. scanner, payment, eCommerce, content management) • production site selection • budget	• customized packaging and shipment • define partner for shipment • speed • costs • quality • budget	• hotline • satisfaction panel • returns/replacement • next steps • new offers • ensure enduring customer-brand-relationship	• clarify types of payment: →online (credit card) →credit card at event location →invoice →currencies →accounting and billing

Figure 15.1 Working breakdown structure plan

Source: Company information.

however, Berger had to draw implementation support from the various functions and use external contractors to complement his team (refer to Figure 15.1 for a project breakdown). Mi adidas was launched at the beginning of the new millennium to provide consumers with the chance to create unique athletic footwear produced to their personal specifications. The idea was not entirely new, as adidas had provided tailor-made shoes to top athletes for many years. Now mi adidas could be experienced by many consumers at top sporting events and select retailers. The project initially offered only soccer boots but was to be expanded in 2001 to offer running shoes. For 2002 the plan was to build volume further and expand the offering into the customization of basketball and tennis footwear.

Phase I: the mi adidas pilot

The first phase of the mi adidas project was a small pilot to evaluate the feasibility and prospects of mass customizing athletic shoes. The objectives were clear-cut: offer a customized product, test consumers' demands for customized products, and fulfil their expectations as far as possible. The pilot allowed both project team and functions to gain hands-on experience in marketing, information management, production, distribution, and after-service of customized shoes. It also provided a basis for a rough cost–benefit analysis and future budgeting.

Product selection

The pilot mandate was soccer boots. A Predator® precision boot already in production was offered for customization with regard to fit (size and width), performance (outsole types, materials, and support), and design (colour combinations and embroidery), as shown in Figure 15.2.

Marketing: event concept and communication

The pilot was 100% event based. Over a two-month period in 2000, six events were held in different European cities: Newcastle, Hamburg, Madrid, Marseille, Milan, and Amsterdam. Consumer recruitment was very selective, using local market research agencies, phone calls, written invitations, and pre- and post-event questionnaires. The target group was 50 participants per event and country. The MC unit was designed in a

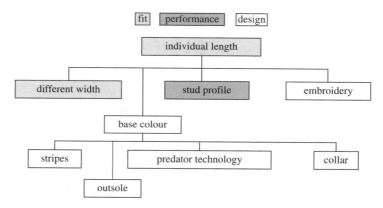

Figure 15.2 Combination logic of Predator® precision soccer boot

rather neutral technology-oriented style stressing the brand's tradition as the athlete's support. A white cocoon (evoking a mysterious atmosphere with its shape and colour) housed the three-dimensional foot scanner, the heart of the unit. A newly developed matching matrix software supported scanning and fitting. At a separate fitting terminal, a selection of sample boots was available for testing fit preferences. In addition, a design terminal had a laptop on which the participants, assisted by adidas experts, could customize their soccer boot in terms of materials and design. The stations also displayed material and colour samples to facilitate the decision-making process.

Consumer feedback

Adidas consumers greeted mi adidas with tremendous excitement.

> Consumers loved the product. 100 % want a customization service available in the future.

Shortly after the introduction of mi adidas, even adidas headquarters started to receive direct inquiries from interested consumers who wanted to purchase a customized shoe. Franck Denglos, marketing coordinator, reflected on his experience with the mi adidas pilot:

The concept and its execution gave consumers a strong positive impression of the brand. They left with the perception that adidas was acting as a leader. However, we have to keep in mind that their perception was highly influenced by the impressive tool, run by highly qualified adidas experts. Plus, during the pilot, the shoe was free.

Competitors' footwear customization initiatives

Several key competitors offered a similar service: Nike Inc. decided to bring MC to the web in November 1999. Nike's NIKEiD program enabled online customers to choose the colour of their shoe and add a personal name of up to eight characters.[10] For this service, Nike asked the regular retail price for the shoe plus a $10 custom design fee and shipping charges. Delivery of the footwear was advertised as being within three weeks for the US market. To keep fulfilment and distribution under control, however, Nike imposed an artificial ceiling and only accepted up to 400 US-based orders per day.[11] As of 2001, Reebok had not launched (or announced) its own mass customization initiative. Instead, it marketed its full foot cushion for its top-of-the-range running shoe, the Fusion C DMX 10. Utilizing DMX®10 technology and three-dimensional ultralite sole material, Reebok provided 10 air pods to help distribute air for custom cushioning and to achieve the ultimate in shock absorption.[12]

New Balance opened its first 'width centre concept unit' at Harrods in London in April 2001. Coming from a long tradition of making arch supports and prescription footwear to improve shoe fit, the US-based company first manufactured a performance running shoe in 1961. By 2001 New Balance featured a range of athletic shoes and outdoor footwear. Although New Balance did not offer a customization of shoes, it typically offered its products in three (at times up to five) different width sizes to optimize shoe fit.[13]

In addition to these usual suspects in the industry, others were also focusing on customized shoes. Custom Foot Corp. was one of the leading pioneers of mass customizing shoes in terms of fit and design. In 1998 Creo Interactive designed a totally new shoe based on a modular concept for the sole, the main body, and the tongue. This shoe could be produced in just 83 working steps compared with Custom Foot's 150 to 300 steps.[14] Leveraging the internet as an interface for configuration, Creo offered pure design customization in terms of colours and patterns. By locating production in Germany, it was possible to swiftly fulfil European market needs. However, three years into the venture, Creo Interactive closed operations in 2001. Based in Santa Cruz, California, Customatix.com allowed consumers to log on to its internet site and choose from a vast array of colours, materials, graphics, and logos to create their own personalized portfolio of designs online: '150 choices you can put on the bottom of your sneakers'.[15] The blueprints were then transmitted to the company's factory in China, where the shoes were manufactured and shipped to the consumer's doorstep within two weeks. The shoes retailed for $70 to $100 per pair, including import duty and delivery charges.

> The biggest problem we have is, people don't believe we can do what we do. Dave Ward, CEO of Customatix.com[16]

Besides intensifying competition, mi adidas was also confronted with substantial uncertainty about the future development of the MC segment.

Phase II: the mi adidas retail tours

> The decision to proceed with the 'Customization Experience' project was made after the successful completion and stringent evaluation of a pilot project conducted in the second half of 2000 in six European countries. During the test project some 400 pairs of the revolutionary adidas Predator® Precision soccer boots were custom built and delivered to a select group of consumers in Germany, France, England, Spain, Italy, and the Netherlands. Delivery time took two weeks on average. Consumer satisfaction was overwhelmingly positive.[17]

The pilot project was mainly seen as a first attempt to evaluate the requirements of 'normal' consumers, as opposed to those of top athletes, with whom adidas had an ongoing relationship. Taking the successful concept of the pilot to the retail channel, however, meant facing different and new challenges (refer to Figure 15.3 for the rollout plan). For the pilot, certain issues to do with back-end processes were adapted to current processes or not covered at all. Now, these would require more attention. In addition, a new retail unit had to be created that was smaller (10 to $20\,m^2$), easier to transport, more durable, and user friendly.

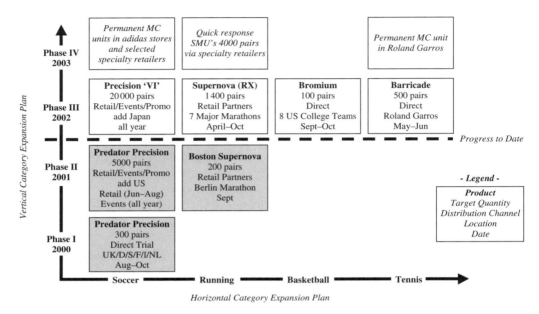

Figure 15.3   Mass customization rollout plan (From C. Berger, 'The Customized Revolution at adidas', *Kundenindividuelle Massenproduktion: Von Businessmodellen zu erfolgreichen Anwendungen* (eds M. Schenk, R. Seelmann-Eggebert, and F. T. Piller), Die dritte deutsche Tagung zur Mass Customization, Frankfurt, 8 November 2000)

Retailers

Retailer interest in mi adidas was overwhelming. In Germany alone, almost 1000 athletics specialty shops wanted to participate. However, only 50 German retail stores could be part of this second phase: the first retail tours in 2001. Soon retailer selection became a sensitive issue within adidas: marketing preferred small athletics specialty shops for a maximal image effect and utmost retailer commitment.[18] Sales, however, favoured big key accounts for reasons of relationship management. In addition, country selection was controversial: in some countries retailers were accustomed to paying a fee to a manufacturer for being able to host a promotion such as mi adidas. In other countries, retailers had never paid a fee for in-store promotions and might even demand a fee from the manufacturer instead. Depending on the final selection verdict, retailer feedback ranged from enormous enthusiasm to vast disappointment (even sporadic threats to withdraw business from adidas altogether).

Once selected, the retailers took care of consumer recruitment. To support them in marketing mi adidas, they were given a package of communication tools: CDs, posters, invitation cards, registration cards, and folders. Some retailers felt that the material was not engaging enough and demanded more support. Subsequently, the countries modified and translated the tools to fit the needs of their consumers more directly. Yet consumer turnout (and order placement) varied greatly from one retail store to another, depending on the commitment to mi adidas. Whereas the pilot was 100% event based, retailers played the central role in the second phase and accounted for roughly 90% of the order volume. Using multiple mi adidas retail units, well over 100 retailers participated across Europe in 2001.

Customization process

The customization process was still run by adidas experts and emphasized the 'brand experience' theme. The three-dimensional foot scanner, however, had been replaced by a simpler Footscan™ unit, which was used in combination with a static measurement device for length and width measures. At the same time, the proprietary matching matrix software continued to evolve and directly conformed to consumer preferences in three out of four cases. The overall process had become very stable: 50 to 80 'customization experiences' could be handled per day during an event while about 15 to 20 were possible at a retail outlet. Recent survey results seemed to confirm European consumers' interest in customized shoes. Although a focus on design customization was much simpler from a configuration perspective, consumers rated a customized design as much less important than a customized fit. In addition, individual preferences varied significantly across different European countries (and to a lesser extent also between men and women), necessitating further research for a targeted offering.[19]

Product and pricing

The athletics footwear market was characterized by rapid product turnover. In 2001 mi adidas already featured its second product generation in soccer boots. The customized version of this soccer boot sold for a 30 to 50% price premium over the catalogue price of €150.[20] In addition, the product offering was expanded into running shoes. After successful internal presentations of mi adidas for running at the adidas global marketing meeting in March 2001 and the Investor Day in July 2001, preparations were made to launch the project in the running market. In September 2001 mi adidas for running was introduced to the market during the Berlin Marathon. Consumers were either recruited or invited by PR, or they were impulse buyers who passed by and became interested. Within three weeks, they received the shoes. For 2002 the plan was for mi adidas for running to be present at all adidas-sponsored marathons (i.e. Paris, Boston, London, Madrid, Rotterdam, Prague, and Berlin) and to go on a retail tour in the relevant country after each event.

Consumers

Consumer feedback was excellent. In particular, the short delivery time and the opportunity to design their own shoes impressed the consumers. Mi adidas also attracted strong interest from the press: two television stations (Bayerischer Rundfunk and Fox TV) and many articles featured adidas's MC initiative and hailed it as a major milestone:

> Although we received this good feedback, there were several technical problems that had to be tackled. These problems caused delays and in some cases wrong production. . . .

Information management

Information management throughout the entire process was critical: basic consumer data, product options, biometric knowledge, and product specifications had to be merged for order taking. In addition, sourcing, production, distribution, payment, and reordering required appropriate IT backing:[21]

> Information is the most important conversion factor of successful mass customization.

Many challenges in terms of the scope and integration of the required IT infrastructure remained:

(a) The mi adidas kiosk system for order creation led to technical problems with synchronizing information-generated offline (e.g. order numbers and customer records), with adidas backbone systems such as the sales system and customer master database.

(b) The traditional sales system was not designed to process orders of individually customized shoes with detailed information on each article.

(c) The IT systems for distribution needed to be extended for an organized distribution and return process.

(d) Consumer data captured via mi adidas could not be transferred to the adidas CRM (customer relationship management) system.

There were ways around these problems, but they resulted in limited centralization and poor accessibility of data:

> The initial rollout was clearly under-budgeted. For example, eRoom was chosen as the web accessible repository for the technical documents. This decision was not entirely supported by Global IT and is seen as a short-term solution until an alternative can be found.

All development, configuration and support for mi adidas had thus far been absorbed by the business and no costs had been charged to the project budget for IT solutions, beyond the mi adidas kiosk application and scanning software. The kiosk application was developed by a contractor. However, no helpdesk was available for support and future system integration. The IT department was worried:

> The speed of implementations, the time needed to support both SAP and non-SAP countries and the limited resources Global IT presently has to support this, leads to the conclusion that we may fail to maximally deliver mi adidas globally.

Mi adidas had progressed fast, calling for a completely new set of requirements:

> mi adidas, even such a small project, has forced the IT department to think about how close we are getting to our consumers and what is needed to support this development.

Production

By 1992 most sporting goods companies had outsourced the main part of their footwear production to the Far East to reduce production costs. Adidas followed suit and outsourced all textile production and 96 % of footwear production during its turnaround in the mid-1990s. The outsourced footwear production was divided between Asia (China, Indonesia, South Korea, Taiwan, Thailand, and Vietnam), Eastern Europe, and North Africa. Depending on the quality of the shoe, between 20 and 40 % of production costs was related to personnel costs, which were the main driver for cost differences between regions.[22] Contract manufacturers focused on footwear assembly and sourced input materials from local suppliers as needed. Adidas maintained a small footwear factory in Germany, in Scheinfeld, near its headquarters. Here, models, prototypes, and made-to-measure performance products could be manufactured and tested. In addition, special shoes for Olympic sports such as fencing, wrestling, weightlifting, and bobsled were made. However, Scheinfeld was not excited at the prospect of taking mi adidas production in-house. Furthermore, material provisioning for a vast set of customization options could be more costly in Scheinfeld because it was too far away from volume production sites and suppliers.

The production processes used for the mass customization shoes were the same basic processes used in mass production. For the MC events, however, a combination of development sample room and mass production facilities was used. This combination was chosen to allow for the highest level of control and quality while providing a minimal 'disruption' to the factory's daily mass production schedule:

> A program like mi adidas, without dedicated facilities, manpower and materials resources, will always be perceived as an interruption to the overall process of creating shoes.

Yet the capacity of the sample rooms was limited[23] and its operational format was not designed for volume scale effects. The mass production facilities, by contrast, were not meant to handle a lot size of one[24] and nor were they set up to allow for close linkage of individual product flow with corresponding customization information. Such a process was not in place and the workers lacked training and language capabilities to handle production according to detailed written product specifications:

> Variability is simply not in our business model!

Although the assembly of a customized shoe was theoretically straightforward, provisioning the required material proved to be time-consuming. Delays were exacerbated when material was needed that was not currently available for in-line production. In this case, special material provisioning resulted in significant inventory costs as materials for the top-of-the-range models in question were expensive. From a production perspective, a better understanding was needed of the value–cost trade-off between the marketing perception of customer value-added versus inventory and production costs for specific customization options. For example, design customization in terms of multiple colours was not ideal from a material provisioning perspective because different shoe sizes already meant different component sizes (e.g. strip length varied with the shoe size), which would now have to be available in a range of colours. These trade-offs and the options available for new shoes should ideally play a much more prominent role right from the start when designing products for MC. Karl-Josef Seldmeyer, vice president and head of global supply-chain management, summarized his experiences:

> For today's volumes, the combined complexity of fit, performance and design is too much.

Distribution

Timely mass customization also depended on proper execution of communications and logistics to meet the seven-day lead-time from order receipt to ex-factory shipping. Starting from July 2001, the mi adidas process was changed from a pilot with deliveries direct to the final consumer to a process that involved the retailers in customization and distribution. After customization at the retailer shops, orders were no longer transferred directly to the sourcing systems. Instead, they were routed from the retailer to the respective subsidiary's sales system and from there to Logistics Ordering Systems, using the subsidiary's regular buying process. The addressee was no longer the final consumer but the individual retailer in whose shop the customization had taken place. The individual retailer was now responsible for distribution to the end consumer.

Communication and competing initiatives

With the push into multiple product categories, communication became more difficult. In particular, the extremely technical and highly advanced customization process could not be adequately promoted as the mi adidas budget did not support targeted messaging by category. However, increasing the marketing spend was not then an option, since marketing saw MC as just one of many initiatives. After all, they already supported top athletes via a special care team and tailor-made shoes made in Scheinfeld. Since it was naturally in competition for resources and management attention with other recent initiatives, mi adidas was often seen as secondary to designated brand concepts such as 'a^{3}'[25] and 'ClimaCool^{TM}'.[26] Hence a^3, 'football never felt better', and Clima acted as overriding messages for the upcoming marathons, Soccer World Cup and Roland Garros, respectively:

> Communication activity and spend needs to be regulated, ensuring that brand concepts are not undermined by ongoing mi adidas activity.

Adidas's own retail activities

To further strengthen its brand, adidas had also just stepped up its own retail activities, increasing the number of its own retail outlets from 37 in 2000 to 65 in 2001. Most notable here was the opening of two concept stores in Paris and Stockholm as well as an Adidas Originals store in Berlin.[27]

Negotiating continued internal support

By October 2001 mi adidas was an established initiative and the generally positive brand image effect was widely accepted within the organization. Although mi adidas had become bigger, the organizational set-up had not substantially evolved. To date, much of the support for the project from different functions of adidas was granted on a goodwill basis. As time progressed and volumes increased, it naturally became more and more difficult to persuade core business units to fully support this initiative, especially out of their own cost centres:

> The annual budget for mi adidas had basically stayed identical during its first years.

The situation was not ideal. Although the functions continued to support mi adidas and took pride in its success to date, the ultimate responsibility for mishaps, of course, rested with the project team. Should mi adidas be elevated and play a more independent role or should it be better integrated into the existing matrix to be in sync with adidas's core business, with the functions in turn assuming more accountability? A clear evaluation was made difficult by the current practice of attributing mi adidas sales to the respective countries, hindering separate accounting.

The Future of mi adidas

Reinschmidt wondered if the time was right to scale mi adidas to the next level. The pilot (Phase I) had been very successful and adidas had developed and refined important new capabilities. Consumer feedback was enthusiastic and retailers fared much better during repeat offerings of mi adidas. Yet the initial retail rollout (Phase II) had been somewhat slower than projected, falling 40 to 50% short of the targets established in the original rollout plan. Reinschmidt had come to the conclusion that mi adidas needed clearer direction. Once again he reviewed the three generic alternatives that the company could embark on:

> mi adidas could be turned into a commercial tool over the course of the next years and now was the time to decide upon this.

Alternative 1: withdraw. Celebrate the success and PR effect accomplished to date but quietly withdraw from MC in order to focus on adidas's core business: mi adidas had been launched two years earlier and now featured a soccer and a running shoe. As the product life for these model cycles ended, so would mi adidas. Current commitments would be honoured but any further investments in the MC initiative were to be avoided. New PR tools would soon take the place of mi adidas.

Alternative 2: maintain. Maintain the developed capabilities and selectively run mi adidas fairs and planned retail tours following top events such as the Soccer World Cup and world marathon series. Mi adidas would continue in its current form and scope and be allowed limited organic growth. Investment would be minimal and MC responsibilities would be more fully integrated into the existing functions. Mi adidas would be part of (and governed by) adidas's annual planning cycle. As new boots were introduced to the market, a customizable derivative of those models would be created for mi adidas; the kiosk application, promotional material, back-end processes, etc. would be adapted accordingly.

Alternative 3: expand. Expand mi adidas to multiple product categories and permanent retail installations; elevate it to brand concept status while further building volume and process expertise. Mi adidas would be scaled up in terms of both volume and product categories. Increased marketing spend and revised back-end processes would support its rollout. Permanent installations at select retail stores would complement the event and retail tour concepts to foster more continuous order flow and steady volumes. Further investments would ensure a degree of independence for mi adidas and help develop MC into a potential business model in its own right for adidas.

Managing complexity in marketing and supply chains

The above 'case' illustrates the complexity challenges faced by adidas management with respect to deciding the future of its mi adidas initiative. Any decision would have to consider a highly interrelated set of issues ranging from strategy, pricing, order taking and after-service, retailer management, information management, configuration, production, distribution, and last, but not least, project management – in the context of the existing operation. With hindsight, deciding in favour of a full rollout may seem to be the obvious choice, but due to the ambiguity and actual number of action steps to be taken, it was not certain the initiative could be scaled up. Indeed, it soon needed redirection and new energy to be turned into a lasting success. Complexity challenges could be mapped along the following dimensions:

1. **Strategy**. Once it has been successfully set up, MC is a great way to deal with diversity. It allows great variety for customers, but it is by no means an ideal or an exclusive way to deliver variety to the marketplace. This readily follows when

considering, for example, watches introduced by Swatch that come in many colours and shapes. In reality, even when mass customizing, choices have to be limited within certain selection bands to control the option space. It is also crucial to understand that MC may be successful in some situations, but not in others. In the footwear market the natural variety of the base product is significantly higher than, for example, desktop PCs, making customization of a standard base product more difficult. MC can thus only be one way to organize work rather than the ultimate goal. Management needs to be clear about the alternatives to and limitations of MC from the outset.

2. **Marketing and branding**. Discussions on MC often focus heavily on operational issues, but market alignment with specific target segments should always be considered first. MC is a new phenomenon in many industries. Thus, the existing customer segmentation and price points may be misleading when trying to gauge the overall market potential. Given the enhanced promises to deliver, it is essential to ensure a flawless execution and an unforgettable experience at the crucial moment. Even if it is done well, it may ultimately change consumer expectations in unwanted ways. Fast flux, being one of the four main complexity drivers, thus deserves special attention. Once MC has been established, the opportunity for rent creation and premium prices vanishes, at least partly; consumers demand more variety but are less willing to pay extra or to wait for it. This can cannibalize standard offerings while increasing overall costs. Often, flux can outdate solutions as soon as they start to be fully operational and MC is no exception.

All this is made even more complex when we ask ourselves: Should an initiative such as mi adidas be considered individually or together with the existing bulk business when launched in a corporate context? This will have major implications not only with regard to dedicated marketing support and branding but also for supply-chain operation and organizational set-up.

3. **Supply-chain operation**. MC may at first appear to be a challenge of smart product configuration, which could be the answer to product variety-related complexity issues. However, there is more to it than simply managing the interface with intelligent product modularity concepts and involving the customer in the product design. Mass customization also involves three other crucial challenges: process flexibility, agile supply networks, and integrated information flows. Process flexibility is the ability to create significant product variety via seamlessly connected processes without introducing added set-up time or cost. Likewise, logistics and final

distribution should not be underestimated when mass volumes have to be delivered to individual consumers within tight time frames. Finally, as part of an integrated business strategy, the IT infrastructure and concept has to ensure accurate information at all stages – from order-taking, production, and delivery through to ongoing customer relationship management and built-in market research. Needless to say, this is a formidable task when multiple parties are involved. Upstream, it is necessary to connect and collaborate with outsourcing partners who run and control their own factories, probably supplying different base products from different locations. Downstream, many retail partners and distribution points need to be woven in – not least from a data management point of view.

Obviously, it is preferable to defer operational and IT-related investment by making use of existing infrastructures. Bridging between processes created for the traditional make-to-stock environment and those required for operating on a make-to-order basis can often translate into severe misalignment problems and added complexities on both sides.

Organizational set-up – putting mi adidas into perspective

In contrast to adidas's choice, other initiatives for launching innovative product concepts have included Nespresso[28] and Tetra Pak's Tetra Recart endeavour.[29] Nespresso Systems is a 100%-owned affiliate deliberately placed outside of Nestlé's main organizational structure. Nespresso was a radical departure from the majority of Nestlé's lines of business targeting the mass market, thus avoiding several of the integration problems and complexities that adidas faced in a similarly large, highly structured organization. Despite not necessarily benefiting from any low-hanging fruits in the early stages, it was thus possible to speed up innovation without making a rather rigid setting more complex.

Tetra Recart was a retortable carton packaging for food suitable for the processing of food contents at temperatures around 120 °C, thus offering food manufacturers a modern alternative to the 150-year-old metal can and extending the reach of Tetra Pak into solid foods. As the project developed and potential materialized, a separate unit was set up, which enjoyed full support from top management and representation of carton as well as food experts. In any new business development, setting up a separate unit can prove to be a very welcome simplifier.

Such entrepreneurial pursuits are often considered strategically imperative to rejuvenate a firm, create value, and sustain competitive advantage.[30] By deliberately introducing what is perceived as entrepreneurial attitude into their organizational cultures, large corporations aim to reduce bureaucracy, increase flexibility, and speed up their product development. As a result, they hope to create more innovative products and services that enable them to stay ahead of the competition. In contrast, if management forgets this softer key success factor, a complexifier of a different type enters the fray. For some organizations, necessary change can happen more easily than for others, as illustrated by the following examples, whose specific goals range from reinventing the entire firm, as illustrated by the Ducati case sample, to 'merely' making a new product introduction more successful, as shown in the Logitech example.

All innovation initiatives, much like small businesses, have to deal with the inherent uncertainty in both new technologies and new markets. In addition, they have to deal with their potential inertia and their size, both impediments to recognizing and exploiting opportunities fully. Ducati, the famous Italian motorcycle manufacturer, explored the renewal of an entire organization and the redefinition of its strategic position when it was facing serious cash issues and declining customer enthusiasm in the second half of the 1990s.[31] Ducati had rested on its laurels for far too long and had fallen behind the competition. Problems pervaded all of its operations, from inefficient production and marketing capabilities to the organizational culture, which at best was being passionate about the company and product, but far from being risk-taking. Federico Minoli had been appointed CEO to turn the company around after it had been taken over by American Venture Capitalist Texas Pacific. Minoli reinstalled the Ducati brand and streamlined its operations. There was no choice.

Logitech took the matter of the right entrepreneurial culture one step further.[32] The company started as a software development company before becoming the well-known specialist of peripheral devices that people use to work, play, and communicate with. In contrast to Ducati, Logitech had consistently flourished up to 2003 when it passed the $1 billion mark in sales and grew its stock price by 580% since 1998. Management started to wonder whether this growth was sustainable and what changes should be envisaged to assure the company's future success. Logitech's senior management understood early on that it needed to put innovation at the core of its business. Logitech's leadership fostered an open, entrepreneurial culture that drove the company to become a champion of innovation. Therefore, even when times were difficult, the strong starting point was an advantage. By ensuring that business opportunities were identified both internally and externally, Logitech were rewarded by another 70 % growth in sales in the 2003 to 2006 period.[33] Corporate values were enforced that allowed risk-taking and even failure while, at the same time, giving the necessary executive support to push projects through. Regular monitoring of organizational cultures, climates, and energies in a proactive way may thus simplify future complexity challenges. While developing organizational cultures can be perceived as a way of relieving the staleness and lack of innovation that big companies can at times suffer from, it can also be a curse that pushes the boundaries of existing structures and hierarchies.[34] Great cultures strive if people living in them understand uncertainty and change not as a threat but as an opportunity. Seizing the opportunities requires out-of-the-box thinking and taking advantage of typically uncontrollable dynamics. At the outset of practically all innovation initiatives, neither the right organizational design nor the market potential or technological feasibility are known. Such ambiguities prompt large firms to apply an explorative and adaptive management style that is typically in contrast with their traditional decision-making process. Organizational inertia plays a crucial role, enabling some firms to deliberately place initiatives outside of the core business, as was the case with Nestlé and Tetra Pak. However, embedded projects can also be successful. Logitech's corporate-wide entrepreneurial culture permitted nurturing the development inside, whereas in the adidas case, the project was championed to respectable growth within very traditional corporate settings. Sooner or later, however, all projects are challenged with taking business to the next level in order to meet high growth expectations. Throughout all these examples, strong leadership support was required to ensure resource availability, to fight organizational inertia, and, last but not least, to act on a vision in order to master complexity, not surrender to it.

References

[1] Cox, M. and Aim, R., Federal Reserve Bank of Dallas, 2005.
[2] Volkswagen/IMD Research.
[3] Nissan Annual Report.
[4] Piller, F. T., 2005, http://www.mass-customization.com/.

[5] This section is based on Ralf Seifert, *The 'mi adidas' Mass Customization Initiative*, IMD case IMD-6-0249, which won a POMS International Case Writing Award in 2004 and an ECCH case award in 2006.

[6] Sporting Goods Intelligence (SGI).

[7] Total market value based on wholesale prices.

[8] The reorganization officially took effect on 1 January 2001. In 2002 the organization was revised again and the Forever Sport Division became the Sport Performance Division.

[9] adidas-Salomon AG, 2001 Annual Report.

[10] http://nikeid.nike.com.

[11] 'Nike Offers Mass Customization Online', *Computerworld*, 23 November 1999.

[12] http://www.reebok.com.

[13] http://www.newbalance.com and New Balance Athletic Shoe, Inc., Press Releases, 20 April 2001.

[14] Piller, F. T., 'The Present and Future of Mass Customization: Do It – Now!', Working Paper, Technical University Munich.

[15] http://www.customatix.com.

[16] Smith, K., 'Fancy Feet', *Entrepreneur's Business Start-Ups*, 7/2001.

[17] adidas-Salomon AG, Press Release, 2 April 2001.

[18] Some specialist stores got very excited about mi adidas and lined up local sponsors to equip entire sports teams with customized shoes while hosting the mi adidas retail unit at their outlet.

[19] Jäger, S., 'Market Trends: From Mass Production to Mass Customization', EURO ShoE Project, 3 March 2002, in Innovation in the European Footwear Sector Conference, Milan, Italy.

[20] 'Individuelle Maßanfertigung von Sportschuhen', *Schuhplus/Infocomma*, 15 October 2001.

[21] Dulio, S., 'Technology Trends: From Rigid Mechanical Manufacturing to Mass Customization', EURO ShoE Project, 3 March 2002, in Innovation in the European Footwear Sector Conference, Milan, Italy.

[22] Horovitz, Jacques, Boissonnas, Giana, and Hilliard, Ursula, *Adidas*, IMD case IMD-3-0743 (GM 743), 1999.

[23] For the mi adidas pilot, volume was limited and production was not a problem. In general, a development sample room, however, could not handle more than 500 to 1000 pairs per month.

[24] Production set-ups were often made only once per day, producing large batches of footwear.

[25] The a^3 was a functional technology combining cushioning, stability, and light weight. It managed the foot's natural movement by dissipating harmful impact forces, stabilizing and guiding the foot through the entire footstrike, and retaining and redirecting energy from the rear foot to the front foot. Adidas planned to introduce the concept for running shoes in 2002 as the most technical, functional design available.

[26] ClimaCool™ was a footwear technology concept offering 360 degrees of ventilation and moisture management. In scientific tests, it produced 20% dryer and 20% cooler feet. Targeting regular and serious athletes, adidas planned for a staggered market introduction across products in 2002.

[27] adidas-Salomon AG, 2001 Annual Report.

[28] Kashani, K. and Miller, J., *Innovation and Renovation: The Nespresso Story*, IMD case IMD-5-0543, 2000.

[29] Deschamps, J.-P. and Pahwa, A., *New Business Creation at Tetra Pak: Reinventing the Food Can*, IMD case IMD-3-1448, 2004.

[30] Covin, J. G. and Miles, M. P., 'Corporate Entrepreneurship and the Pursuit of Competitive Advantage', *Entrepreneurship: Theory and Practice*, 1999, **23**(4), 47–63.

[31] Turpin, D. and Chung, R., *Rebuilding a Passion Brand: The Turnaround of Ducati*, IMD case IMD-5-0666, 2004.

[32] See J. Deschamps and A. Pahwa, *Innovation Leadership at Logitech*, IMD case IMD 3-1337, 2003. The case describes how Logitech tried to spur technological innovation at a constant rate and how it handled a new product introduction in particular.

[33] Logitech's 2006 Annual Report, p. 39.

[34] Thornberry, N., 'Corporate Entrepreneurship: Antidote or Oxymoron', *European Management Journal*, 2001, **19**(5), 526–533.

Part IV
Additional Complexity Challenges

16
The Price Tag of Ignoring Complexity in the Globalization Process

Wolfgang Amann

Introduction

With advances in technology helping to bridge geographic distance and market boundaries vanishing, it could easily be assumed that picking low-hanging fruit internationally is becoming easier for companies. The targeted fruit come in various forms, such as access to new customers abroad, low costs, highly skilled HR, advantageous locations, access to critical resources, access to capital on international stock markets or from investors, spread risks, and learning opportunities, to name but a few motives for expanding abroad. Multinationals furthermore enjoy a substantial power basis. The 800 largest businesses employ only 1 % of the 3 billion people on Earth, but generate as much value as the 144 poorest countries together. They even represent 60 % of global capitalization in contrast to the 6 % attributed to the 144 poorest countries. This power, their access to capital and key talent from around the world, their core competencies, and dynamic capabilities as well as the brands they own, should provide them with ample opportunities to harvest international opportunities successfully. Gaining global competitiveness and becoming a global player are therefore major strategic directives, also for the emerging multinationals from developing countries such as China, India, or Brazil. Internationalization may thus appear to be a road to the Promised Land, until strategists and managers realize that the reality may be different. In the following, two idiosyncratic paths to becoming a truly global player are scrutinized as well as their impact on performance from a complexity perspective.

The road to the Promised Land revisited

For the purpose of this analysis, let us differentiate between two archetypical scenarios. Company A had the opportunity to expand abroad into rather familiar terrain. This could have been a US company starting to sell first to Canada, then perhaps the UK and Australia, overall rather familiar and culturally similar markets. The legal systems and the way the business worlds tick are rather similar. While minor adaptations were necessary, it was a relatively easy journey. More difficult markets would only later emerge on the radar screen.

The notion 'global' deserves further thought. As Ghemawat rightly points out,[1] globalization today is semi-globalization at best. There are very few companies with extreme degrees of internationalization, e.g. in terms of a very high percentage of sales abroad and the percentage of foreign assets to total assets. So-called 'born globals' are still only a small fraction of internationally active companies and more than half of the world's population is not integrated into the web of globalization benefits and its related value creation. Many countries and even regions have not been developed. There is vast potential left for further international growth – and more complexity.

In contrast, company B could have been one located in Germany. Switzerland and Austria may be culturally related to Germany, but are rather small countries and, according to the UNCTAD data that was collected, have never really played a major role as far as foreign sales are concerned. Even though EU integration lowered transaction costs somewhat, company B still had to deal with a considerable variety of cultures in its surrounding and distant markets. Difficulty and complexity thus hit company B much earlier than they did company A. When looking at cross-company patterns on how internationalization – measured according to the ratio of foreign sales to total sales – impacts overall corporate performance in hundreds of the largest companies, interesting patterns emerge, as shown in Figure 16.1.

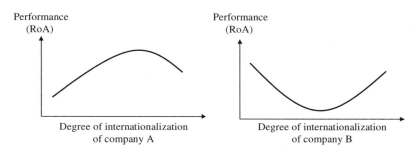

Figure 16.1 Two paths to internationalization (RoA, return on assets)

Interestingly enough, these are the dominant patterns that are part of reality. Consequently, several insights become clear. Companies could indeed overexpand abroad, thus sacrificing performance. This holds true for several ways of measuring performance, e.g. according to return on sales, return on assets, return on capital employed, and operational efficiency. Such companies are often unaware of having overexpanded. Complexity overwhelms many companies with high degrees of internationalization when the quantity and quality of problems to solve increase. The sheer number and heterogeneity of the various markets stretch companies' information processing capability. Market positions, financial flows, the movement of people, information, and goods within the internal and cross-company value webs ultimately become so interdependent, while simultaneously being in constant flux, that it is sometimes a miracle that such complex systems still continue to function. Too much information, the lack of clarity regarding some information, and the constant evolution of elements and parts of the organization that render information outdated at an increasingly rapid pace, eventually strain the organization beyond what it can bear.

Company B was exposed to greater diversity and challenging environments far earlier while internationalizing. Internal solutions had to be changed and learning had to occur to adapt to the new realities, performance pressures being the catalyst that drove such adaptations. Company B therefore built up the capability to cope with complexity much earlier, while company A missed out on this opportunity and did not prepare for higher degrees of complexity. However, if company B does not implement further performance enhancement, returns could diminish due to too much complexity, and its ongoing quest to expand further abroad could simply lack business logic. In fact, as far as the financial bottom line and performance ratios are concerned, company B benefited from internationalization rather late. Internal adaptations, which seem to be inevitable, were, however, implemented and have paid off, as portrayed on the right side of Figure 16.1.

Does going global always lead to a more complex environment? There are a few examples of companies for which this adversity in their business environment appears to matter less. Swiss companies, for example, enjoy high degrees of diversity in their small domestic market by simply having to cope with four official languages. The domestic Chinese market is held to be so challenging that if a Chinese player manages to conquer the Chinese market, foreign expansion appears to be less of a problem. The situation changes, though, once Chinese companies evolve beyond doing contract manufacturing for foreign companies and take on all the design and marketing tasks themselves. The same holds true when Chinese companies move beyond their current attempt to acquire technologies globally by merely repatriating them. Chinese companies have invested US$30 billion in foreign firms since 1986; US$10 billion of this was invested in just the last 2 years. However, integrating foreign acquisitions and management fully into Chinese companies often lags behind expectations, as diversity complexifies such deals overproportionally.

Companies that employ foreign partners to assist them frequently experience the 'double whammy of globalization' (cf. Zacharakis[2]). They face the challenge of a double-layered acculturation to the culture of different countries as well as foreign partners. In the short term, this boils down to the performance being at risk as well as a drastically heightened need for learning. Partnering therefore does not decrease the overall level of the challenges faced through globalization.

Wal-Mart's frustration in Germany as a case in point

Wal-Mart's recent exit from Germany serves as a worthwhile case to study complexity in action. The retail giant operates 2700 stores in 14 countries outside the US, generating US$80 billion of its total of US$300 billion abroad. Sales abroad increased by a hefty 12 % in the recent past. In mid-2006, Wal-Mart sold its underperforming German stores to the country's leading retail chain Metro after an unrewarding eight-year slog.

The sale marked a major retreat that cost the company about US$1 billion. In 2003, Wal-Mart lost 20 cents for every euro of sales in Germany, and thereafter refused to disclose its losses.

Even though Germany is the third biggest market for retail goods in the world, the relative diversity of the market and its customer was overwhelming. The US business model could not be applied in Germany. The wages were too high and the workers resisted management's demands when they felt that these were unjust, especially when, for example, Wal-Mart's American managers pressured their German executives to enforce American-style management practices in the workplace. Employees were, for instance, forbidden to date colleagues in positions of influence. Workers were also told not to flirt with one another. This code of conduct was so incompatible with acceptable local norms and, simultaneously, contrary to German legislation that employees were driven to sue the company. In addition, in 2005, a German court ruled against the company's attempt to introduce a telephone hotline that employees could use to inform on their colleagues.

Another example of Wal-Mart's problems with diversity in Germany is related to the actual products that the company sold. Wal-Mart employed American buyers for the German market with so little knowledge of local conditions that they ordered piles and piles of pillowcases that couldn't be sold because German pillows differ in size from those in the US. As salaries are quite high in Germany compared to those in the US, the customers did not accept or appreciate the greeter at the door who welcomed them or the staff who packed their purchases, as they assumed that they would eventually pay for these hidden costs.

Wal-Mart furthermore took over two second-tier chains with nothing in common and tried to merge them, thus imposing organizational culture traits incompatible with the ones in place – in a market with razor-thin margins and zero tolerance for mistakes. Besides Germany, Wal-Mart also exited South Korea, another quite large market, after turnaround attempts failed.

Is complexity fatal?

A quick glance at the massive amount of quantitative data on a variety of countries ranging from the US to Germany and Japan is sufficient to reveal the risk of overexpansion and the fact that companies suffer from lower performance ratios at some point in time in the internationalization process. There are solid, generalizable patterns that are found across companies, depending on whether they embark on company A or B's archetypical growth path. Globalization comes with a price tag that is too often ignored, but the cost of learning could eventually provide companies with a better-developed absorptive capacity to cope with complexity.

Complexity is by no means fatal. Companies have several means of coping with it. It has already been mentioned that various opportunities to simplify, e.g. through standardized processes, can prevent new processes from just being added to existing ones and not replacing them. The proactive development of an organizational culture emerges as a second key to success. In this context, organizational cultures are not a 'garbage variable' (if there is no other way of explaining a problem, it is ascribed to the culture). Organizational cultures should rather be understood as histories of learning leading to behaviours, values, and assumptions that are worthwhile passing on within the organization. They are solutions that have worked in the past. During the globalization journey, new challenges and diverse problems emerge. Only organizational cultures that are open to learning and adaptation will survive. Traditional ways of working in teams, designing and organizing systems, structures, and processes, must be scrutinized to see how well they hold up in a more global company – usually, previous patterns have to evolve drastically. Performance downturns often accelerate adaptations, but what if companies proactively embark on organizational culture programmes before traditional solutions become outdated and performance starts to suffer? Cross-company learning and teaming up with top business schools or consultants to trigger such programmes could pay off handsomely. Artificial crises and simulations are tools that can be successfully used before problems become a reality. The liabilities of foreignness could cost a company much more than learning – as the Wal-Mart in Germany example has illustrated.

Conclusion

The warnings have now been issued. Globalization is a journey during which, sooner or later, complexity challenges impact performance negatively. Companies have to manage the balance between continuously building their absorptive capacity to cope with more complexity and the actual adversities faced in their globalized market arena. It is a matter of accepting and embracing the complexity of the globalization process and of carefully simplifying it and increasing the ability to cope with it. There is no other alternative.

References

[1] Ghemawat, P., 'Semiglobalization and International Business Strategy', *Journal of International Business Studies*, 2003, **34**, 138–152.

[2] Zacharakis, A. L., 'The Double Whammy of Globalization: Differing Country and Foreign Partner Cultures', *Academy of Management Executive*, 1996, **10**(4), 109–110.

17

Managing Complexity in Mergers and Alliances

Ulrich Steger

B y all counts, 2005 was a record year for mergers and acquisitions (M&As), hitting the trillion dollar limit once again for the first time since 2000.[1] Although still significantly below the 'merger-mania' years of 1998 to 2000 (with $1.7 trillion at its peak), it is a remarkable recovery, because study after study indicates that the (significant) majority of M&As deals fail to create value.[2]

The amazing fact is that most of the studies do not come from academic M&A critics, but from traditional proponents like investment banks and consultants. Sometimes the studies are vaguely linked to their 'new' concepts that will avoid the old mistakes; sometimes they blame the managers, but they always ignore the role of the selfsame banks or consultants.

The new wave of M&As today is driven by private equity companies, which are awash with cash as a result of the low returns in a still low interest rate environment and more foreign – that is non-US – buyers, including some from emerging markets. In addition, a variety of industries – from IT and telecommunications to steel – are on the path of further consolidation.

The cyclical M&A dynamics once again show all the signs of an inflating bubble: frenzied bidding wars, with the 'winner's curse' – no chance to recover the premium paid; and demand driving up prices so that sellers are now starting to think more rigorously about how to get rid of units they do not want or are unable to manage successfully. Are companies doomed to repeat the mistakes of the past? Not necessarily – and this is the central thesis of this chapter – if we start to understand better what causes complexity in M&A transactions (from 'pre-' to post-') and create a learning process that takes out the hype, as well as introducing more transparency by using the simplifiers.

What causes complexity?

Generally it can be said that complexity increases from the pre- to the post-M&A phase, with distinct complexity drivers in each phase.

The offer phase

Whereas the selection of the target can still be done confidentially by a small set of decision makers and their advisors, as soon as the offer is made, the M&A becomes public – whether intentionally or by leaks (which are never unintentional, but might be done by a player with a hidden agenda). Contrary to the cliché of the all-powerful CEO bulldozing the deal through, from that moment on, a broad range of stakeholders has to be managed in order to avoid the deal being aborted early.[3] Figure 17.1 gives an idea of the many players involved, and it is plausible to assume that the number of players and their interdependence is the most relevant driver of complexity.

Basically six groups of stakeholders can be identified:

1. Internal stakeholders, including the broader management levels and (organized) employees, all of whom have a degree of leverage on the decision makers. Potential internal resistance should not be underestimated, as M&As are notoriously regarded with skepticism even by managers, who fear – rightly or wrongly – rationalization, cost-cutting, the impact on career opportunities, and the like.[4]
2. External advisers, who want to be associated with a bold 'big bang' M&A and would like to earn their fee as quickly as possible. They do a lot to push the deal

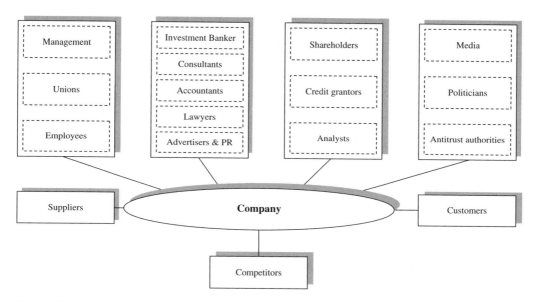

Figure 17.1 Stakeholders in the M&A environment

through and try to create a dynamic by which the offer is an unstoppable, obvious 'no-brainer'.

3. The financial market community, from the noisy financial analyst who likes to comment (more skeptically than positively) on the deal in the media – as long as he is not involved – to the shareholders and creditors who assess the deal in terms of their own interests (e.g. impact on credit taking).

4. 'Nonbusiness' stakeholders, including (anti-trust) authorities, the media, and politicians, who are sensitive to the deal for reasons of employment concerns, national pride, removing competition from the market, and the like.

5. 'Supply-chain' partners, such as customers and suppliers, who may resist the deal because of concerns about being 'ripped off' due to increased market power of the merged entity.

6. Competitors, who may respond with a counter-bid or, in Europe, mobilize anti-trust authorities (unlike the situation in the US, competitors get an extensive hearing from EU monopoly busters).

The interdependence of the players and the diversity of the interests may lead to a 'fast flux' situation: an internal player who opposes the deal leaks negative information to the media, which start to report negatively; financial analysts jump on the bandwagon, influencing shareholders. The declining share price is then used as an argument against the deal, with customers and competitors chipping in; this in turn alerts the politicians, which increases the media criticism, and so on. (Siemens' attempt to acquire Austrian VA Technologie AG, which failed in its first two rounds, might serve as an example here.) The more hostile the bid is perceived to be, the greater the risk that a coalition of players might want to attempt to derail the deal as soon as possible.

The due diligence/negotiation phase

Here, uncertainty is the main driver of complexity. As all players are jockeying for the best position, the interactions are intense, and small errors can have huge impacts. As a lot of money is at stake, there is no trust between the players. The bidder is suspicious as it is in a position of information asymmetry: the seller knows the company/unit much better and any due diligence can only compensate to a certain degree for this disadvantage. All too often, after the deal the bidder claims that the seller misrepresented certain issues (e.g. environmental liabilities). The advisors pile on psychological pressure: 'no deal' is a failure, and a last-minute move might derail any agreement achieved so far. This is a particular risk when the bid is hostile and the target is desperately looking for a 'white knight'.

Above all, the pressure to succeed often leads in this phase to increases in the buying price that are hard to justify in economic terms. The expected 'synergies' are exaggerated beyond any reasonable chance of delivery after the deal is done. The many subsequent write-offs of 'goodwill' are telling. This has led to shareholder suspicion that the seller is capturing all the value of the deal and even more. This explains the often seen pattern in listed companies of the bidder's share price declining after an offer, and the target's share price going beyond the offer price – a sure sign that the dynamics of the negotiation will lead to a higher price than the current offer.

The high uncertainty of the outcome puts tremendous pressure on all players involved and therefore ensures that the outcome is – with hindsight – often less than 'economically rational'.

The post-M&A phase

The main complexity driver of the post-M&A phase is diversity. No matter how bruising the battle was before, the target company/unit now has to be integrated and the new entity made competitive. This is easier said than done because there are a number of diversities that have not been recognized – or not sufficiently – in the M&A transaction so far:[5]

- Diversity of cultures. This not only relates to different corporate cultures but also – in the (not untypical) case of a foreign acquisition – to different national cultures. Cultures are, beyond the visible artifacts, difficult to detect and even more difficult to change. In many M&As it is still possible to observe a 'them and us' mentality, even after years. These issues have become more relevant as M&As increasingly involve not only companies from the same industry but also – and this is rapidly expanding – institutional investors, especially private equity companies and even hedge funds. The diversity in core values, attitudes, and worldview could not be greater than between the professional or even technically driven culture in the target company and the financially driven culture of institutional investors. The latter are sophisticated in financial restructuring, but usually lack any practical industrial and leadership experience.
- Diversity of business models. Even within the same industry, the relevant drivers of success can differ significantly. This is often overlooked, especially in the due diligence phase. 'Harmonizing' diverse business models often leads to the worst of both worlds. The difficulties in many 'mergers of equals' can be traced back to these differences. It is difficult to find not only equals in power but also companies with equal value drivers for their business.
- Diversity of 'personal' interests. As M&A transactions are often followed by cost cutting and layoffs, the top priority of the managers and employees involved is to 'save their skin' and ensure that the axe falls elsewhere. This leads to a lot of politics, infighting, and blocked decisions. Competitors are tempted to accelerate

their efforts while the newly merged or acquired unit is struggling to keep the focus off internal fights and on the customer.

As argued throughout this book, the more global the activity, the greater the complexity. This is also true for M&A transactions. A cross-border M&A easily doubles the number of stakeholders/players involved and increases the diversity. The potential for an emotional, not to say nationalistic, blowout is not negligible (just try as a Chinese company to buy a US oil company or as a 'Yankee' a French food company).

What are the simplifiers?

As seen from the analysis above, first it would help if a company managed to inject more common sense, a more sober decision-making process, and more transparency about success factors and ways to avoid failures in the M&A process. Second, there are specific simplifiers for M&A transactions: understanding the business model, being specific about synergies, integrating negotiation and operation teams, and creating a common glue of shared values.

Common sense simplifiers

These seem a bit like 'Forrest Gump of Management' recommendations – pretty simple, but how often has it been violated? Remember all the smart consultants and investment bankers who explained that in the 'new economy' the basic rules of the 'old economy' no longer applied (especially that a company's costs should be lower than its revenues)? How could a board approve an acquisition with a price based on a multiplier of exactly 123 of the average operating profit over the last five years – as in the case of Monsanto? The key is to restrain the external deal promoters, such as consultants and investment bankers, and remove the psychological pressure that 'no deal' is a failure. In almost any business situation other than M&A, it seems to be accepted that 'no deal' can be good business. One effective practice is for the board to set guidelines for M&As, e.g. about market segments and size, with clear price restrictions in advance and on a general level, so that negotiators – and the CEO – know how far they can go. The Danish food ingredient company Danisco is one of the few examples known to have – and implement – such clear guidelines.

The other recommendation in this context is to create transparency in the results of M&A and document the learning from previous activities. However, M&A are high-stake games, usually involving the CEO, and if things go wrong, the game is often then focused on finding scapegoats. However, it would definitely help if a post-M&A review were carried out. It would have to be done by a neutral, competent source (e.g. internal audit) and would have to go straight to the board[6] as everyone involved would claim the M&A to be a success. (Normally the result is not black or white, but various shades of grey and, since nobody can prove what would have happened without the M&A transaction, it could be a never-ending discussion.) The purpose of such a review is not a 'Monday morning quarterback' assessment, with the benefit of hindsight, but more to make transparent the knowledge gained in the whole process from pre- to post-M&A. What worked, what did not and what could be done better next time?

The last 'common sense' recommendation is: avoid herd behaviour. If everybody is rushing toward the promised land, you should not go there. Prices are rising, the best deals are already done, and everybody knows it. It is obviously hard to avoid the pressure that is created. As one CEO put it in a personal interview, 'If you make a mistake that everybody has done, you get away with it. My nightmare is that I am the only one who made that mistake.' Put another way, we all disclaim the herd behaviour of lemmings, but could not single out an individual lemming for criticism.

Specific simplifiers

Of the more specific simplifiers of complexity in M&A transactions, the first is a detailed analysis of the business model – of both the acquiring and the target companies. A detailed comparison of the value drivers gives a much more precise understanding of the value-added of an M&A transaction than the more elusive concept of 'synergy'. Generally, there is at best a synergy potential, and the most underestimated task post-M&A is the actual realization. A focus on value drivers often leads to an emphasis on growth and innovation potential, instead of cost cutting (with the positive side effect that the collateral damage in the post-M&A phase is significantly lower). Knowledge of the business model gives negotiators clearer guidelines for the negotiations and an appreciation of what is really important: it 'narrows the territory' on the value-adding features and the strategic fit of this specific M&A deal and gives a clear idea of the upper price limit.

We stress this factor, as it is sometimes surprising how vague and general the arguments in favour of an M&A deal are (and probably not only for the purposes of keeping the competition in the dark). However, the present research has shown that there are specific strategic intents, as shown in Figure 17.2, which can be identified by analysing the business model and which help to keep the players focused on the important issues instead of 'covering the waterfront'.

The second specific simplifier deals with the issue of team – and incentive – alignment. Often the negotiation team for acquisitions is separate from the team that has to run

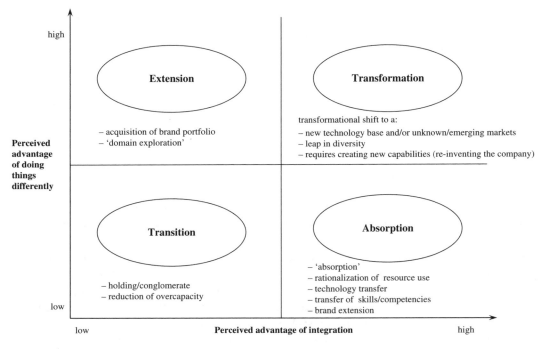

Figure 17.2 Options for capability application and growth

the (combined) units later. The focus for the negotiation team is to get the deal done, and their incentives also depend on this. They are not involved with what follows afterwards, and this can be the cause of many costly mistakes. It simplifies the internal coordination tremendously if the executive who will later be in charge is also the head of the negotiation team. His incentive structure is different from the 'negotiator only' case. He has to make the newly merged company work and, especially, earn a decent profit. This serves to counter the temptation to get the deal done at all costs, especially in the case of a bidding war.

The third and most important simplifier post-M&A is to create a common glue of shared values and purpose – underpinned with appropriate processes – even if the values of the acquiring unit are imposed on the target: the following process makes sense, even when it is transferred.[7] The values and purposes include what performance is expected and the core behaviours (do's and dont's); the standardized processes make this operationally viable. They give a sense of direction and create transparency in the core operations as the standardized processes generate the information needed for a timely evaluation of performance. This releases headquarters from too much intervention in the new unit – as known, any specific intervention in a subsidiary, especially a newly acquired one, is easily perceived as meddlesome.

Conclusion

The basic simplifiers of complexity – focus on the important shared purpose and values, standardize processes – plus a good dose of common sense and readiness to learn are in principle not different in M&A than in other business areas. However, it seems that they are most urgently needed here.

References

[1] Rosenbush, S., 'M&A: Back with a Vengeance', *Business Week Online*, 6 December 2005.

[2] For an overview, see, for example, C. Kummer, 'Internationale Fusions- und Akquisitionsaktivität: Eine historische Untersuchung der Entwicklung in Deutschland und eine empirische Untersuchung anhand der pharmazeutischen Industrie', Dissertation, Technische Universitaet Berlin, 2005.

[3] For an in-depth analysis of the different stakeholders and their agendas see U. Steger and C. Kummer, 'M&A Activity in the New Competitive Milieu', in *Managing Complex Mergers* (eds U. Steger and P. Morosini), London: Prentice-Hall, 2004, pp. 3–27.

[4] Steger, U. and Lachmann, H.-D., 'Performing under Pressure: Managers Embracing New Realities', *European Management Journal*, August 2002.

[5] Steger, U. and Kummer, C., 'M&A Activity in the New Competitive Milieu', *Managing Complex Mergers* (eds U. Steger and P. Morosini), London: Prentice-Hall, 2004, pp. 21–23.

[6] For the roles of boards, see U. Steger and C. Kummer, 'Challenges of Governance Structures in International Mergers and Acquisitions', *Managing Complex Mergers* (eds U. Steger and P. Morosini), London: Prentice-Hall, 2004, pp. 21–23, 137–146.

[7] Morosini, P., 'Are Mergers and Acquisitions Creating Value?', *Managing Complex Mergers* (eds U. Steger and P. Morosini), London: Prentice-Hall, 2004, pp. 41–45.

18
Managing Complexity: The Family Business Experience

John Ward

Introduction

The world of family-controlled firms provides an important laboratory to examine, extend, and enhance the insights and prescriptions of this book. First, if the principles presented previously have validity, they must stand up to the test in that part of the business universe that represents 40 to 50 % of all significant companies. Second, family-controlled firms provide examples of firms that are relatively very successful in coping with the complex reality of today. Third, family-controlled firms illustrate particularly well the complexity that comes from dilemmas and ambiguity. What can be learnt from the experiences of successful, global family firms?

Successful firms: the empirical evidence

Global family firms are relatively successful, and there are many of them. Recent business school research has begun to study the performance of family companies and their role in the economy. Surprising to many, the evidence is mounting that family firms, despite their extra challenges, perform at least as well as non-family firms – those widely held by anonymous, atomistic shareholders. A look at stock market indices in the US (S&P 500), France (CAC 40), Italy, Germany, and the like reveals that family-controlled firms make up 20 to 40% of the indices and have, over the past 10 years, outperformed them.

In my own research I examined the 1000 largest quoted companies in the world.[1] Eighty were controlled by families in the second or later generation of ownership. (It is estimated that there are at least as many totally private family companies of equivalent size, suggesting about 15% of the largest firms in the world are family controlled.) In that research, the family-controlled companies had an average return on invested capital 30% greater than the widely held firms.

Family firms are not only a relevant category of corporate experience but can also possibly – because of their impressive performance – shed light on the challenging questions of this book. Table 18.1 shows some of the world's largest family firms.

Table 18.1   Large global family businesses

Quoted	Private
Wal-Mart	Cargill
Ford	Koch Industries
Samsung	Mars
News Corp.	IKEA
BMW	Bertelsmann
Metro	Tetra Laval
H&M	Bechtel

Special challenges

A core thesis – perhaps the most fundamental core thesis – is that firms are confronted with more dilemmas than ever before. Family-controlled firms have long lived with difficult dilemmas. Most profoundly, they have had to digest the powerfully pervasive dilemma of mixing the family's interests and welfare with those of the business. That dilemma is often emphasized as the most serious vulnerability of family firms. It is a close-run contest as to whether satisfying family needs damages the business's effectiveness more than 'running the business first and foremost as a business' negates the advantages of stable long-term family ownership.

This dilemma is complicated by the variety of powerful conflicts of interest for a family firm, as Figure 18.1 illustrates. Different family owners have different, even opposite, objective functions. Some significant owners seek to maximize near-term shareholder value, even liquidity. Others feel more strongly about growing and protecting the business in order to serve their managerial cares and commitments. Still others may put the interests of employees or the community first. What makes these conflicts of interest especially pronounced is that they are held deeply on an emotional level by substantial blocks of ownership.

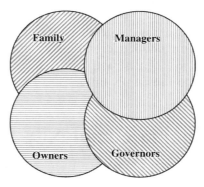

Figure 18.1   Conflicts of interest in a family firm

Often different views relate to the different roles family members play in the company. Some may be executives who know the business inside out, the competitive imperatives, and the goals to be achieved. Some are involved in governance roles, e.g. as members of the oversight board, and know at least the fundamentals of the business, even if their own professional experience is in other areas. Some are more or less passive investors with no business expertise, who may or may not depend personally on the cash the business is generating. The more generations a family business is away from the founder, the more fragmented these roles are. The solution is not to simply let shareholders who think differently liquidate their holdings. That usually results in chaos and/or dissolution.

There is another layer of complexity more apparent in large family firms. On average, family firms are more often more diversified and more vertically integrated in their strategies than their nonfamily counterparts.[2] Further, they are, on average, successfully so. Other research shows that the more diversified and vertically integrated family firms are even more profitable than those that are not – counter to most strategy research for nonfamily firms. For family business this makes sense because a large percentage of the wealth of a family – sometimes all – is tied up in the business. Therefore, another risk-diversification approach is needed than what a portfolio investor can take in the stock market. It will be seen that this approach increases internal complexity, but reduces external complexity.

Another classic dilemma that family firms in particular face is how to change with the times for growth, even survival. Family-controlled companies have cultures that are more firmly steeped in past ways. The shadow of the heroic founder lasts long. Top management teams have much longer tenures. Successor leaders are likely to be reluctant to discard or even criticize the past. Inflexibility and resistance to change are widely viewed as more common in family firms.

Principles of reducing complexity

In this section, family firms' basic approaches to managing and reducing complexity will be described. It explains why family businesses are more successful, despite the fact that they, as global companies, have to manage the same business complexity as other companies, along with the additional drivers explained above.

Paradoxical thinking

If there is one overarching lesson to be learnt from the way successful family firms address complexity, it is that they tackle the challenging underlying dilemmas with paradoxical thinking. They find ways to keep two seemingly contradictory truths in mind simultaneously. The basic simplicity of their approach is not to compromise their ideals or overcommit to any one choice. In other words, accepting complexity with relative equanimity and using the complexity of dilemmas to spur new ways of thinking are the clear messages from the field of family firms. However, this is easier said than done. A review of some of the dilemmas and paradoxical principles of family business experience are outlined in Table 18.2.

Table 18.2   Family business paradoxes

- Business first versus family first? Neither. Family firms seek the synergistic win–win of both goals, discovering alignment between family and business visions.
- Preserve tradition versus innovate change? Both. Family firms reconceptualize the problem to be 'innovation and change *are* the tradition to preserve and promote'.
- Emphasize headquarters' culture and values versus integrate regional culture and values of global locations? Not a contradiction. 'Home values' are common and meaningful the world over.
- Grow for global scale versus conserve financial resources for long-term security and opportunity? Both. Conserving for security offers even better future growth opportunities than maximizing current growth opportunities.

Patience and perspective

Facing change, the fear of the unknown, the pressures to project certainty and clarity, and the likely expectations of others to act decisively requires a certain patience and perspective. Where does this faith that it will work out, in spite of everything, come from?

There are two insights to this question from successful family firms. The first is that they emphasize a culture of trust. Trust allows confidence and tolerance of uncertainty. Trust encourages 'doing the right thing' rather than taking actions to appear decisive and in control. Trust promises personal rewards that are more in line with the welfare of the business. Trust lubricates efficiency and effectiveness in imperfect and complex organizational designs. Trust empowers decentralization. Trust encourages investment in and reliance on nonbureaucratic processes. Trust protects commitment to a sense of purpose in difficult times.

The second insight is the paradoxical focus on both the past and future at the same time – even more so than the present. Confidence to take action in the present is obviously essential, despite the environment of complexity, confusion, and contradiction.

However, family firms exemplify what behaviour research has preached for some time: better decisions, especially in uncertainty, are taken if there is a good sense of the past and a focus on the future.

Understanding the past strengthens the ability to understand the future. Respect for the past and respect for the future assure more calculated risk taking and less speculation. Focus on the future reduces dissonance over current dilemmas.

Another feature of patience is that rules stay in place for a long time, normally more than a generation. It is not only that it might be difficult to change rules in a larger family but also the recognition that fundamental rules should not be bent opportunistically. For example, the Haniel family business is Germany's eleventh largest company and has been going for more than 350 years. For over 100 years there has been a clear division between ownership and management. Family owners do not take jobs in company management. Not that there has been a shortage of entrepreneurial talent in the family – many members of the family have started their own businesses or risen to the top of other big companies. However, the rule has never been seriously challenged. The stability of rules gives the major decision makers a kind of guard-rail, which increases the predictability and consistency of decisions and reduces infighting and politics in the organization.

Finally, patience – the long-term view – lessens the immediate pressure to resolve dilemmas. The family business perspective, that secure continuity supersedes all other objectives, allows time to reveal more information before decisions must be taken.[3]

Personal, not functional, values

Trust and long-term orientation represent a special type of value found more distinctively in family companies. Family firms, much more than nonfamily firms, shape their culture around very human, very personally attractive values.[4] The most common are personal integrity, mutual respect, personal passion, personal commitment, and personal freedom. As it has been argued throughout the book, values that are lived and shared are the most important simplifiers in a complex and uncertain business environment, and are vital for an effective but lean organization.

Nonfamily firms, by contrast, typically define their company values more function-ally, such as innovation, teamwork, empowerment, and change. These values are less personally directive in times of uncertainty and less compelling for long-term commit-ment. Family firms' values, by their very nature, create fewer new dilemmas and contradictions. For example, more personal values are more universal throughout a global organization. They create less strain on the dilemma of stability versus flexi-bility. They more easily reconcile the contradictions of individualism and collectivism. Two examples of global family values are shown in Table 18.3.

Table 18.3 Values in two global family firms

Zegna (Italy)	Levi Strauss (US)
Self-respect	Integrity
Discipline	Courage
Hard work	Empathy
Honesty	Originality
Trust	Perseverance

Reducing complexity in practice

Dilemmas create strategy

The primary insights from family businesses in this chapter put the spotlight on culture: values, purpose, future orientation. Developing strategy during waves of dilemmas may seem problematic. Paradoxically, perhaps it is keeping the dilemmas alive and top of the mind that helps create strategic insights and opportunities. The IMD case on Beretta illustrates this idea.[5] Beretta, the Italian gun maker, is a nearly 500-year-old private family company. It is adding to its complexity by diversifying its business lines and markets, by having more revenues from out of Europe than in, and by facing an ever-more challenging sociopolitical environment. It struggles perpetually with a series of strategic dilemmas:

- preserving art, craft, and design, yet benefiting from technology and mass manufac-turing;

- designing and coordinating an organization to assure attention to very different products, for very different markets, all in very different countries;
- acting prudently, yet also audaciously;
- emphasizing teamwork, yet also believing in individual freedom.

Many of these dilemmas have been with the company for decades. Rather than artificially or unilaterally resolving these dilemmas, Beretta, not insecurely, lets them all continue to fester. Its belief – and its success – has been that this ambiguity makes it more open to opportunities, and the tension in the unresolved dilemmas sharpens its continual experimentation with the new opportunities. Beretta has a clear culture for the long, long term and a loyal, trusting, empowered organization. At Beretta culture creates strategy more than strategy defines culture.

Culture drives strategy

The IMD Hilti case study offers the perspective of the 50-year-old global construction tool company.[6] Hilti had long had a crisp distribution and sales strategy, though – like Beretta – it was in constant strategic tension over a dilemma. In this case the dilemma was product innovation for every customer need versus standardized offerings for organizations and cost efficiency. Global coverage, size, industry recession, product expansion, and, in particular, new opportunities in the distribution network that put long-time core values and ways of doing business in conflict with each other deeply concerned the company. The resolve? To dig deeper into the core values to find the synthesis of the dilemma by rededicating themselves to their personal, individual sense of commitment and responsibility, rather than imposing a structural strategic solution top-down. For Hilti, culture – especially in complex times – drives strategy. The most fundamental values of that culture are personal commitment, personal responsibility, and also personal courage to take the chance to innovate and make mistakes.

Stretch time, not targets

Earlier it was suggested that the more and further a company focuses on the future, the better the choices it will make in a confusing present. Successful family firms work to stretch the organization's perspective into the longer-run future. What they do not do, typically, is create BHAGs – the quantitative 'Big Hairy Audacious Goals' promoted by authors Jim Collins and Jerry Porras in *Built to Last*.[7] While almost all of the other lessons in *Built to Last* are relevant to and reaffirmed by successful family firms, BHAGs are not.[8] To define an arbitrary, organization-challenging, operational long-term goal does not fit the inclinations of family businesses to stress values and let culture create opportunities. Open dilemmas and environmental challenges seem to provide ample tension for innovation and change. BHAGs are not necessary and are an affront to the sincerity of the company's culture.

When a commitment to the long-term future is the primary purpose, a different approach to opportunity analysis is recommended. Rather than relying on discounted cash flows and expected monetary value tools as the dominant decision-making analytical frameworks, the 'options' analysis framework is better suited to future thinking, especially in times of ambiguous uncertainty. Options thinking keeps alternatives open, stimulates more examination of the future, and helps family owners stay more committed to the business. Options thinking comes naturally to family-controlled companies as they remember their entrepreneurial heritage, which thrived on keeping options open yet limiting downside risk.

Governance assures clarity

With dilemmas inevitably come disputes. For family firms these conflicts are particularly intense: ownership stakes are very large and the values are very personal. The conflicts are compounded by the role conflicts between family members described at the opening of this chapter. The risk that family conflicts transfer into business risk and vice versa is the Achilles heel of family business. To address this risk, family firms set up special governance structures. In the boardroom, at owners' assemblies, and on board committees, they look to blend family and external members. Among the external members they seek a particular diversity of perspectives – some who are sympathetic to the value differences of family firms and others who are experienced champions of the discipline of shareholder capitalism.

Family firms will utilize these governing bodies to help bring clarity to dilemmas and resolution to conflicts. The business depends on the externals to keep the dilemmas in balanced perspective. Externals are asked to provide forums for healthy debate and to keep the focus on process, not personality. The governance bodies are often designed into mediation roles and, sometimes, arbitration roles. These roles are especially critical around leadership succession decisions that may include family-owner candidates.

Family firms also assure perspectives on differences and conflicts by designing governance to represent the variety of ownership perspectives. Sometimes different owner roles are represented structurally (e.g. Merck, Germany's largest pharmaceutical company), while sometimes governance representatives need a 'cross-family-tribes' (or branches) vote of confidence.

As long as the business runs smoothly, the precise provisions of the family governance contract are unknown, but when things get tough, the roots are discovered quickly and the clarity of the decision-making power solves major issues. It is then, seen what the quality of the contract is and whether it allows adjustment to new circumstances with the same basic rules. When and how to amend these ownership and governance contracts – like national constitutions – is another complex dilemma particularly affecting family firms.

Conclusion

As highlighted throughout this book, purpose, values, and profound simplicity are critical capabilities for coping with the increasing complexity of a rapidly changing and increasingly global environment. Family-controlled firms present a special laboratory in which to explore these elements of success. In several ways family firms face even more heightened circumstances of ambiguity and intense dilemmas.

The relative success of family firms, despite their extra complexities and challenges, sharpens this examination. That family firms reinforce the messages of this book is reaffirming. That they demonstrate that they – even more than nonfamily firms – have the prescribed behaviours, coupled with their above-average performance, further strengthens the messages.

How family firms are managed differently to achieve these behaviours provides enhanced insight. Family firms define purpose as continuity, not financial results or stretched strategic intent. Family firms emphasize personal, fundamental values more than impersonal, functional values. Family firms attempt to learn from the past, yet focus on the longer-term future. They manage to strengthen the sense of future for the organization. Successful family firms customize their governance systems to reflect their challenges and to address their conflicts.

Family firms are a reminder that these powerful messages are, basically, simple. Doing the right thing, with a base of core personal values and a focus on and commitment to the future, offers empowering solace in complex and changing times.

References

[1] Ward, J., 'Live Long and Prospers', *Families in Business*, March–April 2004, p. 86.

[2] Ward, John L., *Unconventional Wisdom: Counterintuitive Insights for Successful Family Firms*, Chichester, West Sussex: John Wiley & Sons, Ltd, 2006.

[3] Chaponnière, C. and Ward, J., *Family Business through Darwin's Theory of the Species*, Geneva: Lombard Odier Darier Hentsch and Co., 2003.

[4] Denison, Daniel R., Lief, Colleen and Ward, John L., 'Culture in Family-Owned Enterprises: Recognizing and Leveraging Unique Strengths', *Family Business Review*, 2004, pp. 61–70.

[5] Ward, John L. and Lief, Colleen, *Prudence and Audacity: The House of Beretta*, IMD case IMD-3-1495, 2005.

[6] Ward, John L. and Lief, Colleen, *Hilti: Our Culture Journey*, IMD case IMD-3-1434, 2005.

[7] Collins, J. and Porras, J., *Built to hast*, Harper Business, 2002.

[8] Ward, J., 'Better Built to Last Longer', *Families in Business*, January–February 2006, p. 71.

19

The Future of Managing Complexity

Wolfgang Amann, Ulrich Steger, and Martha Maznevski

This book discussed how drivers of complexity render management more challenging. After describing developments on the macro-level, we outlined what managing complexity in different industries and functions comprised. We pointed to further complexities arising in special ownership structures, M&A, and internationalization endeavours.

Based on the key lessons from these chapters, it can be seen that there are three major tasks crystallizing how managing complexity can be achieved in the future. As outlined in Figure 19.1, this consists of embracing complexity differently. The times of a predictable future are definitely over. In the past, through careful extrapolation of trends and the consideration of a few wild cards, two to four main scenarios could be identified. However, scenarios that were of great help in environments with some degree of uncertainty fail when environments become hyperturbulent, technological advances accelerate, and more players decide to drive markets rather than to be market driven. Evolutionary thinking and strategy become increasingly helpful, as they are the equivalent of being prepared.

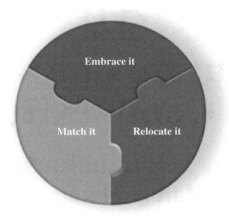

Figure 19.1   A holistic approach to managing complexity

Unpredictability frequently causes a feeling of unease. As traditional solutions that may have worked well in the past become outdated, constant learning and simultaneous unlearning are crucial. Constantly turning parts of previous efforts into sunk cost may lead to a feeling of unhappiness as well. In times of constant change and mounting complexity, we therefore suggest a mental switch from temporarily accepting complexity to achieve goals to an attitude of embracing it. In conditions where the external environment, the company, as well as technology are continuously in fast flux, we suggest starting the analysis with one of the few aspects that you can still control and know best – yourself. What are you willing to invest or sacrifice in hyperturbulent environments? How much complexity are you willing to accept? Which *a priori* decisions do you have to take to avoid dilemmas? How can you proactively prepare for times of ambiguity, diversity, interdependence, and flux?

Figure 19.1 picks up this thought of matching complexity with the ability to cope with it. However, the related demands not only hold true for the individual; they encompass teams, units, functions, joint ventures, M&A, and entire companies. Many examples could be cited where marketing in foreign and unknown markets failed because the cultures were too diverse. With a success rate below 30 %, M&As continue to be challenging and, worst of all, this success rate is not improving – this, despite an overabundance of consultants, managers with own M&A experience, and a next generation of leaders and managers who were exposed to M&A dilemmas in their education. As outlined, realizing the benefits of a truly global reach is often harder than managers admit, as there are considerable liabilities associated with a presence in foreign places. However, if companies continuously develop the ability to cope with complexity at the right pace, they can avoid substantial performance downturns.

An additional avenue for the future of managing complexity lies in its relocation. We have already outlined simplifiers' enormous potential. Addressing and counterbalancing increasing complexity with (sometimes) radical cuts in complexity prevents a company from being overwhelmed. Focused energy is still relevant.

Complexity is not, however, always bad. The essential condition is found in the under-lying economies. Do the customers not only appreciate the offered variety and service levels but are they also willing to pay for them? Or, what are other forms of desired behaviours, such as sharing information, getting involved in the quality design or inno-vation process, showing loyalty, etc.? At the same time, there is a side of complexity that may offer noticeable internal advantages. Early awareness systems, management information systems, diverse pools of talents, the capability to master distributed inno-vation, and the possibility of responding quickly to emerging trends and shaping them by driving hot spots and opinion leaders around the globe are just some examples of when overcomplexifying is a truly worthwhile investment. Relocating complexity thus includes crucial aspects of simplifying and overcomplexifying.

Relocating complexity, along with matching and embracing it in the first place, demands a new set of skills. When everything becomes increasingly interdependent, when globally active companies try to tap synergies through internal integration, inter-esting network structures emerge. Hence, network fitness, e.g. in the form of detecting and altering network patterns, the attractiveness of connecting or being connected, strong and weak links (with the largest potential probably in weak links as they can be developed more), and communication skills, will become even more invaluable in the future than they are today.

Index

Index compiled by Terry Halliday

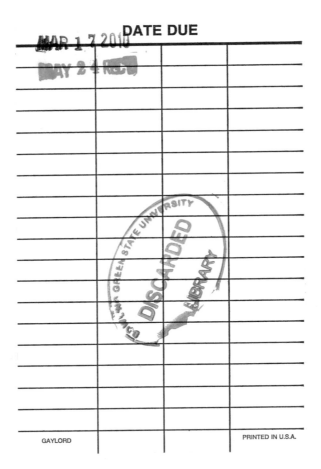